Songs of the Women *Trouvères*

Locating the
Women Trouvères

Songs of the Women *Trouvères*

Edited, Translated, and Introduced by

EGLAL DOSS-QUINBY

JOAN TASKER GRIMBERT

WENDY PFEFFER

ELIZABETH AUBREY

Yale University Press
New Haven
& London

Designed by Mary Valencia.
Set in Meridien type by Tseng Information Systems, Inc.
Printed in the United States of America by R. R. Donnelley & Sons.

ISBN 0-300-08412-9 (cloth); ISBN 0-300-08413-7 (pbk.).

A catalogue record for this book is available from the British Library.

The paper in this book meets the guidelines for permanence and durability of the
Committee on Production Guidelines for Book Longevity of the Council on Library
Resources.

10 9 8 7 6 5 4 3 2 1

To Samuel Rosenberg and William Paden, for their vision, encouragement, and support

Contents

Plainte

Chansons d'ami

Chansons de croisade

Aubes

Chansons de malmariée

Chansons pieuses

A CIRCLE OF VOICES: RONDEAUX   179

Motet for Four Voices

Motet Texts without Music

Illustrations

Attributions are cited as they appear in the manuscripts.

FIGURES

MAPS

Acknowledgments

We wish to offer special thanks to the friends and colleagues who have been generous with advice and encouragement, and who have allowed us to benefit from their editorial and translating expertise on more than one occasion: Samuel Rosenberg, Rupert Pickens, William Kibler, Keith Busby, William Paden, and Matilda Bruckner. We are grateful to Rebecca Baltzer for advice concerning transcription of the motets. We also thank Brigitte Buettner, Mark Cable, Alain Corbellari, Kerstin Gaddy, David Quinby, and Kerry Spiers for their help with various aspects of this project. We wish to recognize the subscribers to medtextl@postoffice.cso.uiuc.edu who kindly answered our queries. Joseph Duggan, who reviewed our manuscript for Yale University Press, has our deep appreciation for his unequivocal support of our work.

We take pleasure in expressing our gratitude to the Institut de Recherche et d'Histoire des Textes, the Bibliothèque Nationale de France, the Bibliothèque de l'Arsenal, the Biblioteca Apostolica Vaticana, the Biblioteca Medicea Laurenziana, the Bodleian Library, and the Burgerbibliothek Bern for providing us with reproductions of manuscript material. We are particularly indebted to Mireille Vial, Conservateur en Chef, Bibliothèque Interuniversitaire de Montpellier, for her unstinting cooperation in tracking down every item we needed.

We acknowledge the generous financial support of Smith College. Faculty development grants and a Presidential Faculty Fellowship for ED-Q greatly facilitated bringing this project to completion. We also acknowledge the research funds awarded to JTG by the Catholic University of America, to WP by the University of Louisville, and to EA by the University of Iowa.

We are grateful to the publishers and editors who granted us permission to reprint various material. The Old French texts and critical apparatus of song nos. 3, 10, 14, 18-19, 22-23, 27-28, 30-31, 33, 35, and 39 appeared originally in S. N. Rosenberg and H. Tischler, *Chanter m'estuet* (1981) and are reprinted here by courtesy of Samuel N. Rosenberg. Song no. 4 is reprinted by permission of Librairie Droz from Fresco 1988. Song no. 16 is reprinted by permission of Éditions de l'Université d'Ottawa from Lepage 1981. Song no. 29 is reprinted by permission of Garland Publishing from Rosenberg, Danon, and van der Werf

1985. Song no. 37 is reprinted by permission of the Académie des Inscriptions et Belles-Lettres from Långfors 1932. Manuscript facsimiles are reproduced by permission of the Bibliothèque Nationale de France, the Biblioteca Apostolica Vaticana, and the Burgerbibliothek Bern.

Our translations owe much to those of our predecessors. We acknowledge with gratitude Samuel Rosenberg and Marie-Geneviève Grossel (Rosenberg, Tischler, and Grossel 1995; Rosenberg, Switten, and Le Vot 1998), Robyn Smith (in Anderson 1977 and Smith 1997), Susan Stakel (in Tischler 1985), Elizabeth Close (Anderson and Close 1975), and Brian Woledge (1961).

Abbreviations

BIBLIOGRAPHIC DATA

B	Boogaard 1969 (refrain)
B rond.	Boogaard 1969 (rondeau)
G rond.	Gennrich 1921-27
L	Linker 1979
M	Mass (motet tenor)
MW	Mölk and Wolfzettel 1972
O	Office (motet tenor)
PC	Pillet and Carstens 1933
RS	Spanke 1955

MANUSCRIPTS

fol.	folio
r	recto
v	verso
♪	music

CRITICAL APPARATUS

DF	Dialectal Features
MC	Musical Commentary
ME	Musical Emendations
MV	Musical Variants
RR	Rejected Readings
TN	Textual Notes
TV	Textual Variants
cond.	conditional
conj.	conjunction
em.	emendation
fut.	future
imp.	imperfect
ind.	indicative

inf.	infinitive
nom.	nominative
part.	participle
pers.	person
pl.	plural
pres.	present
pret.	preterit
rel.	relative
sing.	singular
subj.	subjunctive

MOTET VOICES

Mot	Motetus
Q	Quadruplum
T	Tenor
Tr	Triplum

MUSICAL TERMINOLOGY

B	*brevis*
L	*longa*
N	*nota simplex* without rhythmic distinction
R	rest
S	*semibrevis*
2li	two-note neume or ligature
3li	three-note neume or ligature
4li	four-note neume or ligature
c.o.p.	ligature *cum opposita proprietate*
c.perf.	ligature *cum perfectio*
s.perf.	ligature *sine perfectio*
P following a note	ascending plica
p following a note	descending plica

Manuscripts Consulted

The manuscripts listed below are those to which reference is made in abbreviated form in this book. A complete listing and a bibliography may be found in Linker 1979: 23–69. See also Jeanroy 1918, Spanke 1955, and Aubrey 2000. For sources that preserve polyphonic music, see Ludwig 1910, Gennrich 1958a, Everist 1989, and van der Werf 1989.

A	Arras, Bibliothèque Municipale, 657
Ba	Bamberg, Staatsbibliothek, Lit. 115 (olim Ed. IV. 6)
C	Bern, Burgerbibliothek, 389
Cl	Paris, Bibliothèque Nationale de France, n. a. fr. 13521
E^n	Einsiedeln, Biblioteca Monasterii, 364 (385)
H	Modena, Biblioteca Estense, R4, 4
Her	Leuven, Universiteitsbibliotheek, Herentals fragment (Göttingen, Niedersächsische Staats- und Universitätsbibliothek, Ludwig Nachlass, IX, 14)
I	Oxford, Bodleian Library, Douce 308
K	Paris, Bibliothèque de l'Arsenal, 5198
M	Paris, Bibliothèque Nationale de France, fr. 844
Mo	Montpellier, Bibliothèque Interuniversitaire, Section Médecine, H 196
M^t	Insertion in M (fols. 13r-v and 59r-77r)
N	Paris, Bibliothèque Nationale de France, fr. 845
O	Paris, Bibliothèque Nationale de France, fr. 846
P	Paris, Bibliothèque Nationale de France, fr. 847
S	Paris, Bibliothèque Nationale de France, fr. 12581
StV	Paris, Bibliothèque Nationale de France, lat. 15139
T	Paris, Bibliothèque Nationale de France, fr. 12615
Tu	Turin, Biblioteca Reale, vari 42
U	Paris, Bibliothèque Nationale de France, fr. 20050
V	Paris, Bibliothèque Nationale de France, fr. 24406
W2	Wolfenbüttel, Herzog August Bibliothek, Helmstedt 1099 (Heinemann 1206)

X   Paris, Bibliothèque Nationale de France, n. a. fr. 1050

a   Rome, Biblioteca Apostolica Vaticana, Regina 1490

b   Rome, Biblioteca Apostolica Vaticana, Regina 1522

c   Bern, Burgerbibliothek, A. 95

f   Montpellier, Bibliothèque Interuniversitaire, Section Médecine, 236

i   Paris, Bibliothèque Nationale de France, fr. 12483

j   Paris, Bibliothèque Nationale de France, n. a. fr. 21677

k   Paris, Bibliothèque Nationale de France, fr. 12786

Ψ   Paris, Bibliothèque Nationale de France, lat. 11266

Introduction

The Case for the Women Trouvères

We bring together here the songs of all medieval women whose names are recorded in the rubrics or tables of contents of various Old French manuscripts as composers of songs or as participants in *jeux-partis* and *tensons* (debate poems). The songs by women whose names are known are relatively few in number, but there were undoubtedly many more women composers, and whereas their names are lost to us, some of their songs are probably still extant, though bereft of proper attribution. Accordingly, we have chosen to include a generous sampling of anonymous works—*chansons de femme* (women's songs), *rondeaux,* and motets—both because they offer a wide variety of female voices and because some of these pieces may well have been composed by women. We hope in this way to rectify a situation that for many years has denied women their rightful place in the pantheon of Old French medieval lyric poets.

For, as surprising as it may seem, the very title of our anthology, *Songs of the Women Trouvères,* makes a bold, even controversial, statement. Although nearly all scholars now acknowledge the existence of medieval women who composed poetry in other romance languages (Occitan, Spanish, Italian, Galician-Portuguese), most have accepted without question Pierre Bec's contention that none of the songs composed in northern France in the twelfth or thirteenth centuries are the product of a woman *trouvère* (Bec 1979: 236). A number of Old French songs feature women's voices (*féminité textuelle*), particularly in the lyric type known as the chanson de femme. However, féminité textuelle does not necessarily imply female authorship (*féminité génétique*), to use a distinction introduced by Bec himself (1979: 235-36). The majority of these songs are anonymous, but because most of the ones that are attributed in the manuscripts are credited to a male author, Bec has concluded that no Old French songs of the period in question were composed by women.[1] Although many have agreed with Bec, the literary history of the past 125 years includes a few dissenters who base their opinion on evidence that until recently was either ignored or not seriously considered. A brief summary of that history is instructive, as it highlights the major arguments for and against the historical existence of the women trouvères.

One of the first scholars to enter the fray was Alfred Jeanroy (1889). Stating that medieval sources mention French women trouvères only infrequently, he went on to express his conviction that none had actually existed. Citing the unreliability of manuscript rubrics and the probability of false attribution, he found it implausible, moreover, that a woman should have surrendered so wholeheartedly her traditional role by deciding to compose poetry. Why should she have wished to step down from the pedestal to which the male courtly poets had raised her? In any case, he thought, women poets would have infused their poems with more tenderness, emotion, and especially discretion.[2] Clearly, Jeanroy's refusal to acknowledge the existence of women poets reflected an attitude he owed to his time—the Victorian conception of a woman's place in society.[3] Joseph Bédier apparently shared that attitude: he offered specious arguments similar to Jeanroy's to deny the existence of women trouvères, and he worked hard to explain away certain manuscript attributions to women (Bédier 1910: 912–15).[4]

Some scholars have simply abstained from debating the issue, seeing no reason to question the validity of manuscript attributions. As early as 1581, the humanist Claude Fauchet entered "Doete de Troies chanteresse & Trouverre" and "*Damoiselle* Sainte des Prez" in his repertory of French poets living before 1300 (Fauchet 158, 192). In 1780, Jean-Benjamin de Laborde listed "Dregnau, de Lille, (Marotte ou Marie)" among the known trouvères. He presented the text of "Mout m'abelist quant je voi revenir" (our song no. 15) by matter-of-factly noting: "Il nous reste une seule chanson d'elle, que l'on trouve dans le manuscrit du Roi & dans celui de Noailles" (Only a single song of hers has come down to us; it is found in the manuscrit du Roi and that of Noailles) (Laborde 1780, 2: 185). In 1839, Arthur Dinaux was pleased to include in his anthology of trouvères from Flanders and Tournai "Marie Dregnau" (Maroie de Diergnau), whom he characterized as one of the few women who had been willing to take up "the bards' lyre." Although he regretted that only one piece had been preserved (song no. 15), he was convinced that Marie must have composed several others.[5] Arthur Långfors, who published his edition of jeux-partis in 1926, expressed even greater confidence in the existence of women poets, for he believed that all the parts in jeux-partis giving voice to both sexes had been composed by actual male and female poets alternating as speakers and interlocutors.[6]

Manuscript rubrics and tables of contents indicating female authorship have seemed credible as well to a few scholars publishing in the late twentieth century. In his study devoted to the lyric death-lament, Samuel Rosenberg (1983) included an analysis of a *plainte* attributed to the Duchesse de Lorraine (song no. 18); the piece appears in all three of his anthologies (Rosenberg and Tischler

1981; Rosenberg, Tischler, and Grossel 1995; Rosenberg, Switten, and Le Vot 1998). The first two also incorporate two jeux-partis featuring three named women participants: the Dame de la Chaucie and Sainte des Prez (song no. 3), and the Dame de Gosnai (song no. 4).

Musicologist Maria Coldwell (1986), secure in her knowledge of documentary evidence attesting to the existence of female musicians in France in the twelfth and thirteenth centuries, accepts as a natural corollary that there were women who composed songs, and she sees no reason to question the manuscript attributions of various songs and jeux-partis to women trouvères.[7] Because her focus is primarily on music, she highlights the songs for which music is extant and publishes transcriptions of the melodies of a love lyric by Maroie de Diergnau (song no. 15), a prayer to the Virgin by Blanche de Castille (song no. 36), and a jeu-parti between Dame Margot and Dame Maroie (song no. 1).

In the late 1970s and the 1980s, in the midst of the debate regarding the existence of the *trobairitz* (women troubadours in Occitania), a new wave of predominantly French critics challenged the validity of female authorship in medieval France in the twelfth and thirteenth centuries and endeavored to prove not only that there had been no women trouvères but even that all female voices in the lyric poetry of northern France during that period were constructs by male poets.[8] In a highly influential article on the trobairitz, Pierre Bec formulated two apparent paradoxes: first, that women wrote "troubadour" songs (that is, songs in conformity with a male-dominated lyric system) while men wrote women's songs (chansons de femme); and second, that there were in Occitania several women poets but very few chansons de femme, while in northern France there were a number of chansons de femme but no women poets (Bec 1979: 236). Bec's argument aimed not only to erase the women trouvères but also to diminish the accomplishment of the women troubadours, because he sought to prove that the trobairitz' originality resided almost exclusively in their exploitation of themes from chansons de femme—and all these pieces, according to Bec, were composed by men. Although Bec cited isolated cases of women who composed poetry in other Romance languages, he was adamant about the absence (or at least silence) of women trouvères in northern France; indeed, he did not so much as allude to the cases where a few songs and jeux-partis are attributed to women, nor did he mention the anonymous women partners and named judges in several jeux-partis. In his anthology of the lyric poetry of northern France, which he had published a year earlier, not only did he not attribute a single song to a woman, he failed to mention in his notes cases where the various manuscripts containing a particular song offered contradictory attributions. For example, if a song was attributed to a woman in one manuscript, to a man in another, and remained anonymous in a third, he routinely chose to attribute it to the male poet and did not mention the other manuscripts.

Like Bec, Peter Dronke states in his *Women Writers of the Middle Ages* (1984: 97) that there are no extant poems by women from northern France, England, Spain, or Portugal. (As he does not mention the manuscript attributions to women, it is not clear whether he finds this evidence unconvincing or is simply ignorant of it.) Nevertheless, he asserts that because there were *jograresas* in the Iberian peninsula, there must have been women who composed poems, adding that if these pieces were not chosen for preservation, it is because "we are much at the mercy of the selectors—the predominantly male world of chroniclers and copyists" (98). Apparently, he did not know about the French *jougleresses* discussed in Coldwell's essay (which postdates his book by two years), but if he had, presumably he would have had to posit the existence of women trouvères in northern France. For although he notes that the extant *cantigas de amigo* from Spain and Portugal were composed by male *trovadores,* he is convinced that such pieces were often performed by women (jograresas), adding that "it seems wholly unlikely that the *jograresas* did not compose as well: nowhere in Europe do we know of any hard and fast demarcation between composing and performing" (98). Indeed, Dronke believes that women of all classes composed poetry, and he laments that the "love-poetry that women of the people composed" is lost to us: "Yet it is certain that they too composed, as well as recited and sang" (105). Nevertheless, he hesitates to attribute to women poets the female voices of the Occitan debate poems (*tensos*) that alternate male and female voices or feature only female voices, because "it is hard to identify characteristic women's thoughts and feelings or to distinguish these from the rôle-playing which is inseparable from genres of poetic debate" (98). He does not mention the northern French jeux-partis featuring women's voices, but if he had known of them, he would presumably have had the same hesitation about attributing those voices to women trouvères.

For some reason, the role-playing to which Dronke alludes seems in the minds of most scholars to be the province of male poets only, as Carol Nappholz and Simon Gaunt point out. Nappholz argues that the anonymous female voice in troubadour poetry was often the product of unacknowledged women poets (the "unsung women" of her book's title); she builds on Gaunt's observation that critics display little objectivity when assessing the status of anonymous voices in male-female tensos: male voices are considered to be real, while female voices are dismissed as fictional (Nappholz 1994: 7–8; Gaunt 1988: 302). Yet if men were able to invent women's voices, it stands to reason that women were just as capable of doing so (Bruckner et al. 1995: xli). After all, the trobai-ritz, according to Bec (1979, 1995), drew on themes they found in the chansons de femme—a natural choice, as these songs evoked situations of women in love. Most critics, even those who believe that the chansons de femme were all composed by men, concede that these songs were originally inspired by more archaic forms composed by women (Jeanroy 1889: 445; Dronke 1984: 98) and that women must have played an important role in the preservation and propagation of songs in which they were the central figure.[9]

Although Bec's 1979 article on the trobairitz and the chansons de femme has attracted much attention over the past twenty years, it has been cited mostly by trobairitz scholars. Not until the 1990s did scholars begin to challenge Bec's contention that there were no women trouvères.[10] This initiative was fueled in part by the appearance of a number of studies and critical editions devoted to the trobairitz. Indeed, it was in an article entitled "Some Recent Studies of Women in the Middle Ages, Especially in Southern France" that William Paden issued his plaintive challenge: "Who will provide us with a monograph on the women *trouvères,* including a study, all the texts (edited from the manu-scripts), and the music?" (Paden 1992: 117 n. 24). In an article published that same year, Madeleine Tyssens made a major step in that direction. Noting the remarkable resurgence of interest in the women troubadours, she turned her attention to the women trouvères, whom she, too, felt had been unjustly ne-glected. Specifically, she objected to Bec's reduction of the Old French corpus of women's voices to the category of féminité textuelle, with utter disregard for the information furnished by the texts and the manuscript rubrics and indices that point occasionally to a female author (Tyssens 1992: 377). After analyzing this evidence, she came up with a corpus of twenty-five texts (thirteen *chan-sons d'amour* and *chansons de départie* and twelve jeux-partis and tensons).[11] It is curious that while protesting Bec's reduction of historical women to the ab-straction of féminité textuelle, she chose to exclude from her corpus any texts that feature a male narrator or that do not include linguistic evidence (for ex-ample, inflections) of female authorship.[12]

Another promising sign that the women trouvères are gaining recognition is that although they were not included in the twenty-volume *New Grove Dic-tionary of Music and Musicians* (Sadie 1980), the more recent *Norton/Grove Dic-tionary of Women Composers* devotes separate entries to five of them (all con-tributed by Maria Coldwell), namely, Blanche de Castille, the Duchesse de Lorraine (identified by Coldwell as Gertrude, wife of Thibaut I, Duke of Lor-raine),[13] Dame Margot and Dame Maroie (localized as *"trouvères* from Arras"), and Maroie de Dregnau de Lille (Sadie and Samuel 1994: 66, 289, 313, 315).

Our anthology, *Songs of the Women Trouvères,* which is at least a partial response to William Paden's challenge, is the latest contribution to the modest corpus of studies devoted to the women trouvères. Although this brief history has identified only a few scholars who have affirmed the existence of women poet-composers in northern France, a number of studies published in the past few decades on behalf of their counterparts in Occitania have prepared the way. Indeed, many of the arguments advanced to prove or disprove the existence of the trobairitz or to calculate their number are pertinent as well to a discussion of the women trouvères.

There are several criteria for arguing female authorship (féminité génétique) of a medieval work: (1) a woman is named within the poem as the author (signature); (2) a woman is referred to, by name or not, as the interlocutor in a debate poem with another woman or a man; (3) a woman is named in the rubric or table of contents of a manuscript; (4) a woman is the speaking subject—the lyric "I"—of the poem (féminité textuelle).[14] In the case of the women trouvères, the first criterion is inapplicable, because there are no extant songs from the period in question in which a woman explicitly claims authorship by naming herself.[15] In this anthology, all of the songs for which we have identified a female author meet the second or third criterion, or both, and all but two also meet the last criterion. This last criterion is the only one that justifies our inclusion of all the songs listed as anonymous.—*JTG*

THE FEMALE VOICE IN THE OLD FRENCH LYRIC

Although the songs known to have been composed by women in the Middle Ages are not numerous, there is a large body of lyrics that give voice to women and explore the whole spectrum of feelings and behavior said to be characteristic of them. The great majority of these pieces fall into the group known as "women's songs," which were produced all over medieval Europe. In the Middle Ages there was no precise term to distinguish these songs from other types, but since the nineteenth century they have been known generally as chansons de femme or *Frauenlieder,* and sometimes as cantigas de amigo. Remarkably varied, they include the Germanic *winileodas* attested in a tenth-century manuscript, the Romance *kharjas* appended to Arabic *muwashshaḥāt* composed between 1000 and 1150, the Latin songs of the Cambridge manuscript, the Spanish *villancicos,* and especially the Galician-Portuguese cantigas de amigo, of which more than five hundred are extant. The considerable place accorded the woman's voice in these songs could alone justify our decision to include a number of Old French chansons de femme in our collection. But our initiative is fueled as well by the desire to challenge two assumptions that have become commonplace: the first is that these songs were all composed by men; the other is that they belong in the "popular" or "popularizing" register, which is often opposed to the aristocratic register.[16] In the following discussion, centered on the chanson de femme, we shall explore these two widespread assumptions, particularly as they are applied to Old French lyric.

Féminité textuelle

The chanson de femme is not a genre, but rather "a conceptual set" (Rosenberg 1995b: 987) or "lyric type" (Bec 1977: 57) that includes several more or less clearly defined genres, such as *chanson d'ami, chanson de malmariée, aube, chanson de croisade,* and *chanson de toile*. The chanson de femme has been variously defined. Doris Earnshaw's definition (1988: 3) is no doubt the most all-inclusive: "a song with the woman's voice in all or in part of its lines." Although all critics agree that the female voice is the sine qua non, most nuance Earnshaw's definition by specifying that this voice constitutes the lyric subject ("I") of the song. Pierre Bec states that the dominant theme is love in all its emotional manifestations and most diverse situations,[17] and he specifies that the songs are mournful in tone; accordingly, he defines the chanson de femme as "a lyric monologue in a woman's voice with a sorrowful undertone."[18] Rosenberg's definition complements Bec's: "Love here tends to be forthright, sensual, shadowed by pain, and unencumbered with the artifices of *fin'amors;* its basic vehicle is the monologue." But he cautions that "these characteristics are all subject . . . to considerable modification" (Rosenberg 1995b: 987), an assertion that is amply borne out by the variety of chansons de femme represented in our collection. Ingrid Kasten, who defines Frauenlieder simply as "songs whose lyric subject is a woman,"[19] observes nonetheless that the songs present the same basic situation, that of a loving woman separated from the man she loves. The tension between the yearning for love and the pain of separation is explored in various ways: "laments about the pain of separation, assurances of love and faithfulness, expressions of yearning for the man, promises of steadfastness in the face of separation, complaints about exterior obstacles that hinder the relationship, recollections of past happiness in love, and finally the worry that the man will turn to another woman, a rival."[20]

Many scholars—indeed most—see the chanson de femme in opposition to the courtly love lyric, the *canso*. Pilar Lorenzo Gradín, at the end of her study exploring the various manifestations of the *canción de mujer* in medieval lyric, concludes that this *código,* or poetic scheme, was part of the competence of every medieval *trovador;* it is "a stylistic alternative in which are introduced particular themes and motifs always from a particular narrative focus, that of the woman, which causes this type to be differentiated from the rest of medi-eval lyric production and to present itself as the reverse of the *canso*." [21] Implicit in this opposition between the chanson de femme and the canso is the perva-sive belief that women's songs belong to the lower—noncourtly or "popular"—register. The first scholars who studied the medieval Frauenlieder believed they contained palpable traces of the *älteste Volkspoesie*, of ancient songs sponta-neously composed in a popular milieu; emanating from the soul of the people, they were "the grandiose expression of its deepest and most ardent feelings." [22] Although, as Jeanroy (1889) demonstrated, the extant medieval chansons de femme were generally composed by court poets who drew inspiration from preliterate female-voiced songs, these earlier pieces—of which no examples remain—were assigned to a register (*populaire*) at the opposite end of the spec-trum from the aristocratic or cultivated register (*savant*), which included pre-dominantly male-voiced pieces associated with the *grand chant courtois* or the *troubadouresque* canso. Consequently, the chanson de femme, in its medieval as well as its earlier forms, has remained associated with the "popular" regis-ter, despite widespread recognition that the extant songs display many traits associated with the courtly register.

Doubtless the term "popular" still retained some of its Romantic cachet in 1889, when Jeanroy proposed his celebrated theory that European popu-lar lyric had originated in preliterate French dance songs, remnants of which he believed could be found in the extant chansons de femme. In 1969, and then again in 1977, when Bec undertook his analysis of medieval French lyric, he was careful to reject the stark opposition (populaire-savant) that had taken hold. In its place, he has proposed a new terminology—*aristocratisant-popularisant*—designed to blur the distinction, as the suffix -*isant* indicates a tendency rather than a clear-cut category. Yet Bec's discussion of the various genres covered by the chanson de femme uncovers a remarkably high inci-dence of what he calls *interférences registrales* (borrowing between registers) (Bec 1977: 57-119). His analysis shows, in fact, that the songs preserved in thirteenth-century manuscripts are so replete with elements borrowed from the courtly register that it is really only with reference to their *origins* that these songs can be considered "popular" or even "popularizing." Indeed, in order to justify assigning the chanson de femme to the noncourtly register, Bec is obliged to devote an inordinate amount of space to the "prehistory" of each of the different genres related to that lyric type, even though he specifically states that his analysis is grounded in the formal characteristics of the songs rather than in their origins. (The subtitle of his 1977 study promises a "contribution to a typology of medieval poetic genres.")

Medieval poets had no terminology to discriminate between learned (aristo-cratisant or troubadouresque) and unlearned (popularisant or *jongleuresque*) registers, although they were aware of levels of style, a notion they inherited from Antiquity. Classical and medieval theoreticians distinguished three levels, high (*grandiloquus*), middle (*mediocris*), and low (*humilis*), differentiated on the basis of language, poetic voice, and the social status of the speaker, subject, and audience.[23] Medieval poets were familiar with these recommendations, but they had no compunction about mixing various levels of style within a single composition, whether they were composing epic, romance, or lyric; in-deed, they seemed to delight in doing so. Consequently, such notions as register and genre are relatively fluid and likely to lead to erroneous perceptions when rigidly defined and applied. Nevertheless, modern scholars often find such dis-tinctions useful tools for analysis.[24] Roger Dragonetti (1960) was the first to identify the courtly love lyric (which he called the grand chant courtois) with the "high" style (15–20), and both literary critics and musicologists have found it helpful to differentiate between at least two levels of style or registers, such as those defined by Bec. Christopher Page (1986), for example, distinguishes between the "High Style," associated with troubadouresque qualities, and the "Low Style," a jongleuresque category that includes more popular forms such as dance songs, *pastourelles,* and songs with refrains; according to Page, each of these "styles" implies whether or not musical instruments were used as ac-companiment to the singers. (See the discussion and critique of this theory in "Introduction to the Music," later in this introduction.)

However useful the registral dichotomy may appear to be, when it is applied to medieval lyric, and specifically to the chanson de femme, it often seems to constitute more of a hindrance than a help. Bec, for example, claims support for his registral distinction by pointing out that manuscript *I,* one of the few Old French *chansonniers* that classify their contents by genre, sets the trouba-douresque *grans chans* (cansos) apart from the other genres: *estampies,* pastou-relles, *ballettes, sottes chansons,* most of which belong to the *registre popularisant* (Bec 1977: 34 n. 39). However, the third section of the manuscript comprises nearly forty jeux-partis, and this section—of eminently courtly pieces—fol-lows the estampies, not the cansos, where one might expect to find it if the scribe-compiler of the manuscript had thought the registral distinction was meaningful. Paul Zumthor (1972) clearly felt uneasy about certain distinctions invented by modern critics. Although he believed that the courtly register, which he called the *requête d'amour,* could be defined on the basis of the char-acteristics specific to the grand chant courtois or canso, he admitted that his other register (the *bonne vie*) was by the thirteenth century composed of so many heterogeneous elements that it had lost its expressive coherence (251, 254). He articulated even more clearly his discomfort with a scheme based on register alone by proposing to classify the extant lyrics in a way that cut across registral boundaries: thus, he distinguished three groups of texts according to whether they present (1) chanson form with the register of the bonne vie; (2) a form other than that of the chanson with the register of the requête d'amour; and (3) chanson form with indeterminate nonregistral content (for example, *chansons bachiques*) (255–56).

As every anthology of medieval women's songs makes clear, the distinction between the two registers is difficult to defend on the basis of the extant chansons de femme of the high Middle Ages. Indeed, although Ulrich Mölk calls for a redefinition of the Frauenlied based exclusively on formal criteria, he contradicts his own definition ("a love song in the popular register in which the woman's perspective is realized as a monologue, dialogue, or reported speech")[25] by including in his 1989 anthology songs that do not correspond to any but the broadest concept of the Frauenlied (that is, féminité textuelle). In fact, Bec reproaches him for including certain pieces composed in the "elevated" style, such as trobairitz lyrics and even sonnets (Bec 1995: 46 n. 3). Similarly, Kasten's anthology (1990) embraces songs clearly composed in the courtly mode, including all four of the Comtessa de Dia's cansos. She explains that this choice is dictated by the desire to trace and document the impact of the Frauenlied on the German love lyric and the main stages of its development, especially its central place in the songs of the first *Minnesänger* (ca. 1160) and its transformation under the influence of the Occitan troubadours (23–25). Although the concept of the indifferent and aloof Lady found in troubadour lyric clashed with the Frauenlied concept of a loving woman filled with yearning for a man, the Minnesänger drew on both images in composing their lyrics (18). Thus, Kasten states that the clear-cut registral distinction on which Bec insists in his analysis of the Old French chanson de femme does not really apply to German lyric, for even the earliest Frauenlieder allude in their stylistic conception to the knightly-courtly world and are integral components of the courtly lyric throughout the Middle Ages (21). As we have just seen, Bec's registral scheme is ill-suited to a discussion even of the chansons de femme preserved in Old French.

Because the chanson de femme focuses generally on love and most often involves yearning for a love past, present, or future, it echoes many of the themes characteristic of the register of the requête d'amour. Indeed, most scholars accept Bec's theory that when the trobairitz adapted the troubadour cansos to the female voice, they drew on themes they found in the chansons de femme (Bec

1979; Blakeslee 1989; Bruckner et al. 1995). Antoine Tavera (1978: 142) has re-marked that many of the trobairitz lyrics echo the troubadour theme of the *mal aimé,* and Kasten (1990: 21), in speculating on the function that the Frauenlied fulfilled in the range of lyric genres, observes that it poeticizes a basic human experience in love, that of separation. Moreover, as Cynthia Bagley (1966) has demonstrated, very little distinguishes the female-voiced cantiga de amigo from its male-voiced counterpart, the *cantiga de amor.* Given these similarities between the canso and the chanson de femme in all the medieval languages of Western Europe, one might well wonder if the registral distinction is not frankly meaningless with respect to theme. Rather than assigning the canso to the registre aristocratisant and relegating the chanson de femme to the registre popularisant, as Bec does, it might be more logical to envisage a register of the lyric "I" encompassing love lyrics with both male and female voices and sub-divide it by genre such as the canso, chanson de malmariée, aube, and so on. If this idea seems counterintuitive, it may be because critics are so used to de-fining fin'amors from the male perspective that the female viewpoint tends to be seen as derivative and somehow inferior. But if it is true, as the evidence suggests, that the chanson de femme existed before and simultaneously with the troubadour canso, would it not be fairer to consider the woman's voice as an equal and active partner in the creation as well as the development of the game of courtly love? Perhaps then we could redefine fin'amors according to whether the lyric "I" is masculine or feminine.

Féminité génétique

Whereas all the current definitions of the chanson de femme specify féminité textuelle, they steer clear of postulating female authorship (féminité géné-tique). As Kasten (1990: 13) points out, "women's songs" are not necessarily songs by women, adding that, on the contrary, most were composed by men, who in the Middle Ages were the major transmitters of culture.[26] But there is no reason to conclude that women were excluded from composing and per-forming either in the courts or in the marketplace. Kasten cites the case of the trobairitz who clearly performed in a court setting (13),[27] and she mentions that there were also women—the *spilwîp*—among the itinerant musicians who performed in more public places (16). It is likely that such women, like the jou-gleresses discussed by Coldwell and the jograresas mentioned by Dronke, com-posed as well as performed. If most scholars firmly believe that all the chansons de femme preserved in Old French were composed by men, it may be owing in part to the existence of the large corpus of Galician-Portuguese cantigas de amigo, which contains a number of songs attributed to the same male court poets who composed the cantigas de amor. However, the situation is quite different for northern France, where the overwhelming majority of chansons de femme are anonymous, and this very anonymity might well indicate female authorship (see the section "Manuscripts and Transmission," later in this introduction). But because all the Old French chansons de femme that are ascribed are attributed to male trouvères,[28] many critics assume (with Bec) that "anonymous" was a man, and some have speculated as to why male trouvères might have wanted to appropriate female discourse. For example, Kasten (1990: 22) has suggested that male poets who composed Frauenlieder may have been projecting their own wish or angst onto the female figure and thus using the songs as a means of self-portrayal. More than a century ago, Jeanroy (1889: 96-100) speculated that they sought a kind of poetic justice, compensating for the suffering inflicted by a cruel or indifferent mistress by portraying a woman who had to beg mercy from an insensitive lover. More recently, Michel Zink (1996: 142-43) has postulated that since adherence to fin'amors was an experience of frustrated desire, male poets were pleased to create chansons de femme in which guileless women responded eagerly and passionately to sexual desire. The title of Zink's book, *Le moyen âge et ses chansons, ou Un passé en trompe-l'œil,* encapsulates his theory that the archaic quality of the extant Old French chansons de femme is simply an illusion created by twelfth- and thirteenth-century male trouvères who exploited this "simpler" register to construct a different kind of female persona from the indifferent, haughty "Dame" of the grand chant courtois. According to this theory, the chansons de femme that have been preserved were invented as a contrast to the courtly lyric, and the "popularizing" tone exists only by opposition to the "poésie savante" (146-47).

In spite of the prevailing view that all the extant Old French chansons de femme were composed by men, it is generally assumed that their distant origins are to be found in preliterate songs composed by women. Jeanroy traced the roots of the noncourtly genres back to dance songs, no doubt composed during the *maieroles* or *fêtes de mai,* as described in the *Carmina Burana,* the *Roman de la Rose ou de Guillaume de Dole,* and *Flamenca.* Because in the Middle Ages dance was primarily a feminine pastime, Jeanroy theorized that young women composed songs for their own use, giving voice to their own feelings.[29] He claimed further that the earliest songs were essentially chansons de malmariée. Indeed, the maieroles, whose roots could be found in pagan celebrations of Venus' domination, often featured a May Queen who led the dance with her female companions, excluding the *gelos*—the husband and all those who did not love (Paris 1892: 416). This festival encouraged exuberant role reversal, giving women the initiative in love, which would account for the passionate, sensual, outspoken, often obscene nature of the discourse.[30]

The theory positing the existence of a preliterate traditional poetry received new impetus in 1948, following Samuel Stern's spectacular "discovery"—or, more precisely, his deciphering and identification—of the Mozarabic kharjas, the earliest surviving secular lyrics in a Romance vernacular. These texts, which appear as the refrain or final strophe of the muwashshaha, give voice to women expressing frank and passionate yearnings. Although they offer a stunning contrast to the refined language and imagery of the preceding (male-voiced) strophes, there is internal unity in that both parts of the poem are an expression of unrequited love; together they embody the different poetic traditions that had come together in al-Andalus (see Menocal 1987: 83-113). But the kharjas are important not simply for what they reveal about the poetic traditions of Moslem Spain, for they offer tangible proof that the chanson de femme as it appears in thirteenth-century chansonniers has deep roots in the past. They attest to the existence of an oral vernacular lyric tradition south of the Pyrenees and perhaps in all of Romania as early as 1000 at least—a tradition vigorous enough to influence the poetry of the troubadours and subsequently to compete with it. Significantly, the earliest kharjas predate the first compositions of Guilhem IX, and they develop themes that were unknown to classical Arab poetry and are precisely those found in the extant chansons de femme (Le Gentil 1963: 216-17). It is also worth noting that although the earliest muwashshahāt preserving the kharjas were composed around 1000, the muwashshaha as a literary genre was introduced in Moslem Spain around 900, and there is no reason to believe that the Romance songs presumably known by the earliest practitioners of the muwashshaha were a novelty at that time (Dronke 1996: 89-90).

Indeed, there is documented evidence that women were composing even earlier in the Middle Ages: indecent women's songs were denounced by churchmen already in the fourth century. They were condemned by the Council of Châlons in 650 (Zink 1996: 143), and a capitulary of Charlemagne dating from 789 prevails on abbesses to prevent nuns in their charge from composing or sending winileodas from the convent (Dronke 1996: 91). Now, if women were capable of composing—and indeed *were* composing—chansons de femme from the earliest times, why should they have suddenly lost that ability and initiative in the twelfth and thirteenth centuries? Dronke believes that they were indeed composing at that time, even though in his opinion no songs have survived in Old French. He notes that themes found in the kharjas "can already be found in Egyptian collections of love-songs from the late second millennium B.C., and in Chinese songs contemporary with Sappho" (90) and concludes: "So too, many poets and poetesses of medieval Europe turned to the ancient and universal themes of women's love-songs and made new poetry out of them in a fascinating variety of ways" (91).

Because there is evidence that European women were indeed composing songs in the high Middle Ages as in earlier periods, by what logic does it follow that none of the extant anonymous chansons de femme were composed by women? We will doubtless never know who composed these songs, which is why many scholars, like Lorenzo Gradín, prefer to avoid the question altogether by concerning themselves only with formal aspects of the songs. Mölk, too, professes little interest (even where the trobairitz are concerned) in the question of attribution, which he sees as a matter of social history; he opts instead to concentrate on how the feminine "I" is treated in lyric texts (Mölk 1990: 143). But if we are content to reduce the many female voices in the chansons de femme to the status of féminité textuelle alone, we run the risk of denying women a place in the pantheon of medieval lyric poets. It is a risk of no minor consequence. —*JTG*

WOMEN AS POETS AND MUSICIANS

There is ample evidence in literature, iconography, and historical documents that women were active poets and musicians in the twelfth and thirteenth centuries. To fully appreciate this evidence, it is important to remember that, for most songs, poet and composer were the same person and, as an important corollary, that in the essentially oral culture of the Middle Ages the line between composition and performance was fluid. The poet-composer created her song for an immediate hearing by a live audience—she did not simply hand her song over to a "professional" performer, but she herself sang it, perhaps even while she was composing. In many literary works, the word *chanter* seems to mean either singing or composing, depending on the context. Women as well as men are portrayed composing and performing both poetry and music, as in Thomas de Bretagne's *Roman de Tristan* (ca. 1170-75), where Yseut composes and performs the *Lai de Guiron:*

> En sa chambre se set un jor
> E fait un lai pitus d'amur:
>
> . . . .
>
> La reïne chante dulcement,
> La voiz acorde a l'estrument.

Les mainz sunt beles, li lais buons
Dulce la voiz, bas li tons. (Wind 1960: Sneyd 1, ll. 781–94)

In her room she sits one day
And composes a sad *lai* of love:

. . . .

The queen sings sweetly,
She accords her voice with the instrument.
Her hands are lovely, the lai is fine,
Her voice sweet, the tone low.

In the compositions anthologized in this volume, references to women singing are many, and in them the line between singing and composing is vague.[31] In her death-lament (song no. 18), the Duchesse de Lorraine explicitly refers to her poetic activity, and although she does not give us her name, she clearly is aware of her reputation:

Par maintes fois avrai esteit requise
C'ains ne chantai ansi con je soloie. (ll. 1–2)

Many a time I have been asked
Why I no longer sing as I used to.

The act of authorship embraced many possibilities: deliberate invention of original poetry and musical designs; outright borrowing of forms, themes, motifs, figurative images, and melodies from other authors (during the Middle Ages, such borrowing was seen as an honorable exercise in homage); and re-creation and adaptation of pre-existing poetic and musical materials. A song could be improvised on the spot or worked out over a period of time. Several of these processes can be seen at work in the *Roman de Tristan en prose* (ca. 1230–40), a veritable mine of information regarding musical practices in the thirteenth century. Several of Arthur's knights can compose and perform lais, but the best musician by far is Tristan, whose lais are performed by a number of anonymous young women. Yseut herself composes a lai on two different occasions. When she hears the false news of her lover's death, she tells Brangien to bring her Tristan's harp:

"Il a fait por moi lai novel de ses max et de ses dolors, et je aprés por l'amor de li voudrai un lai trover d'autel guise et d'autel semblance, se je onques puis, com il fist le Lai Mortal. Ausi ai je bien achoison de trover com il ot, et por ce vel je trover un lai d'autretel maniere com fu celi lai qu'il fist."

Brangien li aporte la harpe sanz delai. Et sachiez que la roïne en savoit assez, car ele l'avoit apris de mesire Tristan en ce termine qu'il demoroient ou Morroiz. La roïne reçoit la harpe et la vet sonant et atrampant au mieuz qu'ele set, et vait trovant chant por son lai. Le dit trove ele en brief termine, mes li chanz la vait plus grevant assez que li diz. (Curtis 1985, 3: 896)

"He composed for me a new lai from his grief and sorrow, and now I, for love of him, would like to compose one for him in the same form and manner, if only I can, as he made his Mortal Lai. For I have good reason to compose, just as he did, and so I wish to compose a lai with the same form as the lai he composed."

Brangien brings her the harp straightaway. And know that the queen was quite skilled, because she had learned to play the harp from Tristan when they lived in the Morrois. The queen takes the harp and concentrates on tuning it as best she can and begins composing a melody for her lai. She composes the lyrics in a short time, but the melody is harder to compose than the words.[32]

Yseut takes great pains to compose her lai, then, richly attired, she goes out to the garden to sing it, intending afterward to kill herself with Tristan's sword. But King Mark, who has witnessed this scene, stops her. Yseut composes a second piece after Kahedin, desperately in love with her, sends a harpist to her to sing the lai that he has composed in which he begs Amour to intercede in his favor. She then composes a short lai with the same versification and to the same music ("vers d'autretel maniere et d'autretel cant") for the harpist to take back to Kahedin as her response (Ménard 1987, 1: 233).

The differences between monophony and polyphony color our understanding of the ways and venues in which women worked and were educated and the various strata they occupied in medieval society. With the exception of *chansons pieuses,* monophonic song was a secular repertoire, created for entertainment. A chanson d'amour was performed by a single singer, a jeu-parti presumably by two, while dancing songs, such as rondeaux and ballettes, and other refrain songs, such as *rotrouenges,* probably were sung by a community of singers. Late thirteenth-century Parisian academic Johannes de Grocheio, the only music theorist of the time to give serious attention to secular music, places different kinds of vernacular song in various environments: *chansons de geste* among "the elderly, working citizens, and those of middle station when they rest from their usual toil";[33] "crowned songs," or chansons which have received a prize from "masters and students," to be sung by "kings and nobles";[34]

rondeaux sung "by girls and by young men as an adornment to holiday cele-brations and to great banquets";[35] estampies and dancing songs by "young men and girls" who because of the "difficulty" of such songs are led "away from depraved thoughts" and whose erotic passions are controlled[36] (Page 1993b: 23-27).

Grocheio's descriptions are amplified by evidence in literature, sermons, and other religious and historical documents. Striking in so many of these texts are indications that chansons de geste, courtly love songs, dancing songs, in-deed songs from all genres, evidently were sung among and by members of every class of society—the nobility, teachers and students, bourgeois, and peas-ants—and by males and females, young and old (see Page 1989). Long nar-rative works, as Grocheio says, were sung by minstrels in rural lanes and on city bridges, to audiences moved to tears by tales of the exploits of heroes and saints (Page 1989: 176-78). Such a song is found within the story of *Aucassin et Nicolette* (from the end of the twelfth or the beginning of the thirteenth cen-tury), a charming *chantefable* composed of passages in verse and prose intended to be sung and recited alternately. It ends with a performance by the heroine, who has avoided marrying the man her parents had chosen for her by fleeing to the country of her long-lost love. There, disguised as a minstrel, she takes out her fiddle and recounts in song to her lover the highlights of their love story. Whether she presents herself as a male or female minstrel is unclear; it is also immaterial: the story suggests not only that women were capable of com-posing, but also—and more important—that for a woman to compose a song was perfectly natural and commonplace.

Courtly love songs were the province not only of princes or of "masters and students" but also of young retainers of a household, men and women who might be called upon to sing a song composed by a trouvère to enter-tain members of the noble family or their visitors (Page 1989: 97-104). Songs for circle dances, the *rondets de carole,* in particular, as well as other seemingly rustic songs such as pastourelles, are found among both sexes and all levels of the populace, gliding easily from rural fields to the public square to the court, and playing a part even in civic celebrations that involved everyone from the king to the most illiterate farmer (Page 1989: 86-92, 116-18). In the Old French pastourelle, a lyric genre that stages the chance encounter of a poet-narrator (typically a knight) and a shepherdess in a remote bucolic setting and relates his attempted seduction of the young girl, the knight sometimes espies the *pastoure* alternately singing and playing the flute or pipes, as in this example ascribed to Jocelin de Bruges:

L'autrier pastoure seoit
Lonc un buisson,
Aignials gardoit, si avoit
Flaiol pipe et baston:
En haut dist et si notoit
Un novel son,
En sa pipe refraignoit
Le ver d'une chanson. (RS 1848=1854, ll. 1-8, Bartsch 1870: 316)

The other day a shepherdess was sitting
Near a bush,
Watching her lambs; she had
A flageolet and a stick:
She was singing out loud and was playing
A new song,
With her flute she was repeating
The verse of a song.

In Jean Renart's *Roman de la rose ou de Guillaume de Dole*, the earliest narrative with lyric insertions (variously dated from ca. 1200 to ca. 1228), ladies and knights sing either alone or in groups in a variety of circumstances. In their chamber, Liënor and her mother sing chansons de toile as they embroider and while they entertain the emperor's envoy (ll. 1159-1216). With the *jongleur* Jouglet accompanying on his fiddle, the innkeeper's daughter sings a rondeau in the masculine voice (B. rond. 10, designated a *chançonete novele*, ll. 1846-51). Jouglet's sister performs a *laisse* from an epic about Gerbert de Metz:

Cel jor fesoit chanter la suer
A un jougleor mout apert
Qui chante cest vers de Gerbert. (Lecoy 1979: ll. 1332-34)

That day he had the sister
Of a very gifted jongleur
Sing these lines about Gerbert.

In Gerbert de Montreuil's *Roman de la Violette* (ca. 1227-30), modeled on Jean Renart's *Roman de la Rose ou de Guillaume de Dole*, Euriaut sings a stanza from a courtly Occitan canso ("un vier d'un boin son poitevin") by the troubadour Bernart de Ventadorn (ll. 319-31) [37] and the first stanza of a chanson de malmariée ascribed to Moniot d'Arras (ll. 441-49).[38] Note that in this instance a woman performs songs that are in the masculine voice.

The weight of this type of evidence—literary, historical, theoretical—casts doubt on the validity of any registral distinctions, whatever their content, in the function or use of vernacular songs, whether the singer or composer was male or female.

The creation of a monophonic song of whatever type required certain kinds of poetic and musical skills, most of them probably learned informally, whether within a domestic situation, from a seasoned trouvère, or in a community. There was no "conservatory" to which trouvères were sent, although they had to learn such poetic techniques as versification, and such musical ones as how to sing and to fit a melody to a text. Judging from the many intertextual allusions in the courtly repertoires, most trouvères were familiar with a wide variety of literary works—other lyric songs, but also Latin and vernacular texts.

Girls in wealthy families learned to read (the vernacular as well as Latin) alongside their brothers as part of their preparation for a leisured aristocratic life (Ferrante 1980; Page 1989: 120-25), as depicted in *Floire et Blancheflor* (ca. 1150-60):

> Et quant a l'escole venoient,
> Leur tables d'ivoire prenoient.
> Adont lor veïssiez escrire
> Letres et vers d'amours en cire.
>
> . . . .
>
> Letres et saluz font d'amours,
> Du chant des oisiaus et des flours.
>
> . . . .
>
> En seul cinc anz et quinze dis
> Furent andeus si bien apris
> Que bien sorent parler latin
> Et bien escrivre en parchemin. (Pelan 1956: ll. 253-66)

> And when they went to school
> They took their ivory tablets.
> Then you should have seen them write
> Love letters and songs in wax.
>
> . . . .
>
> They composed letters and epistles on love,
> Birdsong, and flowers.
>
> . . . .

In only five years and fifteen days
They both became so well educated
That they could speak Latin well
And write ably on parchment.

Sometimes this education included singing and playing fiddle or harp or
another stringed instrument (Coldwell 1986: 41; Page 1989: 102-6). Thirteenth-
century visual representations of women singing and holding instruments are
not uncommon, especially manuscript illuminations, some of which depict
female harp, fiddle, rebec, and gittern players.[39] An anonymous vernacular re-
daction of Ovid's *Ars amatoria, La clef d'amors* (ca. 1280) enjoins girls that they
should learn many skills, including singing and playing instruments:

Chanter est noble chose et bele,
Especiäument a pucele.
. . . .
Le seri chant de le sereine
Tret a soy les nes et ameine:
Aussi poueiz vous enchanter
Les amourous par bien chanter.
. . . .
Chantez a vois melodiose,
Simple, plesant et graciose.
. . . .
Metre doiz ton entencion
A sonner le psalterion
Ou timbre ou guiterne ou citole;
C'est cen qui du tout nous afole.
Semblablement te doiz adieure
A rommans fetichement lieure. (Doutrepont 1890: ll. 2589-610)

Singing is a fair and noble thing,
Especially for a young woman.
. . . .
The harmonious song of the siren
Lures ships and leads them to her;
In the same way you can enchant
Lovers by singing artfully.
. . . .

Sing in a melodious voice,
Clear, pleasing, and charming.
. . . .
You should apply yourself
To playing the psaltery,
The timbrel, gittern, or citole.
It is what drives us totally mad.
Similarly you should dedicate yourself
To reading romances properly.

The part-time composing endeavors of such busy political personages as Blanche de Castille and Richard Cœur-de-Lion and other members of the aristocracy, who did not depend upon it for their livelihood, contrasts with the full-time efforts of professional poet-musicians, who were paid in some fashion—by money, goods, food or housing, commissions, or a prize—for their talents. In Jean de le Mote's *Le parfait du paon*, redacted in 1340, men and women alike compose and perform *ballades* for a poetic competition (laisses 30-52). Indeed, first prize is awarded to a woman (Clarete, one of Melidus' four daughters) whose poetic and musical skills surpass those of the mighty Alexander—who ranks second. Before presenting his or her ballade, each participant is asked to affirm that it is an original composition:

". . . vous jurés sans boidie
Par la foy que devés Venus et Dyanie
Que ceste balade est par vous faite et furnie
Et qu'ailleurs autres fois ne fu dicte n'oÿe?" (Carey 1972: ll. 1046-49)

". . . do you swear without deceit
By the faith you owe Venus and Diana
That you have composed and completed this ballade
And that it has never been recited or heard elsewhere?"

At the end of her turn, Clarete further declares that she composed both the text and the melody of her ballade:

"Seigneur, dist la pucelle, je m'en sui acquitee
Et vez ci ma balade bien escripte et notee." (Carey 1972: ll. 1370-71)

"Lord," said the young girl, "I have acquitted my task,
And here is my ballade carefully written and notated."

References to the writing ability of women are relatively scarce; references to their ability to write down musical notes are even more exceptional. Clarete's claim that she has set down both the words and the music of her ballade is all the more remarkable, even for this relatively late text.

The activities of several female musicians working in Paris are attested in thirteenth-century tax records of the city, while thirteenth- and fourteenth-century household accounts record payments to women performers (Coldwell 1986: 46). The *Statuts de la corporation des ménestrels de Paris,* which dates from 1321, lists eight professional jougleresses and one female vocalist among the guild's thirty-seven members, and the women evidently were given the same privileges as men. Such a professional minstrel appears in Jean Renart's *Roman de la rose ou de Guillaume de Dole* to entertain the emperor Conrad:

> L'en i chantë et sons et lais,
> Li menestrel de mainte terre
> Qui erent venu por aquerre.
> De Troies la Bele Doete
> I chantoit ceste chançonete. (Lecoy 1979: ll. 4563–67)

> Minstrels from many lands
> Who had come to earn money
> Were singing songs and lais.
> Fair Doete of Troyes
> Was singing this little song.

The *chançonete* Bele Doete performs, "Quant revient la sesons" (RS 1914b), is the first stanza of a pastourelle in the masculine voice.

The lively city of Arras rivaled Paris as a center of the composition of trouvère song. Whereas none of the manuscripts that transmit the songs of the trouvères can be shown to have been produced in Paris, a significant number of them are from Arras or the region around it, including *M* and *T,* which notably contain French motets as well as monophony (see Everist 1989: 175–87). The literary life of Arras centered around two organizations, the *puy* (or literary academy) and the confraternity of professional jongleurs and bourgeois that was one of many guilds (including those of bakers, butchers, tapestry makers, and shoemakers) in existence in the city since the early twelfth century (Berger 1981: 83–88). From at least as early as 1224 the guild convened three times a year. The *Puy d'Arras* held yearly competitions beginning around 1245; bourgeois, clerics, knights, and professional musician-poets (both local and from outside the city) presented their chansons and jeux-partis to the assembled juries, which "crowned" the best works. A surviving necrology of the confraternity lists many women, and several women were associated with the puy, including the Dame de Fouencamps, wife of an important landowner in the area; Demisele Oede, wife of a wealthy financier known to have composed jeux-partis; and the Dame de Gosnay (see the section "Introduction to the Authors: What We Know, What We Can Surmise," later in this introduction).

Arras occupied a pivotal point between monophony and polyphony. Its most famous trouvère, Adam de la Halle (d. ca. 1288), composed in both idioms, and two of the most important repositories of trouvère songs, Artesian manuscripts *M* and *T*, contain both French monophony and motets. In contrast to the origins of monophony, those of the motet were sacred rather than secular; the earliest motets, which date from the early decades of the thirteenth century, were created when upper parts of *organum* were given Latin tropes on plainchant (see the discussion of the motet's evolution in the section "Introduction to the Music," later in this introduction). These first motets probably were destined for and sung during the celebration of liturgical rites by secular canons (the uncloistered clerics; see Page 1989: 144–48), first in the cathedral of Notre Dame in Paris but within a few years beyond the Île de France in England, Scotland, Italy, and the Iberian peninsula (Wright 1989: 244, 268). The composition and performance of motets required some improvisatory skills, as did monophony, but a knowledge of counterpoint and harmony was also necessary. The opportunity to learn these rules and experiment with new compositions, at least in the formative years, was limited to a few churches and monasteries with large enough clerical and musical institutions to provide apprenticeship situations.

Cloistered nuns received some formal education, and several women's monasteries produced manuscripts, including liturgical books. They were taught to sing plainchant so that they could pursue the *opus Dei*, the celebration of the daily Office and the Mass, and although their command of Latin in general was not as good as that of men (Yardley 1986: 17), nuns at some convents did sing sacred polyphony. Several manuscripts of the twelfth, thirteenth, and fourteenth centuries written at nunneries contain two- and occasional three-voice settings of various liturgical items, including parts of the Mass Ordinary, *conductus*, sequences, hymns, antiphons, and a few motets (Yardley 1986: 26–27). Most of these institutions were in regions east, northeast, and south of the Île de France, including Alsace, the Netherlands, Germany, Switzerland, and Italy, but the wealthy double monastery of Fontevrault, just south of the Loire, in the fourteenth century produced a manuscript that contains three two-voice liturgical works. Proof that nuns sang not only polyphony but specifically motets can be found in a 1261 dictum of Archbishop Rigaud of Rouen, which enjoined the nuns of Montivilliers *not* to sing such "scurrilous songs" (Yardley 1986: 24).[40]

Only a scant few motets are found in manuscripts produced in convents, with one extravagant exception. Thanks to the pilgrimage route to Santiago de Compostela, Parisian polyphony, including motets, found its way to the Iberian peninsula, where it was cultivated at the large Cistercian convent at Las Huelgas de Burgos. This monastery, founded in 1187 by King Alfonso VIII of Castile to serve as a burial place for the royal family, represented a significant challenge to the authorities of the Cistercians, who up to that time had not countenanced the acceptance of women into the order. Las Huelgas, because of the royal patronage, soon aggressively assumed authority in ecclesiastical, civil, and social affairs throughout Castile and León, and it became a model for the foundation of other Cistercian convents all over Europe.[41] A manuscript of liturgical music sung there, including plainchant, conductus, Latin motets, and other polyphonic sacred works, was copied around the beginning of the fourteenth century; it remains housed at the monastery to this day. Much of the music it contains is found in other manuscripts as well, but some of it was composed locally, including one piece in honor of abbess Maria González. A community of priests in the monastery celebrated Mass and probably sang much of the liturgical music. But there is evidence that at least a small group of virtuoso nuns—mirroring the soloistic practices in Paris and elsewhere (see Wright 1989: 338-44)—was trained to sing polyphony as well as plainchant (Yardley 1986: 24-25).

University training accelerated during the thirteenth century, supplanting that of the cloister, and this brought with it a decline in the education of women, who were excluded from the universities. The rules of counterpoint became increasingly sophisticated and eventually were written down by university-educated theorists during the second half of the thirteenth century. The exposure of women to polyphony and to the rapidly changing genre of the motet might have remained limited but for a startling development, the emergence of the motet from its liturgical environment into the wider world. Poets began using Latin motets as a forum for treating nonliturgical, even nonsacred, themes—political, satirical, and topical—and presumably these motets were sung outside of religious circles (Wright 1989: 32-33; see also Page 1989: 136-37).

Even more striking, French texts began appearing in motets. Although the skills that were required to compose French motets were similar to those found at first within the clerical establishment, their texts and ultimately the music itself came from outside the cloister and the cathedral. Such pieces represent a consequential departure from the Latin works. They formed a bridge between the sacred and secular worlds, introducing the techniques of polyphony into the latter and a decidedly secular flavor into the former, with abundant interférences registrales across all boundaries—courtly and popular as well as sacred and secular. The texts of French motets drew from the conventions of popular rondeaux and refrains and of courtly chansons (Page 1989: 118-19; see also Aubrey 1997: 6-31). This conflation of registers might seem jarring to a modern ear, but distinctions between the sacred and the secular and among genres were not as sharply drawn then as they are today.

Whereas the sacred Latin motet was limited to ecclesiastics in its creation and performance, the French motet was open to anyone with enough learning to participate—male or female. Although the church remained the most important educational environment for music composition for several centuries to come, the growing repertoire of secular polyphonic music was directed not to an audience congregated before a high altar during public religious ceremonies but to a learned audience of clergy and other educated people gathered in a more intimate setting. Johannes de Grocheio described the proper venue: "This kind of music should not be set before a lay public because they are not alert to its refinement nor are they delighted by hearing it, but before the clergy [perhaps also those who are 'lettered'] and those who look for the refinements of skills. It is the custom for the motet to be sung in their holiday festivities to adorn them." [42]

Women probably were members of such an audience and evidently sometimes were among the singers—and probably composers—as well. A thirteenth-century monk of Saint Denis, Guillaume de Nangis, in his chronicle of the life of Philippe III provides a glimpse of the free mixture of songs and motets during a public gathering of 1275:

Les bourgois de Paris firent feste grant et solempnel, et encourtinerent la ville de riches dras de diverses couleurs et de pailes et de cendaulx. Lez dames et les pucelles sesbaudissoient en chantant diverses chançons et diverses motès. (Cited in Page 1989: 228 n. 41)

The bourgeois of Paris held a magnificent and solemn celebration, and they draped the city in rich cloth of various colors, and in embroidered silk tapestries and taffetas. Ladies and maidens entertained themselves by singing a variety of songs and motets.

This type of evidence, of which the preceding is only a small sampling, renders several points indisputable. First, although women had access to different kinds of training and opportunities than did men, they nonetheless were active as singers, composers, and poets during the twelfth, thirteenth, and fourteenth centuries. Second, women and men at all levels of society composed and performed songs in a variety of genres and forms—including courtly chansons, refrain songs (such as rondeaux and ballades), lais, epic works, and French motets—and in a variety of circumstances, both for public and private enjoyment; registral distinctions are virtually meaningless in actual practice. Third, women sang songs in which the lyric subject could be either masculine or feminine, that is, the gender of the singer did not always correspond to that of the song's lyric subject. The cumulative testimony of all these historical, literary, civic, and ecclesiastical documents to the participation of women in the creation and performance of vernacular song cannot be dismissed lightly.—*EA, ED-Q, and JTG*

INTRODUCTION TO THE AUTHORS:
WHAT WE KNOW, WHAT WE CAN SURMISE

We know of eight named women trouvères: Blanche de Castille, the Dame de Gosnai (L 53), the Dame de la Chaucie (L 54), the Duchesse de Lorraine (L 57), Lorete (L 172), Dame Margot (L 176), Maroie de Diergnau (L 177 and 178), and Sainte des Prez (L 246). The number of names rises to fourteen if we count those women cited as judges in jeux-partis ascribed to either male or female poets (the Comtesse de Linaige, Mahaut de Commercy, Béatrice de Courtrai, the Dame de Fouencamp, the Dame de Danemoi, and Demisele Oede). Compared with the 256 named male trouvères, eight *troveresses*—to adopt a term found in Godefroy's *Dictionnaire* (1880-1902, 8: 94)[43]—is indeed a small count, but the existence of these women becomes significant when it is viewed against the dearth of women poets in medieval Europe.

Three of the named women poets are known only by their given names. The names of the others provide us with information regarding their place of origin.

Dame de Gosnai

Gillebert de Berneville debates with a certain Dame de Gosnai in "Dame de Gosnai, gardez" (song no. 4). Berger (1981: 113) lists her among the members of the Puy d'Arras. Gosnay is in the Pas-de-Calais, *arrondissement* of Béthune, *canton* of Houdain (Petersen Dyggve 1934: 119-20). Nothing further is known regarding this woman.

Lorete, Sainte des Prez, and Dame de la Chaucie

A certain Lorete and her "sister" are partners in "Lorete, suer, par amor" (song no. 2). Sainte des Prez opposes a certain Dame de la Chaucie in "Que ferai je, dame de la Chaucie" (song no. 3). Nothing is known regarding any of these women, except that Sainte des Prez bears the same surname as Gui des Prés who signed a courtly song (RS 2017). According to Petersen Dyggve (1934: 67, 229), Des Prez may designate Les Prés, and La Chaucie is probably La Chaussée, both in the arrondissement of Meaux, canton and *commune* of La Ferté-sous-Jouarre, east of Paris.

Maroie de Diergnau or Dame Maroie

We are slightly better informed regarding Maroie de Diergnau (or Dame Maroie) and Dame Margot. Two compositions can be attributed to Maroie de Diergnau with relative certainty. She debates against Dame Margot in "Je vous pri, dame Maroie" (song no. 1); she is also credited in two manuscripts (*M* and *T*) with a song fragment, "Mout m'abelist quant je voi revenir" (song no. 15), a seven-line stanza, preserved with music. Petersen Dyggve (1934: 82, 176) has identified Dame Maroie as Maroie de Diergnau, from Diergnau, formerly a *faubourg* of Lille with a feudal castle. She is also the addressee of a courtly chanson by Andrieu Contredit d'Arras, "Bonne, belle et avenant" (RS 262), which ends with this *envoi:*

> Chançon, va t'en sans retraire
> Vers Dergan, soiez errans.
> Di Marote la vaillans
> Qu'elle puet de joie faire.

> Song, go without delay
> Toward Diergnau, set out immediately.
> Tell the valiant Marote
> That she can rejoice. (ll. 41–44, Nelson and
>   van der Werf 1992: 113 and 115)

Because Andrieu probably died in 1248 (Nelson and van der Werf 1992: 3), we may assume that Maroie lived in the first half of the thirteenth century.

Dame Margot

The historical existence of Dame Margot likewise seems assured. As previously noted, she debates against Dame Maroie in "Je vous pri, dame Maroie" (song no. 1). According to Långfors (1926: lii), she is in all likelihood the same Margot who figures as a judge, along with Demisele Oede, in a jeu-parti opposing Jehan le Cuvelier and Jehan Bretel (RS 8). She is listed by Berger (1981: 113) among the unidentified members of the Puy d'Arras. Is she the Margot whose name Perrin d'Angicourt inserts in an acrostic, "Mais ne avris ne prinstens" (RS 288)? If so, we may localize her from the reference to Metz in the envoi:

> Tout droit a Mes, per amors,
> T'en vai, chanson, sens tergier,
> Di la belle ke s'amor
> Me fait d'ameir efforcier! (ll. 41-44; Steffens 1905: 272)

> Go straight to Metz, my song,
> In the name of love, do not tarry;
> Tell my beauty that her love
> Spurs me to love.

Duchesse de Lorraine

The rubricator of manuscript *C* ascribes two songs to one *duchaise de lorainne*, "Par maintes fois avrai esteit requise" (song no. 18) and "Un petit davant lou jor" (song no. 34). The fact that he twice inscribes her name—and at a healthy interval—suggests that he had no doubts that this troveresse existed. Yet the *Dictionnaire des lettres françaises*, both first and second editions, deems her authorship of "Par maintes fois avrai esteit requise" "peu vraisemblable" (quite unlikely) and labels "fantaisiste" (fanciful) the attribution in the Bern chansonnier (Hasenohr and Zink 1992: 393, 1460; Bossuat, Pichard, and Raynaud de Lage 1964: 248, 728). It is not entirely certain which Duchesse de Lorraine is referred to in manuscript *C*, as three women held this title over the course of the thirteenth century: Gertrude de Dabo, Catherine de Limbourg, and Marguerite de Champagne.

Achille Jubinal (1838: 54) was first to conjecture that the Duchesse who composed songs was Gertrude (1205-25), daughter of Albert II, Count of Metz and Dagsbourg (today Dabo), who inherited her family's numerous domains after the death of her two brothers. She married three times, first in 1214 to Thibaut I, Duke of Lorraine, a union contracted in 1206, when she was only one year old. Widowed in 1220, she married Thibaut IV, Count of Champagne, that same year.[44] A year after the dissolution of this second union in 1222, on the grounds of either sterility or consanguinity, she married Simon, Count of Linange or Leiningen. She died in 1225 without leaving any children. This Welf (German) milieu is accurately depicted in Jean Renart's *Roman de la rose ou de Guillaume de Dole*.[45] Although Albert of Dagsbourg's court was cultured and certainly open to literary influences, Gertrude held the title of Duchess of Lorraine only briefly—from the age of nine to fifteen—acquiring upon her widowhood the title of Countess of Champagne, followed by that of Countess of Linange after her third marriage. Would she have composed a death-lament at such a young age?

Catherine, daughter of Waleran III, Duke of Limbourg and Count of Luxembourg, acquired the title of Duchess of Lorraine at the age of ten, when she married Mathieu II, Duke of Lorraine, in 1225. She died in 1255. Catherine was also part of a highly cultured milieu, one in which literary patronage was a family tradition; many poets celebrated the patronage of her brother, Henri III, Count of Luxembourg. No one in her family, however, was known to have composed songs.[46] She has been identified as the patron of Colin Muset, but no evidence suggests that she herself was a poet-composer.

Writing a decade after Jubinal, Prosper Tarbé (1850: 25) was the first to posit that the Duchesse de Lorraine who composed songs was not the wife but the daughter of Thibaut IV, Marguerite de Champagne, married in 1255 to Ferri III, Duke of Lorraine. Paulin Paris (1856: 558-59) followed Tarbé's lead. This identification has been accepted by both historians and literary critics, most recently by Grossel (1994, 1: 99-102 and 2: 482-83) and Parisse (1976: 774).[47] If Gertrude de Dabo was too young to compose while she held the title of Duchess of Lorraine, it seems plausible that a woman akin to the prolific trouvère, a woman who grew up surrounded by music and poetry, tried her hand at composing song. It is possible, furthermore, that Marguerite de Champagne was not only a poet in her own right but also a literary patron. Bédier (1912: ix) first identified Catherine de Limbourg as the "bone duchesse" to whom Colin Muset pays tribute in a *descort* (RS 1302), but later preferred to recognize Marguerite de Champagne as his protector (Bédier 1938: xxvi). It should be noted that Grossel (1994: 99, 102) still rallies to Bédier's first hypothesis: Catherine de Limbourg was Colin Muset's protector, whereas Marguerite de Champagne was the troveresse.

The unusually high number of literary allusions found in the death-lament attributed to the Duchesse de Lorraine suggests that she was familiar with courtly romance as well as classical mythology. Mourning the loss of her beloved, she wishes to emulate Dido, who "was slain" for Eneas. She would perform greater deeds for the sake of her love than Anfelise did for Fouque (referring to the hero and heroine of Herbert le Duc de Dammartin's epic poem, *Fouque de Candie*). Her remorse for failing to reward her lover for his service is so great that she irreverently claims to be more repentant for her reserve than Adam was for his sin (note that she compares herself to the male partner of the biblical couple). Finally, showing her familiarity with the literary tradition of the bestiary, she portrays herself as a Phoenix, condemned to resuscitate when all it seeks is to die. This last reference cannot fail to evoke Thibaut de Champagne, who also compares himself to the mythical bird in "Chanter m'estuet, car ne m'en puis tenir" (RS 1476).[48]

In the same way that Thibaut occasionally incorporates popularizing motifs and familiar refrains in his courtly chansons, the Duchesse blends the popularizing and courtly registers in the second song ascribed to her in manuscript *C*, "Un petit davant lou jor" (song no. 34), a hybrid piece that borrows motifs from a variety of genres, including the aube, chanson de malmariée, and *chanson de rencontre,* while preserving the song's decidedly courtly tenor. One thing is clear: whether she was the wife or the daughter of Thibaut de Champagne, this troveresse was associated with the most illustrious of the trouvères and inherited his love for poetry and song.

Blanche de Castille

Li roine blance to whom manuscript *j* attributes a *chanson à la Vierge* (or Marian song), "Amours, u trop tart me sui pris" (song no. 36), is none other than Blanche de Castille (1188-1252), wife of Louis VIII of France and mother of Louis IX (Saint Louis). She was regent of France during her son's minority and during his Crusade (1248-52). Bédier, who was first to edit the song, was amazed by this rubric, "cette rubrique surprenante." He categorically refused to admit Blanche in the "galerie des poétesses françaises" for two reasons: first, on the grounds that the lyric speaker is masculine, and second, that everything we know or can surmise about the queen's taste belies the idea that she would ever have composed verse.[49] He discounts the fact that she is further ascribed a debate poem in manuscript *b,* "Dame, merci, une riens vous demant" (song no. 12), in partnership with Thibaut de Champagne, yielding instead to the evidence furnished by the ten other manuscripts that preserve this piece, where Thibaut's interlocutor remains anonymous. Bédier compares the attribution in *j* with the fanciful ascription of "Chanterai por mon corage" (song no. 27) in manuscript *C* to the fictional *lai dame dou fael,* legendary lover of the Chastelain de Couci. Thibaut's famed love for Blanche would account for the erroneous attributions in both *j* and *b.* Järnström and Långfors (1927: 11), accepting Bédier's reasoning, deny Blanche authorship of the Marian song and refuse to admit her literary partnership with Thibaut.

The persistent legend of Thibaut's love for Blanche was disseminated by the contemporary *Grandes chroniques de France,* in which it is recounted that upon their reconciliation "the count looked at the queen, who was so wise and so fair that her great beauty overwhelmed him. . . . Then he left pensively, and he often remembered the sweet glance of the queen and her beautiful countenance; then a tender, loving thought would enter his heart. But when he remembered that she was so noble a lady, of so good and virtuous a life that he might never possess her, his sweet amorous thought gave way to great sadness. . . . Since profound thoughts engender melancholy, he was advised by wise men to study the beautiful sounds of the fiddle and sweet delectable songs." The chronicle further relates that, with Gace Brulé, Thibaut "composed the most beautiful songs, and the most delectable and melodious that ever were heard in song or on the fiddle." [50] Thibaut's amorous feelings for Blanche have not been confirmed by other sources.

Jean Maillard, who assigns "Amours, u trop tart me sui pris" (song no. 36) to Blanche in his *Anthologie de chants de trouvères*, contends that "une certaine faiblesse de style" (a certain stylistic weakness) could cast doubt on the attribution of this Marian song to Thibaut, but concludes that "s'il s'agit d'une galanterie du Roi de Navarre d'avoir abandonné la paternité de cette œuvre au profit de celle qu'il a pu aimer, nous aurions manqué de courtoisie en annulant de notre propre chef cette rubrique" (if out of galantry the king of Navarre relinquished the paternity of this work to the woman he may well have loved, it would have been discourteous of us to remove this rubric on our own initiative) (Maillard 1967a: 10). In his *Charles d'Anjou, Roi-trouvère du XIIIème siècle,* Maillard dismisses Bédier's first argument as meaningless and cites Blanche's co-authorship of "Dame, merci, une riens vous demant" as justification for accepting the testimony of manuscript *j* (Maillard 1967b: 68). Gérard Sivéry, Blanche's most recent biographer, follows Maillard and accepts her authorship of "Amours, u trop tart me sui pris" (Sivéry 1990: 19).[51]

Bédier's first argument against attributing a song with a masculine lyric speaker to a female author can be countered easily. If it can be argued that a male trouvère could compose a song with a feminine voice when the genre dictated a feminine speaker, it could as easily be argued that a woman could compose in the masculine if she were writing in a genre where that gender was the norm. In fact, it would appear that this is exactly what the Duchesse de Lorraine did in her chanson de malmariée, a genre in which the narrative frame stages a knight's encounter with a lamenting female figure. Bédier's second argument can also be challenged. Admittedly, Thibaut's widely rumored love for Blanche has never been substantiated. One is tempted to ask, all the same, why Blanche has to be the object of Thibaut's affections in order to compose song. The possibility that she could have composed lyrics was certainly not discounted by medieval scribes and rubricators. We follow their lead.

It should be noted that the uncertainty regarding the historical identity of some of the women trouvères is not unlike the uncertainty associated with the identity of many a trobairitz, despite the presence of *vidas* and *razos* that introduce them in a number of manuscripts and of miniatures portraying them (Bruckner et al. 1995; Rieger 1985). In this respect, women trouvères do not differ from many of their male counterparts, who also have names but no personal history. In fact, two of the male trouvères who debate with an anonymous feminine voice, Perrot de Beaumarchais (L 203) and Rolant de Reims (L 242–43, author of eighteen jeux-partis), are known only through manuscript attributions (Hasenohr and Zink 1992: 1304).

Women Judges

Some women appear only as judges of debates. Such is the case of the Comtesse de Linaige and Mahaut de Commercy, who are called upon to render judgment in two debates, one opposing Rolant de Reims and a certain Dame (song no. 5), the other opposing Lorete and her "sister" (song no. 2). They have been identified as Jeanne d'Aspremont and Mahaut d'Aspremont, respectively. Jeanne d'Aspremont held the title of Countess of Linange or Leiningen from 1282 to 1316, her sister Mahaut that of Dame de Commercy from 1305 to 1329 (Delbouille 1933: 138; Parisse 1982: 215). Both women appear in Jacques Bretel's *Le Tournoi de Chauvency,* which chronicles the tournament and appendant festivities organized in Chauvency by Louis de Looz, Count of Chiny, in October 1285 (Delbouille 1932: lxxvi–lxxvii).

The Comtesse who is called upon to judge a jeu-parti opposing Amors and Gillebert de Berneville, "Amors, je vos requier et pri" (RS 1075), is probably Béatrice de Courtrai (d. 1288), sister of Henri III, Duke of Brabant, who in 1247 married Guillaume de Dampierre, heir to the *comté* of Flanders until his death in 1251. The same Béatrice is the addressee of a courtly chanson by Gillebert, "Amors, por ce que mes chanz soit jolis" (RS 1560); she may also be the Bietriz invoked in the refrain of one further song by Gillebert, "J'ai souvent d'Amors chanté" (RS 414) (Fresco 1988: 50–51, 114, 170, 221).

The Dame de Fouencamp who judges a jeu-parti opposing Jehan le Cuvelier and Gamart de Vilers, "Cuvelier, j'aim miex ke moi" (RS 1671), is Jeanne de Fouencamps, wife of Enguerrand de Boves, Lord of Fouencamps from 1247 to 1298. (Fouencamps is in Somme, arrondissement of Amiens, canton of Boves.) Her name appears in a document dated 1273 (Berger 1981: 438). She was apparently associated with the Puy d'Arras (Berger 1981: 113).

A certain Dame de Danemoi is called upon in "Adan, amis, mout savés bien vo roi" (RS 1675) to settle a debate between Adam de la Halle and Jehan Bretel.

The only information we have in this case is that Dannemois is in Seine-et-Oise, arrondissement of Étampes, canton of Milly (Petersen Dyggve 1934: 80-81).

The Demisele Oede who is cited as judge in five jeux-partis (RS 8, RS 667=668, RS 1351, RS 1637, and RS 947=916) is in all likelihood the wife of Audefroi Louchart (d. 1273), a wealthy Artesian financier who is mentioned five times in the *Chansons et dits artésiens*, exchanges two jeux-partis with Jehan Bretel, and judges at least fourteen others (Långfors 1926, 2: 334; Berger 1981: 376). Her name is entered in the necrology of the *Confrérie des jongleurs et des bourgeois d'Arras* for the year 1273 (Berger 1981: 439). What is interesting in the case of Demisele Oede is that her name figures four times in manuscript *a* when versions of the envois preserved in other sources cite different—male—judges. By substituting the name of Demisele Oede, the scribe of manuscript *a* was clearly paying a particular tribute to this woman; he was invoking a noted figure in the literary circles of Arras and perhaps acknowledging a patron. It is assumed that the Demisele Oede participated in the activities of the Puy d'Arras (Berger 1981: 113).

The decisions rendered by these women judges are not recorded in the manuscripts that preserve jeux-partis; their voices are not heard. We enumerate these judges here because their existence further confirms the participation of women in this genre. The existence of these women judges is also evidence of a different kind of literary collaboration between men and women. This collaboration allows us to recognize the possibility that debate poems between men and women are real exchanges, or at least that they reflect a cultural milieu in which such exchanges could and probably did occur.—*ED-Q*

INTRODUCTION TO THE POETRY: GENRES AND FORMS

We use the term *chanson de femme* to refer to compositions in which the lyric or narrative voice is feminine; with the exception of ascribed compositions, we have excluded songs with a masculine narrator even when the song centers on a feminine protagonist (for example, chansons de toile). When the gender of the narrative or lyric voice is indiscernible or ambiguous, we chose not to include the song in our collection (for example, chansons de rencontre and pastourelles). However, we have made a point of including dialogues opposing male and female voices (for example, jeux-partis and motets).

Given the high incidence of contamination between the higher and lower registers, we do not follow the conventional practice of relegating the chanson de femme to the lower register. Within the corpus of chansons de femme, we differentiate between chanson d'ami and chanson d'amour on the basis of versification rather than content, that is, we rely on formal characteristics rather than registral elements for the purpose of these two classifications. We use the label *chanson d'ami* to refer to a lyric composition in the form of a *chanson à refrain* or *chanson avec des refrains,* in which a feminine voice, an apparently unmarried woman, avows her love for a male lover, past or present, regardless of the song's dominant register. We reserve the term *chanson d'amour,* or *grans chans,* for compositions in the form of the courtly canso, that is, for songs that do not have a post-strophic refrain, either repeated or cited.

We present a selection of songs that gives the whole spectrum of women's voices in the Old French lyric in the twelfth and thirteenth centuries. We have selected from among more than thirty chansons de femme, nearly forty motets, and more than twenty rondeaux. Most of the genres practiced by male trouvères are represented in the present anthology: the grans chans (courtly love song), jeu-parti or tenson (debate poem), plainte (death-lament), aube (dawn song), chanson de croisade (crusade lyric), chanson d'ami, chanson de malmariée (unhappy wife's lament), chanson de nonne (nun's lament), and chanson pieuse (devotional song). For a detailed description of each of these genres, see the appropriate section in this anthology. Absent are those genres characterized by political and satirical content (the polemical *sirventes*), non-sense and burlesque genres (the *sotte chanson, resverie, fatras,* and *fatrasie*), such "bourgeois" genres as the *chanson de jongleur,* and the *reverdie*. We have excluded chansons de toile, pastourelles, chansons de rencontre, and *chansons pastorales,* as these genres are defined by the presence of a male narrator (as expounded above, our definition of the chanson de femme is more restrictive than those advanced by Bec, Mölk, and Earnshaw). It would seem that women did not write lyrics in response to social concerns or historico-political events unless these had a direct effect on them as women and as lovers. By way of illustration, the Crusades did not evoke expressions of religious fervor or exhortations to war, rather—to the extent that the Crusades forced the parting of lovers—they led to expressions of pain and sorrow; thus, the crusade song reverts to the feminine experience of the separation motif found in all chansons d'ami. Likewise, an unhappy marital situation leads to invectives against an ugly, old, brutal husband and yearnings for compensation with a young, handsome lover. Why women did not explore the realm of fantasy or revel in celebrations of spring (whether in the form of the reverdie or the traditional springtime *exordium*) is not clear. In the case of the exordium, the situation is much the same in the lyrics of the trobairitz.

With the exception of the estampie and lai-descort, all the forms typical of twelfth- and thirteenth-century trouvère poetry and music are represented in this anthology: the monophonic courtly chanson, the chanson à refrain (a song with a fixed refrain such as the rondeau, ballette, and rotrouenge), and the chanson avec des refrains (a song with variable refrains). Also included are representative examples of polyphonic French motets in which at least one of the voices assumes a feminine persona. For definitions of each of these types, see the appropriate subsection in this anthology.

The works in this anthology are organized according to genre, form, and performance mode; we have not separated ascribed and anonymous compositions. We open with jeux-partis in order to emphasize the constant interaction between men and women through song; jeux-partis, by their very nature, invite an exchange of perspectives. Next, we offer a tapestry of feminine voices found in the Old French chanson. Within this section, we have organized the songs according to their form and content: chansons d'amour, plaintes, chansons d'ami, chansons de croisade, aubes, chansons de malmariée, and chansons pieuses. In the next two sections, we present women's voices heard in some of the oldest as well as some of the most learned types practiced in the twelfth, thirteenth, and early fourteenth centuries: rondeaux and motets.—*ED-Q*

FIN'AMORS AND THE WOMEN TROUVÈRES

Love as it is described in medieval French lyrics is frequently called *fin'amors, amour courtois,* or courtly love by modern scholars. The designation "courtly love" suggests love that takes place in the environment of a noble court; *fin'amors,* which means "refined, true, perfect love" is a less restrictive expression and therefore preferable, for the sorts of love scenarios that occur in medieval lyrics do not always have a court as their setting.[52] Lazar and others have made the case that the term *amour courtois* does not begin to cover all the elements of courtliness, nor does it describe all the variations on love found in medieval literature (see Lazar 1995: 71, referring to Lazar 1964). Regardless of the specific term used, women and men exploited the same motifs and vocabulary to characterize erotic desire, although female authors interacted with the fin'amors ethic in ways that differ from those of men.

The analysis of the love situation in medieval literature was first developed by Gaston Paris (1883), who based his discussion on relatively few medieval romances, Chrétien de Troyes's *Lancelot* in particular. For Paris, the theme he dubbed *amour courtois* had four main characteristics: (1) it is illicit and furtive; (2) the lover is in an inferior position vis-à-vis the lady; (3) the lover strives to perform deeds of prowess to render himself more worthy of his lady; and (4) love is an art, a science, a virtue, with set rules. Paris held that the origins of medieval expressions of love were found in the works of Ovid; the love theme was elaborated by the troubadours of southern France and by courts of love (which we now recognize as fictional), culminating in the court of Marie de Champagne in Troyes (Walsh 1982: 5). However, critics have for years questioned Paris' analysis, and particularly his insistence on adultery. Modern scholars argue convincingly that adultery is not a sine qua non of love in the medieval literary setting, particularly in works set or written in northern France, and historians have affirmed that many of the elements that literary scholars associate with fin'amors had little if any historical reality (Benton 1968; Bloch 1939–40, 2: 41).

The troubadours are credited with creating many of the commonplaces of the theme of love in medieval lyric. These poets sing of a lady they cannot have; they are willing to serve her and act at her command, using vocabulary that is feudal in origin and reminds the listeners of the homage a feudal vassal swears to his lord. Troubadour songs reflect the social nature of love; they often recount a love triangle involving a pair of lovers and a third party who interferes with the amorous couple's wishes. *Fins amants* are concerned that their love will be exposed—hence the importance of secrecy. As Lazar describes love in the troubadour context: "*Fin'amor* exists in a context of sensual longing, verbal love games, separations, frustrated sexual expectations, postponed physical union, temporary satisfactions and stolen looks or kisses, fear of competing lovers" (Lazar 1995: 74).

In addition, fin'amors can be described as embodying courtliness and courtesy, evenhandedness and restraint, the concept of *pretz,* a word whose meaning includes worth and the esteem of others, and what Walsh (1982: 7) describes as "the noble gladness of youth." Although not all of these elements can be found in the songs in this anthology, taken together they do express the sort of behavior that lovers aspiring to fin'amors were expected to display in order to be worthy of the game of love.

Indeed, there existed a word for those who were not courtois, who were not meritorious—they were labeled *vilain,* which connoted lowly class status, moral and physical ugliness, and base, even vile actions. When the word *vilain* entered the English language, its first meaning was that of boor, an uncouth person; subsequently the word came to mean a scoundrel or criminal. The original English meanings suggest just how high the expectations were for fins amants, how strong the condemnation of those who failed to live up to those standards.

Secular Latin poets also sang of love using many of the themes found in troubadour songs, including the perception that love is a positive force, that one should revere the object of one's affections, that prudence and secrecy are necessary, and that love must be freely given (Walsh 1982: 9). Andreas Capellanus is credited with codifying love for the Middle Ages. His *De amore,* often translated—abusively—as *The Art of Courtly Love,* is regularly invoked as the rule book for any medieval love relationship, although its probable date of composition in the 1180s suggests that Andreas simply codified attitudes described in earlier literary works. In this treatise, it is argued that love cannot exist in marriage: "It is clearly known that love cannot claim a place between husband and wife" (Walsh 1982: 366). Andreas' opus, modeled on Ovid's didactic poems on love, *Ars amatoria* and *Remedia amoris,* includes a first book on gaining love, a second on retaining love, and a third arguing against love. Whenever scholars speak of the "rules of love," they are thinking of Andreas' work, for it was he who drafted twelve precepts of love, which include rules such as: "1. Avoid miserliness as a harmful disease," "6. Do not have too many privy to your love," and "7. Be obedient to mistresses' commands in all things, and always be eager to join the service of Love" (Walsh 1982: 117). However, the audience for *De Amore* was limited to those who could read Latin. Only in the late thirteenth century do we find translations of *De Amore* into a vernacular language (Walsh 1982: 14). Most important, however interesting Andreas' work is as one individual's description of the stages of love, we must be leery of applying his rules to all literary love situations. To give but one example, Andreas is frequently cited as the proof of the necessity of adultery in medieval love affairs; however, the theme of adulterous love occurs significantly less often than another, the theme of young lovers, as yet unwed, who are thwarted in their desire to marry each other (see Paden 2001). Medieval romances tend to exalt marriage and fidelity in conjugal relations (Kelly 1993: 125-27).

Many modern critics continue to subscribe to Paris' description of love, although more recent scholars have been inclined rather to hear love celebrated as desire. In a recent effort to correct the misconceptions fostered by Paris, William Paden (2001) has offered a more nuanced view: "Perhaps the troubadours make a spectacle not of their lady, whatever her civil status, but of their love; perhaps this love is not usually identified in relation to marriage at all, but simply as desire; and perhaps this desire, unencumbered by marital impediments, serves as the dominant element of their erotics." While it is true that adultery is not a mandatory feature of the love relationship described by fin'amors, it is a theme that appears in Old French lyrics. Adultery is clearly evoked in the chanson de malmariée in particular (nos. 31-34, 47, 50, 52, 64, and 65 in this anthology).

Northern poets borrowed much from the troubadours' conceptions of love. Rare is the poet who sings of a happy love situation; rather, a commonplace is that the lover is away, whether voluntarily (as on crusade) or not. Poets of fin'amors dream in their lyrics of a return of the lover, or they sing of the happy days now gone when the lover was physically present. Most of the scholarly descriptions and discussions of fin'amors have focused on the male point of view, perhaps because there are so many more extant songs on this theme by men than by women. Yet it would be wrong to assume that there is no female approach to fin'amors. Much has been written in the past two decades on the poetics of the trobairitz, and much of what has been said could be applied to the women trouvères. For when the women do sing, they do not simply switch roles with men (see Shapiro 1978 and Bruckner et al. 1995: xix–xxxii). One of the elements that distinguish women from men lies in the very terms they use to address their beloved. Troubadours use the terms *domna* or *midons* for their lady, terms that suggest the social superiority of the lady over the man. Trouvères tend to address their ladies as *dame*, again a rather formal term that connotes a certain nobility of social status. The women trouvères are more egalitarian in their terms of affection—*ami* is the appellation used most often by the poets of this anthology when they speak of their lover. We cannot identify the lover in question; the only proper name referring to a lover that can be found in our songs is "Robin" (nos. 20, 49, 63, and 75), a name that was relatively common in the Middle Ages and referred to a stock character rather than to a specific individual.

There are numerous other distinctions between the men and women trouvères, just as there are differences between the trobairitz and troubadours. Ferrante (1989: 71) observes that the trobairitz adopt a rhetoric different from that of the troubadours; she sees "a much greater tendency to address the lover directly, to refer to a past state that no longer obtains, a more negative expression of feeling, if not attitude . . . and at the same time an assertion of the female voice in wordplay and rhymes, and in the attacks on the conventions of the courtly game."

At least some of these differences between the trobairitz and troubadours can be found in their French counterparts. Women wrote songs in the same genres as men, using the same themes, motifs, and vocabulary. An examination of the use of some of this vocabulary allows us to perceive more clearly women's attitudes toward love, life, and their situation. The women trouvères invoke *joie* and *joïr* frequently; both terms have strong sexual connotations. The meaning of *joïr* includes "to welcome, to caress, to offer one's love, to enjoy"; the term can also mean, in a very sexual sense, "to come to climax." Likewise, *joie* carries the sense of "joy, enjoyment, sexual climax, (sexual) pleasure."

Any time an Old French author uses one of these terms, or such related ones as *voloir, plaisir,* and *desir,* the language becomes perforce sensual and sexual. For example, in the first song in this book, Dame Maroie uses these terms repeatedly. She assumes that a woman would want to enjoy love, "de l'amor veut joïr" (l. 28), and seek the pleasures associated with it:

> Folie convient avoir
> A boine amour maintenir
> Ki en veut les biens sentir. (ll. 54–56)

And in her last stanza, Maroie insists that a woman should apprise her lover of her desire:

> Bien est cose droituriere
> Dire son plaisir
> A son ami par desir,
> Ains c'on kiece en desespoir.
> Miex vient en joie manoir
> Par proier q'adés langir
> Par trop taire et puis morir. (ll. 78–85)

While women may enjoy love, there are, nonetheless, many obstacles to their doing so. In *"Onqes n'amai tant que jou fui amee"* (song no. 16), the woman despairs that her lover has turned his attention to another. She invokes *mesdisans,* slanderers (l. 14), as partial agents of her current status: because she sought, in accordance with the rules of fin'amors, to keep her love secret, she has now lost her lover. It is as if she is being penalized for having shown restraint in her demonstration of affection. Our author explicitly regrets the moments of passion she could have had with her lover; note her use of several verbs relating to the display of affection and to the sex act:

> . . . baisie et acolee
> M'eüst il or et aveuc moi geü. (ll. 15–16)

She concludes her song with more regrets, recognizing that she has misplayed her hand in this game of love. So in this brief moment—for the song is not long—we find explicit mention of the enemies of lovers, implicit mention of the importance of secrecy, and a suggested questioning of the importance of restraint.

Similar notes are heard in "Lasse, pour quoi refusai" (song no. 22), where a woman decries her cold heart. She sings the praises of her lover: he was sweet and warm (l. 16), in contrast to her own behavior, which she recognizes be-latedly as having been remarkably foolish. In the fourth stanza, although she does not name the slanderers, she does mention people who tormented her lover and invokes a biblically severe punishment on them. The singer hopes, in the final stanza, that her lover will hear her song and return to her. In this song, then, we have a number of the important elements of fin'amors: sensual longing, thwarted love, and frustrated sexual expectations.

The very nature of jeux-partis makes this genre particularly apt for a dis-cussion of the elements of fin'amors. In their debate, Perrot de Beaumarchais and a lady discuss the different merits of potential lovers (song no. 9). Who is better, the man who lacks bravery or the man who is brave but not courtois? Given this choice, the lady prefers the brave man, arguing that bravery lasts forever and that she could refine such a man (ll. 12–18). Perrot makes the case, however, that the man who knows the ways of love is more worthy because he has generosity and wisdom and refinement (l. 24), traits that he will keep whether he is wielding a sword or not. In the arguments of the two speakers, we have a description of the ideal lover—a man who is at the same time gen-erous, wise, refined, handsome, a good and brave knight. One may ask if the lady's reference to a game, *li jus* (l. 35), at the end of this song refers simply to the genre of jeu-parti or if she is suggesting that all of fin'amors is a game.

As stated, love is often hindered by parties bent on thwarting the lovers. Song no. 32, *"Mesdixant, c'an tient a vos,"* features a remarkable list of epithets to describe such enemies. The song opens with an imprecation of the mesdixant, mentioned again as *lozangeours* (scandalmongers who impede true lovers) and described, finally, as envious (l. 24). But the woman is confident that the love she shares will protect her. Indeed, in the refrain she seems to be confronting her enemies head-on:

> *Mesdixant, c'an tient a vos*
> *Se je voil ameir par amours?* (ll. 1–2)

She warns them that she is above reproach if she is, in essence, obeying Love's dictates: she is well loved and loves sincerely and discretely. Moreover, here, as in other songs, the singer refers frankly to sensual pleasure; she invites the listener to consider an unambiguously sexual image when she describes her lover as "the good man who wields the sword" (l. 17) and contemplates the joie (l. 28), the *gueridon* or reward (l. 30), that may soon be hers.[53]

We find the vocabulary and themes of fin'amors in almost every piece in this anthology, even in a chanson pieuse. The singer of *"An paradis bel ami ai"* (song no. 37) praises her ami, who is handsome, sweet, wise, noble, and refined—everything one could want in a lover. But the mention of paradise in the first line alerts the listeners that this lover may be someone other than the man next door. In the final stanza, we learn that the object of this woman's love is God himself, "li rois de paradis" (l. 23). Here the separation of the lovers is caused by the presence of the woman on earth and not in heaven with her lover, but she appears confident that their moment together will come. Blanche de Castille's "Amours, u trop tart me sui pris" (song no. 36) opens with lines that could have begun any love song; it is only in the third line that the listener becomes aware that this is a chanson pieuse addressed to the Virgin. So, too, "Je plains et plors come feme dolente" (song no. 38) begins like many a song by an unhappy lover; in the second stanza we are allowed to think that we are listening to a mother bemoaning the death of her child. Only in the third stanza do we learn that the child in question is Jesus, and the sorrowing mother, Mary. So even chansons pieuses, those farthest removed from the earthly world of secular love, are informed and colored by its imagery, vocabulary, and rhetorical repertoire.

All medieval songs, even those sung by a solo performer, are perforce dialogues, for the performer is in constant relationship with an audience that is hearing the song without benefit of amplification or of recording. Singers could almost always be viewed by their audience, their gestures and facial expressions in clear sight. The lyrics sung represent a conversation between the composer and the audience, as well as a conversation with other works known to the composer and to her listeners. Generally, this is an implicit dialogue, but there are explicit exchanges as well. In motets, a plurality of voices is heard not only in the music but also in the lyrics. In "Qu'ai je forfait ne mespris" (motet no. 61), the male voice asks how he has wronged the lady while the female voice declares that the lover will have compensation for his efforts. In "Je sui jonete et jolie" (motet no. 65), two female speakers express the difficulties of marriage and fin'amors. In one voice, we learn of a jealous husband who may possess the body of his wife but who certainly does not control her thoughts or her desires. In the other, the woman uses the vocabulary of fin'amors to affirm her disdain for her husband. She does not like him because he does not conform to the expectation of a fin amant: she finds no refinement in him, nor any ardor (ll. 3–4). In fact, he is a vilain, that enemy of fin'amors. But the singer takes her revenge: she will find a lover, even as she invites her husband to take a mistress.

Specifically associated with women are the laments of the unhappy wife.

For the malmariée, love songs, Lazar has argued, formed "a compensation for her disappointments, a landscape for repressed desires, and a kind of literary revenge" (Lazar 1995: 63). There is little evidence that the women whose songs are included in this anthology found compensation and revenge through the act of composing and singing. The malmariées whose voices we hear (nos. 31–34, 47, 50, 52, 64–65, 69, and 73–74) have not repressed their desires but sing rather of their frustrations and anger. The wife in *"Au cuer les ai, les jolis malz"* (song no. 31) describes her husband as a boor (vilain) whose breath will kill her, "Vostre alainne m'ocidrait" (l. 10). In *"Por coi me bait mes maris?"* (song no. 33), we have a depiction of wife-beating; the only revenge envisaged by the abused spouse is that she will sleep with her lover. The rondeau *"Vous arez la druerie"* (song no. 52) speaks of the pleasure of love even as mesdissant (slanderers) and a husband are lurking in the shadows. The lover, the ami, will receive the pleasures the husband will never have.

Husbands are frequently condemned to the status of cuckold in medieval love songs because the woman has been obliged to marry a man she has not chosen. In *"Osteis lou moi"* (motet no. 73), for example, we hear the desperation of a wife so unhappy with her state that we can see her pulling her wedding ring off her finger. She describes her husband as vilain and foresees that he is a cuckold in the making, because she has been married off against her will (l. 8). The song is very short as it stands, but the emotions evoked are remarkably strong. We find a reference to cuckoldry in several other songs in this anthology, notably in "Un petit davant lou jor" (song no. 34) by the Duchesse de Lorraine, which combines elements characteristic of the chanson de malmariée and the aube. Here the despairing woman (and we can find a despairing woman whenever we see the terms *vilain* or *mari*) describes her husband in very insulting terms, and the best she can say for him is that he is a cuckold:

Tote la graindre bonteis
C'est de ceu k'il est cous. (ll. 83–84)

She seems to be saying that the only saving grace in her marriage is that she has a lover.

In spite of these references to unhappy marriages, the women trouvères do not find the institution incompatible with love. In two of our jeux-partis, marriage is presented as a perfectly acceptable lot in life. The debate between Lorete and her "sister" on the merits of two different men (song no. 2) is clearly set in the framework of a marriage proposal, "chascuns vos vuelt par mariaige avoir" (l. 7), and nowhere in this song do we hear the marital state disdained. Moreover, the Dame de Gosnai, in song no. 4, is firm in her assertion that marriage is a good thing:

> Amours veult bien et otrie
> Que joie et ses biens doublez
> Ait dame qui se marie. (ll. 32–34)

Her debate with Gillebert de Berneville is concerned more with the public relations surrounding the marriage (should she marry with the approval of her friends or not?), and there is no dismissal of marriage as irreconcilable with love or with a good reputation.

One other element frequently associated with fin'amors is that of love as a sickness without a cure. Male and female trouvères sing of the ills of love, a malady without an antidote. Although it is infrequent that the specific symptoms of love sickness are enumerated in lyrics (such is not the case in longer romances, where the symptoms may be described at some length—see *Cligés* by Chrétien de Troyes, for example), we find an invocation of the ills caused by love in a good number of the songs in this book. Lorete speaks clearly of "d'amor . . . la malaidie" (song no. 2, ll. 17–18). For our singers, fin'amors is a potentially fatal illness—a number of our songs speak of death as an outcome of love. For example, "La froidor ne la jalee" (song no. 14) presents us with a woman feverish from love (l. 3), who states explicitly that love is killing her: "Amours . . . M'ocieis" (ll. 21–22). And if Love does not kill her, her lover can: "Quant li plaist, se m'ocie!" (l. 20). The woman in "Plaine d'ire et de desconfort" (song no. 17) is suicidal because of love, "Ensi ma mort quier et porchaz" (l. 24), as is the Duchesse de Lorraine in her death-lament (song no. 18), "a mien voil moroie" (l. 5). The Duchesse suffers pain and torment, "poinne et travail," as the penalty of love.

Ultimately, fin'amors was a game, one of many that were part of medieval culture. Johan Huizinga (1950) called attention to the importance of games in the Middle Ages, noting that poetry and song are "at one and the same time ritual, entertainment, artistry, riddle-making, doctrine, persuasion, sorcery, soothsaying, prophecy, and competition" (124). Huizinga considered the troubadours, in particular, as proponents of the play function of poetry (135); more recent scholars have also pursued this argument (Rosenstein 1980; Kendrick 1988). French poets recognized the play element of their lyrics as well (Pfeffer 1985), and examples are found in our collection of songs. The lover in "Amis, ki est li muelz vaillans" (song no. 10) uses the vocabulary of games throughout the jeu-parti; it is he who speaks of "li jeus et li gais et li ris" (l. 58).

In the chanson de croisade (song no. 27), the woman laments, "Je n'en ai ne gieu ne ris" (l. 28). The vocabulary of dice games is as likely an image in a love song (see song no. 1) as that of a pining lover. While our fines amantes sang of the pains of love and threatened to die, they were fully cognizant of the ludic function of their work. Now it is our turn to play with their songs.—*WP*

INTRODUCTION TO THE MUSIC

Singing added to a poem an essential dimension that would not have been present if it were recited: the impact on the hearers of the complete song—poetry and music—was surely more than the sum of its parts. The words of the poem spoke to the mind, while the melody, far from being a mere vehicle for the text, had the power to express feelings in a way that transcended the words. In composition, performance, and reception, the manifestly audible songs by women and in the woman's voice were agencies of an overt expression of a feminine view of life that undoubtedly had a powerful presence in French culture of the twelfth and thirteenth centuries.

In style and form, the monophonic melodies included in this anthology are typical of the trouvère repertoire in general. The music is strophic, that is, the melody is repeated for all stanzas of the poem. The forms of most of the melodies follow the verse structure of the poems, and usually one or more of the phrases is repeated at least once as the melody proceeds. Like the vast majority of extant trouvère melodies, most of these are organized according to the scheme *ABAB . . . x,* wherein the music of verses 1 and 2 is repeated for verses 3 and 4, sometimes with slight variation (see, for example, song no. 9).[54] Also like most trouvère melodies, the music of these songs is relatively simple in style, generally flowing in a stepwise manner, with a texture that is syllabic (one note per syllable) or slightly neumatic (two or three notes per syllable). With few exceptions, each melody is modally predictable, meaning that it has a tonal orientation made aurally evident in the prominence of certain notes at cadences and other important points, and pitch intervals (major and minor thirds, whole and half steps) that fall in consistent places within the scale.

Yet there is nothing naïve or reductively formulaic about most of these melodies; many of their features are impressively sophisticated: the exploration of range and contour (song nos. 12 and 13), occasional melismatic textures that are not limited to cadences (song nos. 16 and 35), and subtle manipulation of motivic and structural features that obviates any sense of monotony (for example, song no. 1, in which the music of verse 9 is a variation of that of verse 1; song no. 9, in which verse 6 is a variation of verse 1; and song no. 22, where the melody of verse 1 is varied in verse 5). There are no marked differences in melodic style among debate songs, love songs, crusade songs, chansons de malmariée, devotional songs, or rondeaux.

All rondeaux are distinct from the other genres in one striking respect, their formal scheme, with an identity between poetic and musical structure: poetic rhymes matched by musical rhymes in the form of repetition and recurrent refrains of both verse and music. These regularized, predictable features, which suggest simple musical structures that might have been easy for unlearned people to remember, became increasingly fixed as the end of the thirteenth century approached. One rondeau in this anthology survives with music (song no. 50), a melody that adheres to the conventional form of *ABaAabAB* (where letters graph the rhyme scheme and musical phrases, and uppercase letters indicate identical text and music). Its texture is relatively simple, its range is limited to a fifth from D to A, and its motion is mostly stepwise. The *A* and *B* phrases have a clear antecedent-consequent relationship, with the first phrase moving up the fifth to a half-close on G, the second moving down the fifth and lifting to a final cadence on F. As predictable as the unfolding of this material is, the two phrases are not linked by formulaic or other smaller-scale motivic material, as is common in other extant rondeau melodies, implying perhaps a deliberate working out of the melody's makeup. Further, as transmitted in manuscript *a*, the melody incorporates an infinitesimal but noticeable variation of its *A* phrase, whose fifth and sixth syllables of the refrain are on the pitches G–A, but which in verses 3 and 5 are reversed to A–G. If it had occurred once, one might attribute this variant to scribal error, but its presence in both nonrefrain verses suggests compositional intent.

A relatively limited musical vocabulary, such as in this rondeau, does not by itself mark a melody as either "popular" or "courtly." For example, the straightforward melody of Bernart de Ventadorn's "Can vei la lauzeta mover" invited frequent borrowing (notably, for our song nos. 10 and 17), by male and female trouvères alike, but no one has ventured to suggest that this song falls elsewhere than in the courtly register. Repetition of musical phrases certainly reduces the number of notes that singers had to keep in mind, and in the case of the classic rondeau structure there are only two phrases, distributed among eight verses. But many chansons d'amour in the trouvère repertoire feature musical repetition, sometimes regular as in the *ABAB . . . x* structure, but sometimes even more extensive among all verses of a stanza. Because musical language is not as complex as poetic language, with fewer technical features to mark differences, it is quite difficult to argue registral distinctions on the basis of musical style.

Beginning not from the music itself but from an overall theory about the nature of genre and social or compositional conventions associated with each type, Christopher Page (1986) has argued that the register of a song was an important factor governing certain aspects of its performance. He distinguishes registers partly by poetic theme and language, and also by compositional intent and audience expectations (courtly songs, he says, "lay claim to self-conscious artistry," while the appeal of dances "was not to good taste or judgement, but to the feet" [38]). "Low Style" songs, he maintains—especially pastourelles and songs with dance affinities such as rondeaux—were traditionally associated with instruments and instrumentalists, while "High Style" songs like chansons d'amour never had such associations, and instrumental accompaniment would have been considered inappropriate. He further argues that popular songs, those in the instrumental idiom, would have had a rhythmic pulse that was lacking in the freer, more "rhapsodic" aristocratic songs.

Although enticing, this theory is not without its problems, beginning with its stark separation of genres into "high" and "low," distinguished by their place in society and hence by their function and audience.[55] The concept of "genre" was inexact to medieval theorists, at least until the fourteenth century, and even then there is little direct evidence that a theoretical view of the nature of a song type had any impact on performance in practice; in the twelfth and thirteenth centuries the boundaries between courtly and popular, secular and sacred, monophonic and polyphonic, were fluid. In fact, Page does not attempt to extend his theory of register and its implications for performance to the chansons de femme, but if one accedes to the traditional view discussed (and challenged) above that they belonged to the popular register, his theory should suggest that they would have had a marked rhythm and possibly been sung to the accompaniment of instruments. This, however, would run counter to his own categorization of genres. He does not include chansons de femme in his category of "Low Style" songs, perhaps tacitly acknowledging that most of them belong in the courtly register, if anywhere. Although he offers compelling evidence that the rondet de carole was more closely associated with women than with men (and so in his scheme these dancing songs would be performed with instruments and a lively beat), in the same publication (Page 1989, from which we have cited several examples above) he supplies a great deal of evidence of the participation of women at all levels of composition and performance.

Page's theory of performance has garnered a great deal of support among musicologists, despite its reliance on, at best, indirect evidence. The foregoing is not intended as a rebuttal of the idea that dancing songs, such as the rondeaux in this anthology, were mensural (that is, had a measured rhythm), which they certainly must have been to be functional. One must question, though, whether there is yet enough evidence in the record to argue that such "High Style" songs as the chansons d'amour and the jeux-partis would *not* have had clearly measured rhythms and even been accompanied by instruments on occasion (see Aubrey 1996: 240–62). Many of the passages cited above point to the ubiquity of instruments throughout society, the training that both women and men, from the nobility down to the lowest jongleur or jougleresse, received in playing them, and their presence during performances of all types of songs (see Huot 1989a). And despite Page's attempt to dismiss mensural notation in several of the sources as representing a late "ethos" and therefore not reliable as a witness to earlier practices, the scribe of manuscript *O*, who wrote most of the songs (including the "High Style" tenson, song no. 13) with mensural notation, surely heard *someone* singing courtly songs that way. Furthermore, even though the upper voices of the motets in *M* are written in nonmensural neumes, they *had* to have been more or less precisely measured in performance to accord with the lower voice, or tenor. Scribes simply cannot be relied on for unequivocal information on performance practices.

The French motets in this anthology feature at least one text in the feminine voice. The motet is a curious genre, quite distinct from the monophonic lyric song in its history, function, compositional treatment, structure and style, and performance. A creation of Parisian church musicians, the motet developed through several stages, during each of which new elements were grafted onto old. The roots of the motet are to be found in twelfth-century *organum*, polyphonic part-music created when new voices were added above melismatic sections of plainchant from the Mass or Office of important feast days. The plainchant, called the *tenor*, slowed down considerably, often to a virtual standstill, while the solo singer of the added voice (the *duplum*) spun out a florid and probably rhythmically free line. In the midst of these sometimes quite long stretches of florid organum were occasional brief sections when the tenor moved more quickly, often note-against-note or nearly so against the duplum, and here both voices assumed by necessity a more precise rhythmic movement that enabled them to stay together. These short sections of measured organum, called *clausulas*, began to assume identities as autonomous musical items that could be inserted into the liturgy at appropriate points. The notation of plainchant was adapted to this new measured polyphony, the neumes falling into regular patterns or "modes," which reflected the aural patterns of the sung rhythms.

The earliest of these clausulas consisted of a single voice over the tenor. By the early thirteenth century some three- and even a few four-part clausulas were composed, either by adding new voices (*triplum* and *quadruplum*) to previous two-part clausulas or by the creation of entirely new pieces. Soon there existed a repertoire of several hundred of these compact and animated works whose intermittent emergence from the monophony and unmeasured or irregularly measured organum of the liturgy must surely have been a spectacular auditory sensation in thirteenth-century Paris. Each added voice was designed to agree harmonically with the tenor, and most two-voice clausulas are essentially consonant (revolving around fifths, octaves, and unisons). With the addition of a triplum and a quadruplum in roughly the same range as the duplum, consonance was increasingly difficult to control, and the upper parts often clashed in dissonances of seconds, sevenths, and ninths.

All the voices in a clausula sang the same text, that of the plainchant tenor, but because this was in fact only a few syllables—sometimes only one—a clausula was a virtually textless segment of polyphony, vocalized by a few soloists. The earliest motets apparently developed when a Latin text was added to the duplum of a two-part clausula (see Sanders 1980 and Smith 1989). The added Latin text usually was in a general sense a trope of the liturgical text from which the tenor was extracted. These texted works were called *motets* (or other derivatives of the French word *mot*) in some early sources, including manuscript *M,* and Latin texts soon adopted the term *motetus* for both the genre and the voice that had been called the duplum in a clausula. A three-voice motet resulted from the same process, with the addition of a second Latin text to the triplum of a three-voice clausula.

Soon composers were devising entirely new upper parts over liturgical tenors, creating new polyphonic textures not dependent on pre-existing clausulas. The added texts gave new shape to the polyphony, and motets became full-fledged independent "pieces," apart from the liturgy. Musical phrases were molded to text phrases, while the still practically textless tenor was relegated to a supporting role, almost "instrumental" in sound even if vocalized by singers. Sometimes the tenor notes had to be sung through twice (often slightly altered) in order to accommodate the completion of the upper parts (see motet nos. 53, 55, 59, 60, 63, 65, 66, 67, 68, and 71). The aural effect of a two-voice motet, with a poetic text over the tenor melisma, is that of a solo singer accompanied by the textless notes of the tenor, but a three-voice motet has a strikingly different sound. The added Latin texts for the most part are related to each other in subject matter (and usually also to that of the plainchant), and in the earliest examples the new texts are similar or identical in poetic structure (phrase length, rhyme or assonance). But here the enunciation by two singers of two different texts simultaneously created poetic dissonance, much like the musical clashes between the upper voices. The polyphony of the music was now complemented by a polyphony of poetry (Huot 1989b and 1997).

By the middle of the thirteenth century, French texts had begun appearing in the upper voices of some motets: the motetus in a two-voice motet, and in a three-voice piece either the triplum in combination with a Latin motetus (and hence was born a genre that is polyphonic, polytextual, and polylingual), or both the motetus and the triplum. In some cases these French texts merely replaced Latin ones, using the same notes in the upper parts as the Latin version. And, as musicians had experimented earlier with composing new upper voices for Latin motets, they soon began composing new French songs over a plainchant tenor. Sometimes a French song survives both in monophonic form and as one of the voices in a motet (see, for example, the TN to song no. 16), and in most such cases it cannot be determined which version came first. Nearly all the French texts are secular, most of them love songs of one sort or another. In the later stages of development we encounter a few nonliturgical tenors (such as the tenors of motet nos. 58 and 59, whose sources are as yet unidentified), sometimes even a French song (for example, the tenors of motet nos. 69 and 70), marking a significant and perhaps definitive departure from any sacred association.

The labyrinthine evolution of the motet, with countless new specimens based on or adapted from earlier pieces, means that virtually every thirteenth-century motet shares the music or text of at least one voice with another motet, and often an entire complex or family of motets can be traced through interrelationships among the various parts. Motet nos. 53, 60, 61, and 62 are all based on the tenor "In seculum," which is from the Gradual of the Mass for Easter, "Haec dies"; the family of motets using this tenor is quite large.[56] Motet no. 70, "Dame que je n'os noumer / Amis, dont est engenree / Lonc tans a que ne vi m'amie," is a member of a particularly convoluted complex. Our edition of this piece is based on the version in manuscript *Mo,* fol. 389r–390r, where the text "Lonc tans a que ne vi m'amie" is given as the incipit for the tenor. The same melody, with its full text, is used as the motetus in a different motet with a liturgical Latin tenor and a different French triplum, "Cele m'a tolu la vie / Lonc tens a que ne vi m'amie / Et sperabit," transmitted in a different part of *Mo* (fol. 116v–118v) and in *Cl* and *Ba.* Such motet complexes often involved more than simple borrowing, but rather reworking and adaptation to enable the part to fit its new polyphonic context. In this case, the melody of "Lonc tans a que ne vi m'amie" requires some alteration in order to fulfill different contrapuntal functions, in one motet as the middle voice over a liturgical tenor which provides a harmonic foundation for the counterpoint, and in another motet as the harmonic foundation itself beneath two other melodies.[57]

Each text of a motet is nonstrophic, and the upper parts have no systematic musical repetition. In some three-voice motets the poetic structures of the two upper voices are identical or nearly so, and the musical counterpoint is more or less note-against-note, with phrases cadencing together. In these pieces the poetic counterpoint is somewhat difficult to hear, since the two texts are sung simultaneously. In other cases, including all the motets in this anthology, the poetic structures are not the same, and here the cadences often overlap, so that the phrases of one voice and then the other emerge from the counterpoint. This is especially striking when both the texts and the melodies of the two upper parts echo each other in musical and poetic exchange, as in motet no. 69.

The texts of a motet may be quite divergent, drawing on a wide range of subject matter. They may juxtapose sacred and secular texts, contrasting genres and registers, discourse in both the first and third person, and both masculine and feminine voices. One may attribute this heterogeneity to the often seemingly serendipitous compilation of a motet's components, but in some motets this polyphonic poetry sounds almost like an intentional dialogue, comparable in some respects to a monophonic dialogue but creating an even more complex texture of meaning, allowing simultaneous allegorical and parodic interpretations. Our anthology includes a representation of three-voice motets in which one upper part is in the feminine voice, the other in the masculine (motet nos. 60, 62, 63, 64, 67, 68, and 70). Given the essential musical and textual polyphonic nature of the motet, the femininity of one voice might be best understood as it interacts with the masculinity in another. Feminine as something "other" than masculine is both more sharply defined and more nuanced when it is encountered in dialogue with masculine; the interaction between masculine and feminine in such an elevated literary and musical genre adds a dimension to our understanding of the social fabric within which men and women interacted every day.

A poignant example is motet no. 62, whose triplum, in the masculine voice, is full of optimism, but whose motetus, in the feminine voice, is painfully desperate. Such a contrast of emotions is heightened at times by the arresting musical technique called "hocket" (from the word for "hiccup"), where one voice, then the other, sings one or two notes, back and forth in a quick, choppy manner. So we hear:

He: *She:*
Si

                    Hé!

   grant

                         Diex!

       talent
Together: de chanter que faire un chant . . .   dusqu'adonc que je

                                        vous ravrai?

And, later:

He: *She:*
Que de

                         E!

      tant

                              e!

      me

                                   o!

          puis je
Together: bien vanter . . .   *biaus dous amis* . . .

Music makes this juxtaposition possible, and a performance makes it audible.
Whether hearers perceived the poetic as well as the musical dissonance is impossible to know, but there can be no doubt that the composer of this motet,
and those who sang it, were aware of the extraordinary power of musical
counterpoint to encapsulate divergent, even conflicting poetic themes into a
single riveting moment of time.—*EA*

MANUSCRIPTS AND TRANSMISSION

The manuscripts that transmit the works in our anthology are widely varied in
format, contents, date, provenance, and state of preservation. Some are large
and lavishly decorated, others are small and almost utilitarian in their appearance; most were written in the second half of the thirteenth century, with
a handful from the first few years of the fourteenth. The sources of monophonic chansons are from north and northeast of Paris, the majority having
been produced in Artois or Picardy, several in Lorraine (*C, I,* and *U*), and at least
one in Burgundy (*O*); the scribes' various dialectal propensities are evident in
orthographic and morphological variants. The major motet manuscripts are
Parisian in provenance or inspiration. Manuscripts *Mo, W2, StV,* and *Cl* were
probably produced in the Île de France. Manuscript *Ba,* traditionally viewed

as from eastern France west of the Rhine, recently has also been located in the Île de France region (Norwood 1990). Manuscript *Tu* was produced at the abbey of Saint-Jacques in Liège (Auda 1953, 1: 12–13). The late manuscripts *M* and *T,* from Artois, are principally collections of monophonic songs, with relatively small collections of motets; their importance in the connection between monophony and polyphony has been discussed above. Most of the extant manuscripts remain in the state they assumed when they were first produced, including those that were left incomplete by scribes, but a few survive in fragmentary or damaged form (most dramatically, manuscript *M,* which was dismembered and mutilated at some point in its history by someone enamored of its numerous painted initials).

The monophonic songs are preserved in songbooks (often referred to as chansonniers) that comprise either complete codices devoted exclusively to lyric songs (*K, N, O,* and *U*), or discrete fascicles within manuscripts that also contain other musical works such as motets (*M* and *T*) and liturgical music (*a*), or fascicles within larger miscellanies of nonmusical literary, didactic, historical, philosophical, and religious works (*A, P, V,* and *i*) (see Aubrey 2000). Most of these sources group the chansons together at the beginning, usually arranged by author in descending order of social or aristocratic rank, followed by a section of unattributed chansons, and then jeux-partis, which the scribes also left anonymous. A few manuscripts (*I, a*) group the songs by genre rather than author, and some (*C, O*) give them alphabetically by text incipit, without attributions (Huot 1987).

Among the manuscripts that transmit the monophonic songs that are anthologized in the present volume, two Lorraine compilations, manuscripts *C* and *I,* preserve the most songs: twenty-three compositions appear in manuscript *I*—not an unexpected finding, given that this chansonnier is known for its extensive collection of chansons de femme—and eleven songs are copied in manuscript *C.* Among the thirteen jeux-partis with a feminine voice, seven are found in manuscript *I,* five of which are *unica* (song nos. 2 and 5–8), and four are contained in manuscript *C* (song nos. 9–12). This, too, is not a surprising fact, as it has long been recognized that by the early fourteenth century, after the jeu-parti flourished in Artesian circles under the influence of Jehan Bretel, the genre was transplanted from Picardy to Lorraine (Delbouille 1933: 138–39). Manuscript *C* ascribes four other compositions to women: a chanson d'amour, "La froidor ne la jalee" (song no. 14), is attributed to *une dame;* a crusade song, "Chanterai por mon corage" (song no. 27), is ascribed to the fictitious *lai dame dou fael;* a death-lament, "Par maintes fois avrai esteit requise" (song no. 18), and a chanson de malmariée, "Un petit davant lou jor" (song no. 34), are attributed to the Duchesse de Lorraine. The fact that manuscripts *C* and *I* preserve most of the jeux-partis and chansons with a feminine voice may be indicative of a regional predilection for poetry by women. Also noteworthy is the fact that manuscripts sometimes group songs with a feminine voice. For example, manuscript *b* gathers three jeux-partis with women interlocutors: song nos. 3, 4, and 12, on folios 167r, 168r-v, and 169v-170r, respectively; these three jeux-partis appear in very close proximity with a fourth: song no. 11, on folios 165v-166r. In manuscript *U,* "Plaine d'ire et de desconfort" (song no. 17) follows "L'on dit q'amors est dolce chose" (song no. 23) (Tyssens 1992: 380-82). Manuscript *k* groups four rondeaux with a feminine voice on folio 77r-v (song nos. 41-42 and 49-50). In most instances, however, there appears to be no attempt by compilers of chansonniers to isolate songs with a feminine voice (unlike our own enterprise) or deliberately to exclude women from any collections.

All but a few (*C, I,* and *b*) of these chansonniers contain music. The scribes placed the melody above the verses of the first strophe, with subsequent strophes given below without music. With this layout, a singer would have had to re-create the melody anew for every stanza—perhaps even memorize it, which suggests that singers generally did not sing from written sources. The impracticality of the manuscripts from a performer's point of view is further illustrated by the notation, which in most of the sources (with the exception of *O*) consists of the unmeasured neumes of plainchant.

The motets are found in manuscripts with varied contents, including the two that also contain chansons (*M* and *T*), miscellanies along with nonmusical texts (*Cl* and *StV*), "service books" of liturgical plainchant and other polyphony such as organum and conductus (*W2*), and discrete books of motets (*Ba* and *Tu*) (see Everist 1989). The Montpellier codex (*Mo*) is the most important and extensive source of thirteenth-century motets and the one on which we based most of our editions; in addition to more than three hundred motets for two, three, and four voices with different combinations of Latin and French texts, it contains a number of other polyphonic works.

Unlike monophonic songs, thirteenth-century motets remained anonymous in the manuscript sources. It is possible to infer from indirect evidence the identities of some of the composers of organum, clausulas, and conductus—the most famous names that were associated with them were those of the Parisian cantors Léonin and Pérotin—and some Latin motet texts can be attributed to such luminaries as Philip the Chancellor. A few French motet texts and their melodies are extant as monophonic songs attributed to a particular composer (see, for example, the TN to song no. 16). But because a motet was built up through the overlaying of new texts and melodies onto old ones, in such a combinatorial idiom it is impossible to identify a single individual as composer of both the musical counterpoint and the poetry.

In these sources the voices of a motet are not aligned vertically in score (as in a modern edition) but are laid out as separate parts. Generally in the earlier manuscripts (*W2, Cl, Her,* and *StV*) the voices were written in one continuous stream on a single stave, beginning with the triplum (in a three-voice work), then the motetus, and finally the tenor at the end. Such a layout made it difficult for a group of singers to perform directly from the manuscript, especially if the line continued onto a new opening, requiring the tenor to read from the verso (or back side of a leaf) while the other singers were still singing from the recto (or front side of the same leaf). At this point singers probably were still learning their parts by rote and thus sang more by ear or from memory than from a written source (and not without some rehearsing). As the counterpoint of motets became more complex in the course of the thirteenth century, coordination of rhythm and counterpoint among the voices limited the individual freedom of performers (which a solo singer of a monophonic song enjoyed), and motet singers were forced to rely less on memory and improvisation and more on writing (see Wright 1989: 325–38). Perhaps to accommodate this, scribes began marking out a text block that placed the upper voices at the top of the page and the tenor below, fitting all or nearly all of a motet on one opening. For a three-voice motet, the triplum usually was placed on the left side of the leaf or opening, the motetus on the right, with the tenor stretched on one long staff along the bottom (as in *Ba, Mo,* and *Tu*).

It is possible that authors of monophony and motets engaged the tool of writing as they composed—indeed, the more complex the rhyme scheme, vocabulary and images, development of thematic materials, melody, and counterpoint, the more likely it seems that composers may have sketched out some of their work on parchment or wax tablets. But their reputations did not derive so much from dissemination of their works in writing, which would have met with a limited audience, as from performance. The large codices that do survive were at least one step removed from this process of creation and performance. They were produced for preservation by scribes who were concerned with compiling large collections of a repertoire, much as modern editors do today. Organization by composer necessitated assigning songs to authors, but the large sections of unattributed works (including entire codices) prove that these compilers were not overly concerned with recording the names of composers.

As for the attributions that scribes did give in the chansonniers, it is well known that they are not always reliable, underscoring the fact that scribes did not necessarily receive the songs directly from their authors but collected them from a variety of primary and secondary sources. Whereas scribes probably respected attributions of which they felt sure (which explains the agreement of attribution in a majority of cases), they also doubtless were biased in favor of composers of whom they had heard, and by extension against those of whom they had not heard. Such well-known figures as Gace Brulé and Thibaut de Champagne were ascribed dozens of songs (some of these attributions are now rejected by scholars), whereas less famous trouvères were given credit for only one or two—however likely it is that this is all they produced over a lifetime. It is possible that women, who were almost never ascribed authorship in the sources, themselves declined to claim credit for their works, whether intentionally or by necessity. In such a male-dominated arena it may have been difficult or perhaps merely unlikely for them to assert authorship; perhaps, too, male medieval scribes were less interested in preserving songs by women than those by men. It may also be that many of their songs did not remain active in the repertoire long enough to have been captured by scribes, and those that did may have been kept alive through the voices of men—jongleurs or male trouvères—which could have caused ambiguity about whose songs they were.

The attributions of scribes can be applied more securely to texts than to melodies, which were mobile and adaptable. In the case of Bernart de Ventadorn's "Can vei la lauzeta mover," both men and women engaged in the homage of melody borrowing; whereas the texts of our song nos. 10 and 17 are in the feminine voice and may well have been composed by women, the music is that of a man and was adapted (presumably by the troveresses) to the new texts. But beyond this, there is some evidence of a different tradition of transmitting the monophonic songs composed by women or cast in the female voice. Most of the extant melodies for the chansons de femme survive in only one reading, while a much larger proportion of songs by men are transmitted in more than one manuscript. Ten of the eighteen songs with music that are edited here have only one source for their melodies, and those for three others are found in only two manuscripts. The fact that the two manuscripts that transmit the most texts in a feminine voice, the Lorraine codices *C* and *I*, do not transmit music cannot be ignored. This might mean that these songs were less widely performed than other trouvère songs, which could itself be a positive indicator of female authorship.

With fewer multiple readings of a particular song, the variants that are so ubiquitous and so revealing in the larger trouvère corpus are less enlightening for our repertoire. One especially intriguing case is song no. 34. Although it is found in eight manuscripts, six with music, it is attributed to the Duchesse de

Lorraine only in *C,* which has no music. The text tradition places manuscripts *C, T,* and *a* in one group (although *T* ascribes the song to the Chapelain de Laon) against *K, N,* and *P* in another and *U* in a third; because of the attribution to the Duchesse, *C* has served as the base for the text in our edition. In the *CTa* group, the version in *C* has no melody, and the melody in *T* is incomplete, so we have used the melody found in *a.* This melody, though, is significantly different from the melody given in the *KNP* group. It seems clear that after it was composed this song traveled at least two different paths, one with certain textual features (*CTa*), attributed to a woman in *C* and given a complete melody only in *a,* and another in a recognizably different textual guise as an anonymous work with a different melody (*KNP*). Could it be that the two paths diverged so markedly because the song did indeed originate with a woman and therefore the scribes of what scholars consider to be the more central tradition (the *KNP* group) chose to ignore or suppress the attribution?

Both the monophonic and the polyphonic works of the trouvères (men and women) were collected into codices by scribes who were more interested in the repertoire, and in a few famous authors who epitomized that repertoire, than in giving due credit to individual artists or in providing singers with performance instructions. The later history of the motet is linked inexorably with an impulse toward a precise way to write down music, which became an aid to both performers and composers. We can see in this not only a move toward sight-reading and away from ear-singing, but also the preservation in writing of what appear to be complete "editions" of all the works—musical, lyric, narrative, epistolary, dramatic, and didactic—of a single author, notably Adam de la Halle near the end of the thirteenth century and Guillaume de Machaut in the fourteenth.[58] But, for all of the works in this anthology, indeed for the trouvère repertoire in general, the concept of "authorship" implied not so much a claim to originality fostered in a solitary environment but rather a communal experience of creation, presentation, and hearing, bringing the work audibly to life. Manuscripts were of secondary importance in this cultural phenomenon, and it is important to maintain a healthy skepticism about what they do and do not tell us about authors or the practices of singers—male or female.— *EA and ED-Q*

ON THE DIALECTS

The *langue d'oïl,* or "Old French," comprised a number of dialects used in the various regions of northern France (see the accompanying map). As the central government in Paris began to assert its control over the regional lords in the late twelfth century, the dialect of the Île de France (Francien) became

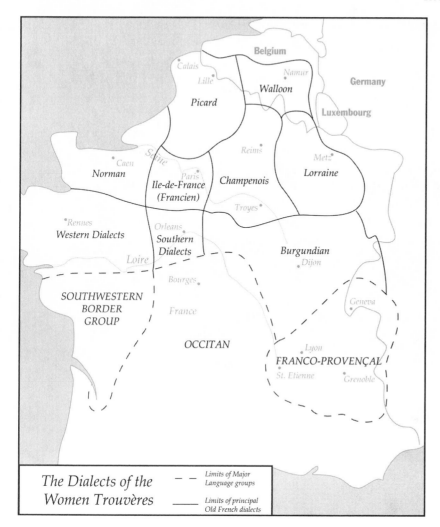

The Dialects of the
Women Trouvères

– – Limits of Major
Language groups

——— Limits of principal
Old French dialects

dominant. Because it is the forerunner of modern French, linguists use it as the
basis of their description of the phonology and morphology of Old French and
generally characterize the other dialects as they relate to Francien. Although
it is usually possible to identify the predominant dialect of a particular text, no
text is a pure example of any one dialect.

Most of the songs in this anthology display traits characteristic of the Lorraine and Picard dialects. For the convenience of readers unfamiliar with these
dialects, we list below the salient features of their phonology and morphology
as compared to Francien.[59] The dialectal features noted after each song in

this volume are characterized in terms of equivalencies, followed by examples found in the text. In the following chart, we have reproduced these equivalencies and added a concise description of the corresponding changes; all the examples illustrating the various traits are taken from our songs.

Lorraine

The dialect of Lorraine is sometimes called Lotharingian or Lorrainese. Classified by Pope (1934) as one of the eastern dialects (along with Burgundian), it shares many traits characteristic of both Picard in the north and Walloon in the northeast. There is a wide range of dialectal features in the geographical area in question, which spans the four modern departments of the Lorraine region (Moselle, Meurthe-et-Moselle, Meuse, and Vosges) and also includes small sections of bordering departments and countries (Bruneau 1925: 349–51). It is not surprising, then, that the dialectal traits found in the Lorraine chansonniers represented in this volume (mainly *C, I,* and *U*) exhibit some variation. However, they do display most of the features identified by Pope (1934) and summarized by Guiraud (1971).

Phonology and Orthography

- *a* for *e:* lowering of countertonic *e* (*davant* = *devant; sarait* = *sera; parsue* = *perçue*)
- *a* for *e:* lowering of *e* before supported *l* (*aus* = *eus; biaus* = *beaus*)
- *ai* (or *e, ei*) for *a:* closing of *a* to *è,* especially before dentals, palatals, and *r* (*ait* = *a; malaidie* = *maladie; saige* = *sage; baicheleir* = *bachelier; pais* = *pas; depairt* = *depart*) [60]
- *au* for *a:* velarization of *a* to *o(u)* before supported *l,* with retention of *l* (*loiauls* = *loiaus*)
- *e* for *ie:* nondiphthongization of tonic open *e* before palatal (*leus* = *lieux*)
- *ei* for *e:* diphthongization of tonic close *e* (*ploreir* = *plorer; volenteit* = *volenté*)
- *i* for *e:* palatalization of countertonic close *e* after *ch* and before palatalized *l* and *n* (*chivaillier* = *chevalier; millour* = *meilleur; signour* = *seigneur*)
- *oi* for *ei* before nasal and preceded by labial (*poinne* = *peine*)
- *oil* for *ueil:* nondiphthongization of open *o* before palatalized *l* (*coillir* = *cueillir; voil* = *vueil*)
- *ou* for *eu:* diphthongization of tonic free *o* to *ou* (spelled *o, ou*) without differentiation to *eu* (*plor* = *pleur; signour* = *seigneur; soule* = *seule*)
- *u* for *ui:* reduction of diphthong (*nut* = *nuit; trus* = *truis; ux* = *huis; desdut* = *desduit*)

- *l* lost before consonant (*aitres = altres; abe = albe; mavais = malvais; magrei = malgré*)
- *nr* for *ndr; lr* for *ldr:* absence of glide (epenthetic) consonant (*devanrons = devendrons; panre = prendre*)
- final *t* retained after vowel (*ameit = amé; povreteit = povreté*)
- *w* for initial *g* or *gu:* retention of initial *w* in Germanic loan-words and in Latin words contaminated with them (*werpis = gorpil, golpil*)
- *w* for initial *v* ou *vu* (*welt = vuelt*) or appearance as intervocalic glide (*druwerie = druerie; juwant = jouant; iawe = eau; lower = louer*)

The following spelling variations are also frequent:

- *an* for *en* (*an = en; volanté = volenté; antant = entent; anvie = envie*)
- *c* for *s* (*panceir = penser*), *s(s)* for *c* (*dessoit = deçoit*), *x* for *s(s)* (*plaixir = plaisir; amaixe = amasse*)
- *k* for *qu* (*ke = que; ki = qui; conkerre = conquerre*)

Morphology

Preferences or frequent substitutions:

- stressed forms *jeu, jou* for *je* and *ceu, çou* for *ce*
- articles *lo, lou* for *le*
- enclitic forms *jou* for *je + lou; dou* for *de + lou; nou* for *ne + lou; sou* for *si + lou*
- relative pronoun *que, ke* for nominative *qui*
- adverb *se* for *si*
- *nuns* for *nus* [61]

Most of the anomalies found in the verb forms can be explained by phonological features listed above. In particular:

- reduction of feminine past participle ending of *-ier* verbs from *-iee* to *-ie* (*otroïe = otroiee; baisie = baisiee; aloingnie = esloigniee*) [62]
- third-person singular present indicative *ait* for *a*
- third-person singular future ending *-ait* for *-a*
- future and conditional stems lacking glide (epenthetic) consonant (*devanrons* for *devendrons*) [63]
- third-person singular imperfect subjunctive in *-est* for *-ast*
- first-person singular present indicative *seu, seux* for *sui;* preterit *fu* for *fui;* imperfect subjunctive *fuxe* for *fusse*

- first-person singular present indicative *pux* for *puis;* present subjunctive *puxe* for *puisse*
- first-person singular preterit *o* for *oi; po* for *poi*

Picard

In today's France, the region of Picardy includes the departments of Aisne, Oise, and Somme. Throughout much of the Middle Ages, however, the area where Picard was spoken corresponded to no feudal or administrative division; rather, it was defined by its dialect and ethnicity (see map).[64] Extending across northern France, it included most notably three large counties: Vermandois, Artois, and Hainaut. For Jean Froissart (1337–after 1404), *la grande Picardie* included the cities of Tournai, Arras, Lille, Douai, Béthune, Saint-Omer, Saint-Quentin, Péronne, Amiens, Corbie, and Abbeville. As a linguistic entity, it distinguished itself from the dialects of neighboring regions: Norman, Francien, Champenois, and Walloon (Gossen 1970: 27–28). Picardy supported a flourishing textile industry that produced a powerful, prosperous group of literary and artistic patrons. Many works of Old French literature are preserved in Picard, and this distinctive dialect has been studied extensively (see especially Gossen 1970).

Some of the songs in this book display traits identified as characteristically Picard, although the range represented in our texts is admittedly quite limited. Moreover, because Picard shares a number of phonological features with Lorraine (and Walloon), there is an overlap that prevents us from identifying certain texts as certifiably Picard. In most cases it would probably be more accurate to claim that a given text is *picardisant* or *picardisé* (flavored with Picard).

Phonology and Orthography

The most striking phonological traits of Picard result from the treatment (reduction or differentiation) of diphthongs and triphthongs. Other features can be explained simply by spellings (such as *oe, oi, ou,* and *u*) used to render a variety of sounds related to the evolution of close and open *e* and *o*.

- *ai* (or *e*) for *a* before palatal (*saige* = *sage; boucaige* = *boschage; theches* = *taches; faice* = *face*)
- *i* for *e:* palatalization of countertonic and initial close *e* after *ch* and before palatalized *l* and *n* (*milleur* = *meilleur; signourie* = *seigneurie*)
- *iau* for *eau:* differentiation of triphthong before supported *l* (*biaus* = *beaus; biauté* = *beauté; vaissiaus* = *vaisseaus; oisiaus* = *oiseaus*) [65]
- *i* for *ie:* reduction of diphthong to first stressed element (*entire* = *entiere*)

- *iu* for *ieu:* reduction of triphthong (*mius = mieux*)
- *oi* for *eu* (*poi = peu*)
- *oi, ou* for *o* before nasal (*boine = bone; noumer = nomer; nounain = nonain*)
- *u* for *ue, eu:* reduction of diphthong (*put = puet; jus = jeux*)

The treatment of the velar consonants is particularly characteristic of Picard: the nonpalatalization of initial *c* and *g* before *a, e, i,* and the shift of initial *c* before Latin *e, i,* and yod to *tch* (*ch, c*) instead of *ts.* These developments account for the following spelling variations, not all of which are a reliable guide to the medieval pronunciation:

- *c, k* for *ch* (*saciés = sachiez; ciere = chere; cose = chose; bouce = bouche; cant canter = chant chanter; boscage = boschage*)
- *ch* for *c* (*deschovrir = descovrir; chuer = cuer; chovrir = covrir; chi = ci; anchois = ainçois; merchi = merci; cheli = celi; chanchon = chançon; commenchai = commençai; pieche = piece*)
- *g* for *j* (*gugier = jugier*)
- *gh* for *g* (*larghece = largesse*)
- *nr* for *ndr:* absence of glide (epenthetic) consonant (*tenrai = tendrai*)
- *s* for final *z:* reduction of sound *ts* to *s* (*sains = sainz; saviés = saviez*)

Other spelling variations include:

- *an* for *en* (*tans = tens; pansé = pensé*)
- *s* for *ss* (*naisance = naissance; mesage = message; deservie = desservie*)
- *ss* for *s* (*pansser = penser; mesdissant = mesdisant*)
- free variation of *c, k, q(u)* (*c'on = qu'on; kar = car; quidoie = cuidoie; kere = quere*)

Morphology

The morphology of Picard is distinctive; it includes most notably a complete set of possessive adjectives and demonstrative pronouns (see Gossen 1970). Only a sampling of these forms is found in this book:

- stressed forms *jou* for *je; mi* for *moi; aus* for *eus; çou* for *ce*
- articles feminine singular *le* or *li* for *la*
- enclitic *me.s* for *les + me* [66]
- possessive adjective *vo, vos* for *vostre*
- demonstrative pronouns masculine *ciz* for *cil; ciaus* for *cels, ceus;* feminine *cheli* for *celi*
- conjunction *u* for *ou*

- alternate infinitive form *seïr* for *seoir*
- first-person singular present indicative in *-c* (*prenc* for *prent; deffenc* for *deffent*)
- present subjunctive forms in *-che, -ce* (*kiece* for *chiee*)
- first-person plural present indicative and future, and present subjunctive in *-omes* (*puissomes, soiomes, herberjomes*)
- second-person plural in *-(i)és* (*saviés* for *saviez*)
- future and conditional stems without glide (epenthetic) consonant (*tenrai* for *tendrai*)
- future and conditional stems with interconsonantal glide in the group *vr* (as in *dr, tr*) (*viverai* for *vivrai; averoit* for *avroit*) or the elimination of *v* (*arez* for *avrez; saroit* for *savroit*)
- reduction of feminine past participle ending of *-ier* verbs from *-iee* to *-ie* (*païe* for *paiee; baisie* for *baisiee; forvoïe* for *forvoiee*)—*JTG*

EDITORIAL POLICY FOR THE TEXTS, TRANSLATIONS, AND MUSIC

This book is aimed at both specialists and students in a broad range of disciplines, including Old French literature, comparative literature, medieval studies, women's studies, and medieval music. Unless otherwise noted, all songs have been re-edited for this volume. When recent authoritative critical editions were available, we chose to reproduce those texts, rejected readings, variants, and dialectal features, by permission of the publisher, as noted in the acknowledgments.

For the texts we edited, we have generally adhered to the principle of minimal intervention. For songs with more than one source, we normally present a single extant version selected for its overall superiority or, in cases of contradictory attribution, the version that ascribes the song to a woman or where it appears as anonymous, with variant readings given in the critical apparatus. We have normally preferred manuscript *M* over *T,* manuscript *M* or *T* over *C, I,* and *U,* and manuscript *U* over *C* and *I;* for the rondeaux, we have given preference to manuscript *I* over *k;* for the motets, we have usually chosen *Mo* over *Ba, Cl, Tu,* and *W2.* Corrections are introduced only when demanded by versification or sense. Square brackets are used to show editorial conjectures of entire words or parts of words. They are not used when a reading is taken from another manuscript. When an emendation other than an evident one is due to a previous editor, credit appears after the rejected reading. For passages marked *missing,* the reading is taken from another manuscript (identified in parentheses) unless an editorial conjecture is specified. Hypermetric and hypometric lines are indicated by numbers preceded by a plus (+) or minus (−) sign. Variants are selective, normally omitting orthographic and dialectal fluctuations; they list readings that differ from the edited text, not necessarily from the base manuscript.

In the use of accents, we followed the recommendations made in Foulet and Speer 1979: 67–73. We have regularized the use of *i, j, u,* and *v* in accordance with modern orthography. Abbreviations are expanded, except that we transcribe final *x* as *x* in every case, as advised by Foulet and Speer (1979: 63), rather than treat it as an abbreviation. Roman numerals are retained as written in the manuscript (except in the musical transcriptions if coordination between words and notes requires expansion). Enclisis is indicated by an internal period. In texts marked by eastern dialectal traits, where the graphies *c* and *s* were often interchanged, we have regularized the spelling in accordance with Old French norms where misunderstanding is possible, for example in the case of demonstrative and possessive adjectives and pronouns, as recommended in Foulet and Speer 1979: 77. Refrains are given in italics. Square brackets denote unrecorded repetitions of fixed refrains. In the case of refrains embedded in motets, we italicize those for which there is a known concordance, but not those that are as yet only postulated. Dialectal features note orthographic, phonological, and morphological characteristics divergent from those of central Old French (Francien). The list of features is not exhaustive.

The aim of our translations is to render the meaning of the texts as faithfully as possible, while giving an accurate sense of the tenor of the pieces. Old French poetry is characterized by its use of a limited number of polysemic, coded terms; throughout the songs, we have varied English equivalents for a particular Old French term: *amis,* for example, is translated as "beloved" in one instance and as "sweetheart," "lover," "love," "my love," "friend," "boyfriend" in others, in order to reflect the wide semantic fields in which these terms function. We have avoided contemporary colloquialisms and have retained terms that pertain to medieval culture (references to the denier or the wimple, for example). Old French syntax can separate relative clauses from their antecedents, use a post-positioned noun subject, omit subject and object pronouns, use pronouns without clear antecedents, or disregard the logical concordance of tenses (notably, switch between past and present). Had we always reproduced the sentence structure of the original or failed to alter the tense sequence, we would not have been able to provide accessible, nuanced, transparent translations. By conveying a measure of the poetic value of the original, our translations are meant to encourage the reader to examine the original.

In the interest of consistency of presentation and interpretation, we have provided new musical editions for all the songs and motets in this anthology for which music survives. For some problematic readings we have been guided by previous editions, and we have supplied occasional explanations where our editions differ from earlier ones. Rather than give synoptic transcriptions of all versions of a melody, as is now typical of critical editions of monophonic music, we give only the version found in the base manuscript for the text or, in the three cases where the text manuscript does not give music (song nos. 10, 11, and 34), from a source whose text reading is compatible with that of the base text manuscript.

Musical emendations, which we have kept to a minimum, are limited mainly to filling lacunae (enclosed in brackets) and correcting apparent errors that cause excessive dissonance in the motets. Some emendations are made following concordant readings, whereas others are derived from comparison with similar or identical musical phrases elsewhere in the piece. Variant readings from sources that give the full melody of the base manuscript are given in the Musical Variants (MV) following the piece. We do not give variant readings for melodies with contrafactum texts, for untexted clausulas of the motets, or for individual motet voices that are found in other polyphonic contexts of a larger motet family.

The pitch levels of the manuscript readings have been maintained without transposition. Although this sometimes seems to place the music quite low for a woman's singing voice, we recognize that written pitch was not necessarily a representation of actual sounding pitch during the Middle Ages, and performers sang songs and motets at whatever pitch fit their voices. Indications of *musica ficta,* or chromatic inflections (flats and sharps) that were not notated but were likely applied by ear during performance, are placed above the note in question; we have been conservative in these editorial suggestions, which should be taken only as a guide.

The manuscripts of monophony for the most part use a notation that does not indicate precise rhythms, so with one exception all the monophony is here transcribed into stemless noteheads. While such notation is not strictly neutral rhythmically, it has the virtue of graphically reflecting the look of the original neumatic notation. All the motets, as well as song no. 13, which is transmitted in mensural notation in manuscript *O,* are transcribed into modern measured values: a *longa* is given as a quarter note or dotted quarter note, a *brevis recta* as an eighth note, a *brevis altera* as a quarter note, a *semibrevis* as a sixteenth note or smaller value if necessary, a *longa maxima* as a half note. We have not used bar lines because of the false impression they give of a regular "meter"; the prevailing motion in mensural music of the thirteenth century is triple, but groups of three breves are not necessarily organized into larger groups of six or nine, which would be implied by a modern time signature of $\frac{6}{8}$ or $\frac{9}{8}$.

In the monophonic songs, neume groups of two or more notes are indicated by a slur above the notes. In the polyphony, all ligatures, including *conjuncturae, currentes,* and ligatures *cum opposita proprietate,* are indicated by a square bracket above the notes. *Plicas,* or notational symbols that originally were derived from special plainchant neumes (liquescents) that did not necessarily have discrete pitch values, are assumed here to have such value and are transcribed as specific pitches; they are indicated by a diagonal slash through the stem of the note (in mensural transcriptions) or by a diagonal slash through the neume slur above the note.

In the Musical Emendations, Musical Variants, and Musical Commentary sections given after the editions, locations within a melody are indicated by line and syllable: for example, 6/7 refers to line 6, syllable 7. For the tenor in motets, location is indicated by "perfection" or *longa perfecta:* for example, 7 refers to the seventh dotted quarter note in the part. A plus sign (+) indicates notes or rests that occur after the last syllable of a verse. Note names are given in lowercase letters: abcdefg. Other symbols used in these sections are found in the list of abbreviations.

In the bibliographic data given with the motets, individual voices are identified according to the system devised by Friedrich Ludwig (1910, revised in Gennrich 1958a). Liturgical tenors are categorized by the plainchant from which they come, preceded by "M" or "O" for Mass or Office. Thus M13 refers to "In seculum" from the Easter Gradual "Haec dies," O46 refers to "Aptatur" from the Office Responsory "Cum in hora," and so on. Each upper voice is identified by the number assigned to it in Ludwig's catalogue, preceded by "Q" for quadruplum, "Tr" for triplum, or "Mot" for motetus.

The songs were selected by ED-Q and JTG. ED-Q was the principal translator of the jeux-partis and tensons; ED-Q and JTG took responsibility for translating the chansons, rondeaux, and motets, although all translations were scrutinized by all three text editors. The critical edition was a collaborative effort: the texts of nos. 2, 7, 9, 11, 17, 20-21, 24-26, 38, 40-52, 54-56, 58, 60, 62, 65-67, and 71 were edited by ED-Q; nos. 5, 8, 12, 32, 53, 57, 59, 61, 63, and 69-70 were edited by JTG; nos. 1, 6, 13, 15, 36, 64, 68, and 72-75 were edited by WP; song no. 34 was a collective undertaking. The dialectal features of the texts were compiled by their respective editors. All editorial interventions in the texts (including rejected readings and emendations) were reviewed by all three text editors. The bibliography and preliminary material (genre and form definitions, identifying data, manuscript sources, previous editions and translations) were prepared chiefly by ED-Q. The textual notes were composed principally by ED-Q, with contributions from JTG and WP. The maps were produced by WP. The musical editions and commentary were prepared by EA. Each section of the introduction, to which all four editors contributed, is followed by the initials of the editor who was primarily responsible for that section.

 For each song in this book, we offer the Old French text, an English translation, and music if available. Following each song, we also provide:

- Attribution, if any.
- Type of song (genre and form).
- Identifying numbers in standard bibliographies (Spanke 1955, Linker 1979, Mölk and Wolfzettel 1972, Boogaard 1969, Ludwig 1910, and Gennrich 1958a). In the case of motets, the data for each individual voice is presented separately.
- Manuscript sources. The first manuscript cited is the base for this edition; other manuscripts (concordances) follow in alphabetical order, all uppercase sigla preceding lowercase sigla. Numbers indicate folios, with the exception of manuscript *K*, which is paginated. In the case of manuscript *I*, we give both the new foliation and the old (in parentheses). Unless otherwise indicated, the manuscript used as the base for the music is the same as that used to establish the text. The presence of music is indicated by an eighth note (♪). Attributions are indicated in parentheses.
- Principal previous editions, listed in chronological order (the first and last are always entered). We include only those that supply the full text. Translations into modern French, English, Spanish, German, and Italian are indicated in parentheses.
- Notes on the texts and translations, including, where applicable, rejected readings, textual variants, dialectal features, and glosses, comments, or clarifications.
- Notes on the music, including, where applicable, emendations, variants, and comments.

For versification data, we refer the reader to Mölk and Wolfzettel 1972. —*ED-Q and EA*

Notes

1. Bec reiterated this position as recently as 1995.
2. "Si ces chansons étaient dues à des femmes on y trouverait sans doute un accent plus tendre, plus ému, plus de discrétion surtout et quelque ombre de pudeur féminine; il n'en est rien" (Jeanroy 1889: 96).

3. Such feminist scholars as E. Jane Burns, Sarah Kay, Roberta Krueger, and Helen Solterer have drawn an analogy between Jeanroy's attitude and Freud's desire to conserve the "idéal de la féminité." They state further that fin'amors as a concept (see the section "Fin'amors and the Women Trouvères," later in this introduction) was readily accepted in the late nineteenth century, because the "notion of disenfranchised women empowered by male mystification corresponded so well to the desires of modern men" (Burns et al. 1996: 229-30). This same attitude survives in the work of more recent critics, such as Frank Chambers, who believes that the bawdiness found in some trobairitz poetry excludes female authorship (Chambers 1989: 45-60).

4. Bédier's arguments are set out in the section "Introduction to the Authors: What We Know, What We Can Surmise," later in this introduction.

5. He does preface his introduction to this trouvère with an observation that anticipates Jeanroy's attitude: "Au moyen-âge, les dames se contentaient de se laisser adorer et chanter: elles abandonnaient aux hommes les luttes poétiques comme les luttes guerrières et se réservaient de juger les coups, et de livrer les palmes aux heureux concurrens, qui trouvaient souvent dans leur reconnaissance un supplément de prix qui devenait le plus beau fleuron de la couronne des vainqueurs" (In the Middle Ages, women were content to allow themselves to be adored and celebrated in song: they left poetic as well as martial contests to men, reserving for themselves the role of judging their efforts and awarding the palms of victory to the winners, who often found in the women's gratitude an additional prize, which became the most beautiful jewel in the victors' crown) (Dinaux 1839: 317).

6. Långfors (1926, 2: 157) even went so far as to propose that a voice referred to as "Amours" in the rubric of one jeu-parti (RS 1075) appeared to designate an actual woman rather than an allegorical figure, as most critics believe.

7. She rejects only the fanciful attribution in one manuscript of "Chanterai por mon corage" to lai dame dou fael, clearly inspired by the heroine (the Dame de Fayel) of Jakemes' Roman du Chastelain de Couci.

8. Jean-Charles Huchet is a particularly extreme case, for he has denied the existence of the trobairitz (Huchet 1983) and has even questioned Marie de France's authorship of the Lais (Huchet 1981). Michel Zink (1978), for his part, has sought to demonstrate that all the chansons de toile were composed by male poets.

9. "La femme (beaucoup plus que l'homme) a dû jouer un rôle important dans la conservation et la propagation de cette lyrique popularisante où elle demeure le personnage essentiel, autour duquel le texte s'articule" (Bec 1995: 49).

10. Although Coldwell cites Bec (1979), she refers only to his discussion of the trobairitz (Coldwell 1986: 60-61 n. 55). Because she does not mention the later discussion of the chansons de femme, she does not question Bec's exclusion of the women trouvères. For a critique of Bec's article, see Grimbert 1999.

11. Tyssens' corpus of debate poems does not include one jeu-parti (song no. 11) between an anonymous Dame and an unnamed Sire because four of the five

manuscripts that preserve it list the participants by name as male poets. For an analysis of this jeu-parti, as well as the ones in Tyssens' corpus, see Doss-Quinby 1999.

12. Thus, for example, she excludes the prayer to the Virgin attributed to Blanche de Castille (song no. 36) and one of the two songs attributed to the Duchesse de Lorraine (song no. 34).

13. For the source of this probably erroneous identification, see the section "Introduction to the Authors: What We Know, What We Can Surmise," later in this introduction.

14. In the case of the trobairitz, a fifth criterion is invoked: a woman is described in a biography (*vida, razo*) that accompanies the poem.

15. However, there are several cases in which the author refers to the activity of creating her song (see the section "Women as Poets and Musicians," later in this introduction).

16. See Grimbert 2001 for a critique of the registral dichotomy as applied by Bec (1977) to the chanson de femme. Klinck (1999) also questions the classification of this lyric type as "popular" or "popularizing."

17. "L'amour règne en maître dans cette poésie, avec toutes ses manifestations sentimentales et ses situations les plus diverses" (Bec 1977: 58).

18. "Un monologue lyrique, à connotation douloureuse, placé dans la bouche d'une femme" (Bec 1977: 57). He specifies that songs in dialogue form are a simple variation on the monologue, because one point of view is dominant.

19. "Es sind Lieder, deren lyrisches Subjekt eine Frau ist" (Kasten 1990: 13).

20. "Klagen der Frau über den Schmerz der Trennung, Liebes- und Treuebekundungen, Äußerungen der Sehnsucht nach dem Mann, Beschwörung der trotz der Trennung bestehenden Gemeinsamkeit mit ihm, Klagen über äußere Hindernisse, die der Verbindung entgegenstehen, Erinnerungen an vergangenes Liebesglück und endlich die Sorge, der Mann werde sich einer anderen Frau, einer 'Rivalin,' zuwenden" (Kasten 1990: 15).

21. "La canción de mujer es una alternativa estilística, en la que se introducen unos temas y motivos particulares siempre desde una focalización narrativa determinada, la femenina, que origina que el código se diferencie del resto de la producción lírica medieval y se presente como el reverso de la cansò" (Lorenzo Gradín 1990: 271).

22. Jeanroy (1889: xvii) characterized thus the views that his predecessors had had of popular poetry: "la grandiose expression de ses sentiments les plus vifs et les plus profonds."

23. Classical theorists such as Cicero (*De Oratore*) and Quintilian (*Institutio oratoria*) based their theory of styles on the circumstances or occasion, the subject matter, and the audience, but as Edmond Faral (1924) pointed out, medieval theorists, such as Geoffroi de Vinsauf (*Poetria nova,* ca. 1208–13) and Jean de Garlande (*Parisiana poetria,* after 1229), asserted that the style should depend as well on the social class of the characters in the composition in question (Dragonetti 1960: 15–16; see also Aubrey 1996: 66–72).

24. See Aubrey's nuanced discussion of these questions (Aubrey 1996: 80-83).

25. "Ein Liebeslied des volkstümlichen Registers . . . in dem die Perspektive der Frau als Monolog, Dialog oder Erzählerbericht realisiert ist" (Mölk 1988: 88; Mölk 1989: 47).

26. Mölk observes that Jeanroy was the first to speak of the chanson de femme as a lyric type (féminité textuelle). Before the appearance of Jeanroy's book (1889), *Frauenlied* designated simply a song composed by a woman, and because Jacob Grimm (1811) and Friedrich Diez (1863) firmly believed that none of the extant women's songs in Middle High German had been composed by women, they did not use the term. It was first used by Wilhelm Scherer when, in a letter written in 1864, he confided to Karl Müllenhoff his belief (which Müllenhoff shared) that some of the female-voiced pieces in Middle High German had been composed by women (Mölk 1990: 135-39).

27. Of course, the songs of the trobairitz are not, strictly speaking, chansons de femme.

28. The Duchesse de Lorraine's "Un petit davant lou jor" (song no. 34), which includes motifs characteristic of both the chanson de malmariée and the aube, might be considered an exception to the rule, if one adopts a broad definition of the chanson de femme, such as that of Earnshaw, for certain parts of it do give voice to a woman. However, we do not classify this piece among the chansons de femme, owing to the presence of a male narrator. (On the tangled transmission of this song, which itself might be an indication of female authorship, see the section "Manuscripts and Transmission," later in this introduction.)

29. "Il est donc à penser que c'étaient les jeunes filles qui composaient à leur usage des chansons où elles avaient d'abord peint leurs propres sentiments. Les premières chansons dont une femme est l'héroïne et le sujet ont donc dû être réellement composées par des femmes, et c'est ainsi à des femmes qu'il faudrait faire remonter les plus anciens essais lyriques en pays roman" (Jeanroy 1889: 445; see also 88-91 and 389-91). On the maieroles, see Bédier 1896.

30. Both Paris (1891-92) and Bédier (1896) endorsed Jeanroy's general theory, with some reservations. Paris (1892: 428) claimed that because the disgraceful attitude toward marriage displayed in these songs could only be conventional, none of the extant materials, not even the refrains, preserved the naïve, spontaneous voice of the people. He also extended Jeanroy's theory dramatically by speculating that dance songs had inspired not just the noncourtly genres but the courtly lyric as well in a seamless and unconscious transition from the peasant milieu to the bourgeois and noble milieux (Paris 1892: 423-27). Bédier (1896: 161), however, believed that this transposition had occurred when a court poet had had the ingenious idea to transform these popular songs into more complex compositions; see his presentation and critique of Jeanroy's and Paris' ideas (Bédier 1896).

31. See nos. 14, 15, 17-19, 21-22, 24, 27, 29, 34, 37, and 71.

32. Baumgartner (1990: 119) notes that Yseut's lai is quite close to a contrafactum: it follows the form of Tristan's *Lai mortel* (monorhymed octosyllabic quatrains) but

not its melody (as it is preserved in Vienna, Nationalbibliothek, Cod. 2542; see Fotitch and Steiner 1974: 144–49). Yseut draws on the lai's inspiration, its genesis, as well as its form.

33. "Cantus autem iste debet antiquis et civibus laborantibus et mediocribus ministrari dum requiescunt ab opere consueto."

34. "Cantus coronatus . . . , qui propter eius bonitatem in dictamine et cantu a magistris et studentibus circa sonos coronatur, . . . qui etiam a regibus et nobilibus solet componi . . ."

35. "Et huiusmodi cantilena . . . solet decantari a puellis et iuvenibus in festis et magnis conviviis ad eorum decorationem."

36. "Haec autem facit animos iuvenum et puellarum propter sui difficultatem circa hanc stare et eos a prava cogitatione divertit"; and "Haec enim ducit corda puellarum et iuvenum et a vanitate removet et contra passionem quae dicitur 'amor hereos' valere dicitur."

37. It is noteworthy that two of the songs edited here, song nos. 10 and 17, were set to Bernart's most famous melody, that of "Can vei la lauzeta mover" (PC 70.43).

38. Buffum 1928: 15–16 and 20–21. For a recent examination of the lyric insertions in Jean Renart's narrative, see Boulton 1997; their melodies are discussed in van der Werf 1997. A study of the practice of quoting songs or song fragments in narrative texts may be found in Boulton 1993. For a broad survey of romances with musical interpolations, including a review of scenes of formal entertainment and dancing toward an analysis of thirteenth-century performance practices, see Coldwell 1981.

39. Foster 1977: 124, 136, 146, 168, 209, 214–15, and 226. See also Smith and Taylor 1997.

40. This may not imply gender discrimination: a similar injunction of the mid-fourteenth century is directed at the choirboys of the Sainte Chapelle in Paris. See Wright 1989: 192.

41. See *New Catholic Encyclopedia,* s.v. "Huelgas de Burgos, Abbey of," and Thompson 1978: 237–38.

42. "Cantus autem iste non debet coram vulgaribus propinari eo quod eius subtilitatem non advertunt nec in eius auditu delectantur sed coram litteratis et illis qui subtilitates artium sunt quaerentes. Et solet in eorum festis decantari ad eorum decorationem" (Page 1993b: 36; the bracketed comment in the translation is added here).

43. Godefroy defines the term as a feminine adjective meaning "celle qui trouve, invente" (she who composes, invents). He cites this example: "Fu *trouverresse* de moult de manieres d'uevres. (*Chron. de Fr.,* ms. Berne 590, f° 6ᵈ.)" The term *troverresse* appears in *Aalma,* a Latin-French dictionary, s.v. "inuentrix. tricis," as preserved in Paris, Bibliothèque Nationale de France, lat. 13032 (end fourteenth century) (Roques 1938: 212).

44. Jubinal rests his identification on the fact that Gertrude's second marriage placed her alongside a most prolific trouvère: "[Thibaut] était un homme d'esprit, un écrivain distingué; il aura voulu épouser une femme dont les qualités

intellectuelles répondissent aux siennes, et celle-ci aura probablement puisé dans ses rapports avec lui le goût de la poésie. La chanson de la duchesse de Lorraine, d'ailleurs, bien qu'il paraisse en certains endroits y être question de la mort de quelqu'un qu'elle regrette, ne serait-elle pas simplement une allusion pure et simple au divorce que l'ambition de son mari fit prononcer, malgré elle et dont elle fut vraisemblablement affligée? La deuxième strophe de notre pièce me paraît singulièrement appuyer cette supposition" ([Thibaut] was a man of wit and a distinguished writer; he would have wanted to marry a woman whose intellectual qualities matched his own, and she would probably have acquired from him a taste for poetry. Indeed, although the Duchesse de Lorraine's song appears in certain places to refer to the death of someone she misses, might it not be a pure and simple allusion to the divorce that her husband's ambition caused him to seek, in spite of her, a divorce that no doubt afflicted her? The second strophe of the song, it seems to me, lends singular credence to this supposition) (Jubinal 1838: 54).

45. For a discussion of the historical context of Jean Renart's romance, including an analysis of the representation of the imperial crisis over succession, see Baldwin 1997.

46. "Catherine sortait d'un milieu très brillant et nombre de poètes ont chanté son frère sous le surnom de *Blondel*" (Grossel 1994: 99). "Le mécénat littéraire était de tradition dans sa famille; mais, précisément, aucun membre, parmi ces seigneurs, ne semble avoir quitté le statut de protecteur pour prendre celui de poète" (102).

47. See also Parisse 1982: 94-95, 375, and 401; and Petersen Dyggve 1934: 85 and 170.

48. For an analysis of the four surviving Old French death-laments occasioned by the death of a lover, see Rosenberg 1983.

49. "Outre que c'est un homme et non une femme . . . qui chante cette louange à la Vierge, tout ce que nous pouvons savoir ou nous représenter des goûts de Blanche de Castille dément l'idée qu'elle aurait jamais composé des vers" (Bédier 1910: 912).

50. "Le conte regarda la royne qui tant estoit sage, et tant belle que de la grant biauté d'elle il fu tout esbahi. . . . D'ilec se parti tout pensis, et ly venoit souvent en remembrance du doux regard la royne et de sa belle contenance; lors si entroit en son cuer une pensée douce et amoureuse. Mais quant il ly souvenoit qu'elle estoit si haute dame, de si bonne vie et de si nete qu'il n'en pourroit jà joïr, si muoit sa douce pensée amoureuse en grant tristesce. . . . Et, pour ce que parfondes pensées engendrent mélancolie, ly fu-il loé d'aucuns sages hommes qu'il s'estudiast en biaux sons de vielle et en doux chans delitables. Si fist entre luy et Gace Brulé les plus belles chançons et les plus délitables et mélodieuses qui oncques fussent oïes en chançon né en vielle" (Paris 1836-38, 4: 254-55).

51. Régine Pernoud does the same. She even cites the entire song in her biography of Blanche (Pernoud 1972: 29).

52. The debate over the use of the term *amour courtois* and its meaning is still raging. Definitions have been advanced and rebuffed; efforts to assess the validity of the

concept and to distinguish the various practices and conventions governed by the designation continue to be made. In exasperation, Henry Kelly (1985: 222) has stated: "The expression courtly love is beyond salvage; my best advice is to terminate it with extreme prejudice: dispatch it, and never let it be resurrected."

53. *Gueridon* is another element of the coded sexual vocabulary of the troubadours and trouvères.

54. Normally, we use the term *verse* to mean "poetry" or "line," but not "stanza" or "strophe."

55. For a discussion of Page's theory, see Aubrey 1996: 257-61.

56. For a catalogue of motets with this tenor see van der Werf 1989: 32-35.

57. For a detailed examination of a similar compositional process at work in motet no. 63, see Pesce 1997.

58. This trend was echoed in the south, where some late troubadours, notably Guiraut Riquier and Joan Esteve, also saw to the preservation of their works.

59. For further information on Lorraine and Picard, see Pope 1934: 486-97; Einhorn 1974: 135-41; Guiraud 1971: 34-39; Kibler 1984: 251-52, 265-67, 275-76, 289-93; and Schwan-Behrens 1932, 3: 5-47.

60. Although the development of *ai* and *ei* occurred in many dialects, it is particularly prevalent in Lorraine. Linguists explain it variously as an early or late palatalization or simply as the insertion of a "parasitic" *i* (Kibler 1984: 238). See Wahlgren 1925 for a thorough discussion and critique of the parasitic *i* theory.

61. This trait is explained by progressive nasalization, seen also in *amins* for *amis* (Pope 1934: §429).

62. This reduction is generally considered a Picard trait, but it is frequently found in Lorraine texts as well. Note that this change does not make the ending monosyllabic. The word *otroïe* in song no. 8, l. 17, rhymes with *druwerie* in l. 18.

63. This trait is also characteristic of Picard texts. Several of our Lorraine chansonniers also display another Picard trait: the development of an interconsonantal glide in the groups *vr, dr, tr,* or the elimination of *v* (*avera* or *ara* for *avra*).

64. As Dubois (1957: 1) notes, people spoke of Picards before speaking of Picardy, a term that first appeared around 1250 in texts related to the Parisian university milieu.

65. Considered characteristically Picard, this trait is nevertheless found in many dialects, including Lorraine and even Francien.

66. "La contraction *mes* . . . renvoie non à *me les,* mais à *les me* par l'intermédiaire de *le mes.* C'est un trait propre au dialecte picard" (Foulet 1928: §203).

Voices in Dialogue
Jeux-partis and Tensons

The jeu-parti is a lyric dialogue between two poet-musicians. The first speaker uses the opening stanza to offer two contradictory solutions to a dilemma—the meaning of *partir* is "to divide"—and to set the rhyme scheme and metric pattern of the song. The respondent is invited to choose one alternative, and the initiator of the debate is committed to defending the remaining position. The two participants then alternate stanzas in expounding their reasons. The song normally comprises six strophes—three for each speaker—and two envois in which each of the participants appeals to a judge to validate his or her opinion; the decisions rendered are never recorded. Given the high incidence of jeu-parti texts associated with multiple melodies, Biancamaria Brumana Pascale (1975-76) has hypothesized that at its initial performance a jeu-parti was sung to two melodies, each partner having composed—or borrowed, in the case of contrafacta—a melody for his or her own verses.

The genre flourished mainly in Arras, a rich center of artistic activity in northern France in the thirteenth century. The great majority of jeux-partis were composed by poet-musicians associated with its puy, its literary academy (for the activities of the Puy d'Arras, including a list of its members and a chronology of the jeux-partis presented at its assemblies, see Berger 1981: 86-88 and 111-14). There are 182 extant Old French jeux-partis, of which 105 occur with music. Setting aside a small number of parodic and burlesque examples, the subject matter of jeux-partis is quite homogeneous, being almost always a point of courtly casuistry. Whereas the tone may be courtly, the participants were most often members of the Artesian bourgeoisie. The genre is characterized by humor and spontaneity. Michèle Gally's (1986) probing examination of the semantic fields combined in the jeu-parti has revealed that the genre respects yet also polemically extends, contaminates, and derides both the discourse and the underlying ethic of courtly chansons d'amour. The jeu-parti had a well-defined social function: it was a highly valued courtly game or *divertissement*, a poetic jousting match that was in essence an exercise in logic and persuasion. Participants had to demonstrate their mastery of a variety of discursive and argumentative strategies, as well as a keen sense of repartee. Georges Lavis (1991) has clarified the various ways the conjunctions *mais* and *ainz* or *ainceis* ("but" and "on the contrary") structure the Old French jeu-parti, linking refutative, contrastive, and concessive sequences. The purpose of the debate was not to display genuine convictions or to settle an authentic controversy but to confront ideas and poetic personas.

Debate regarding authorship of the women's voices in jeux-partis centers on whether these parts were composed by historical women or were simply constructions by male poets. No doubts are expressed by Coldwell (1986: 50), who states that ten of the 182 pieces edited by Långfors (1926) "have women as authors or co-authors" and who publishes the music and first stanza of "Je vous pri, dame Maroie" (song no. 1). Similarly, Rosenberg and Tischler list the Dame de Gosnai, the Dame de la Chaussée, and Sainte des Prés in their index of trouvères, specifying "13th c." and adding for the last "Prob. in Artois poetic circle" (Rosenberg and Tischler 1981: 550 and 552; see also Rosenberg, Tischler, and Grossel 1995: 896 and 901). Tyssens (1992) has no reservations regarding the authorship of parts attributed to named women; her corpus of Old French lyrics composed by women includes all the jeux-partis and tensons in this anthology except song no. 11. She concludes that the actual existence of the seven named women partners in song nos. 1-4 seems assured and that the female authorship of these stanzas is as plausible as that of the *coblas* attributed to the trobairitz Alais, Iselda, Carenza, Iseut de Capio, and Alamanda. She is less persuaded, however, of the historical reality of the partners referred to as "dames anonymes," alluding to a similar debate regarding the anonymous partners of Occitan tensos and *partimens* (Tyssens 1992: 378-79). Bec (1979: 261-62), in contrast, is convinced that all the Old French debate poems were composed by male poets. For an analysis of the perspective offered by the feminine voice in the Old French jeu-parti, see Doss-Quinby 1999.

1 DAME MARGOT & DAME MAROIE
Jeu-parti

I   Je vous pri, dame Maroie,
     Ke respondés contre moi.
     Une dame simple et choie
     Est bien amee de foi,
     Et ele aime bien ausi,
     Ce saciés vous tout de fi;
     Mais cil est de tel maniere
     Ki l'aime ke sa proiiere
     N'ose pas gehir,

     I entreat you, Lady Maroie,
     To debate against me.
     A woman, innocent and tranquil,
     Is loved dearly and faithfully,
     And loves dearly in return,
     This you should know with certainty;
     But the one who loves her is such
     That his desire
     He dares not avow,

1. Je vous pri, dame Maroie
A 141v-142r

Je vous pri, da - me Ma - roi - e,

Ke res - pon - dés con - tre moi.

U - ne da - me simple et choi - e

Est bien a - me - e de foi,

Et ele ai - me bien au - si,

Ce sa - ciés vous tout de fi;

Mais cil est de tel ma - nie - re

Ki l'ai - me ke sa proi - ie - re

N'o - se pas ge - hir,

Et si ne puet a - ve - nir

Ke ja li fai - ce sa - voir.

S'or me vo - liés di - re voir,

S'en doit e - le des - cho - vrir,

U e - le s'en doit ta - sir?

Et si ne puet avenir
Ke ja li faice savoir.
S'or me voliés dire voir,
S'en doit ele deschovrir,
U ele s'en doit tasir?

Thus it can never come to pass
That he will ever admit it to her.
Now, please answer me truthfully,
Should she reveal her feelings
Or should she remain silent?

15 II — Dame Margot, bien vauroie
Droit gugier sans estreloi.
Puis k'Amours si les maistroie
K'il aiment bien ambedoi
De chuer loiaument, je di:
Se cil n'a le cuer hardi
De dire ke il l'ait ciere,
Pas ne doit cele estre fiere,
Ains doit obeïr
Son cuer et sa bouce ouvrir
Pour l'amour faire aparoir.
Puis ke cil n'en a pooir,
Ele le doit parfurnir,
Se de l'amor veut joïr.

— Lady Margot, it is well worth
Judging the truth fairly.
Since Love governs them to such an extent
That they dearly love each other,
Each with a loyal heart, I say
That if he does not have the courage
To tell her he holds her dear,
She should not be proud,
Rather, she should obey
Her heart and speak
To let love appear.
Since he is incapable of it,
She should accomplish it,
If she wants love's joys.

29 III — Vous n'alés pas droite voie,
Dame Marote, je croi.
Trop mesprent dame ki proie
Son ami avant. Pour koi
S'aveilleroit elle si?
Se cil a le cuer falli,
Ne di jou pas k'il afiere
Por ce k'ele le reqiere,
Ains s'en doit chovrir
Et les fais d'Amours soufrir
Sans ja faire percevoir;
Kar feme doit tant valoir
Que n'en doit parole issir
Ki son pris puist amenrir.

— You are going astray,
Lady Marote, I believe.
A grave mistake a lady makes who courts
Her beloved first. Why
Should she demean herself thus?
If he lacks courage,
I do not think it proper
That she should then solicit his love,
Rather, she should conceal her feelings
And suffer Love's pains
Without ever disclosing them;
For a woman should have such high merit
That no word should come from her
That could diminish her worth.

43 IV — Dame Margot, bien quidoie
Miex entendisiés .i. poi
En amours; je vous avoie
Le droit jugé, mais bien voi

— Lady Margot, I really thought
You understood something
Of love; I had
Rendered a judgment to you, but I see clearly

Ke vous estes contre mi	That you argue against me
A vo tort. Je vous afi:	Wrongly. I promise you this:
Boine amour n'ert ja entiere	True love will never be perfect
Q'aucune folours n'i fiere.	Unless struck by a little madness.
Nus n'en puet partir	No one can partake of it
Sans folour, dont face oïr	Without madness, so she should make known
Cele a celui son voloir.	Her desire to him.
Folie convient avoir	Madness is necessary
A boine amour maintenir	To preserve good love
Ki en veut les biens sentir.	If one wants to enjoy its pleasures.

V — Dame Marote, i foloie	— Lady Marote, one is free	57
Ki veut; mais mie n'otroi	To act the fool; but I cannot concede	
Ke d'Amours puist avoir joie	That any lunatic, man or woman,	
Fol ne fole, ki n'ont loi.	Devoid of reason, can possess Love's joy.	
Ne soustenés mais ensi	Uphold no longer, as you have,	
Ke dame prit son ami;	That a lady should entreat her beloved;	
Ke, s'ele en est coustumiere,	Because, if that is her habit,	
Ele se met tant ariere	She does herself such a disservice	
C'on l'en doit haïr.	That one must hate her because of it.	
Autrement s'en doit couvrir:	She should find other means to her end:	
Kere doit par son savoir	She should endeavor through her knowledge	
Ke le puist souvent veoir,	To be able frequently to see him,	
Parler et les lui seïr;	Speak to him, and sit by him;	
Bien s'en doit a tant tenir.	Better that she limit herself to that.	

VI — D'amours ne savés .i. troie,	— You know little about love,	71
Dame Margot, tres bien voi.	Lady Margot, from what I see.	
Cele est fole ki monoie	A woman is mad who grants her favors	
Prent pour faire a li dannoi,	In exchange for money,	
Kar point n'a d'amour en li;	Because there is no love in her;	
Mais qant doi cuer sont saisi	But when two hearts are seized	
D'amours ki n'est losengiere,	By a love that is not deceitful,	
Bien est cose droituriere	It is perfectly right	
Dire son plaisir	To express one's desire	
A son ami par desir,	To one's beloved out of longing,	
Ains c'on kiece en desespoir.	Lest one fall into despair.	
Miex vient en joie manoir	Better it is to live in joy	
Par proier q'adés langir	For having pleaded than to languish now	
Par trop taire et puis morir.	For having been silent and then die.	

RS 1744, L 176-1, MW 2286

Manuscripts: *A* 141v–142r♪ (base), *a* 140r–v♪

Editions: Fiset 1906: 528; Schultz-Gora 1907: 501; Långfors 1926, 2: 171; Coldwell 1986: 54♪ (English translation); Tischler 1997, 11: no. 1005♪

Text: Edited by WP

RR: 4 Et *(em. Långfors)* — 7 manieere *(reading from a)* — 18 Et k'il *(+1)* — 37 se doit *(reading from a)* — 49 entire *(reading from a)* — 59 puis *(em. Långfors)* — 69 seoir *(reading from a)* — 83 proiere *(+1)* *(reading from a)*.

TV: 3 et *missing* — 4 Et — 17 maistroi — 18 Et qu'il — 28 de la mort — 35 jous — 57 folie — 59 puis — 72 b. l'oi.

DF: Picard, including *ai* for *a*, as in *faice* (11); *c* for *ch*, as in *saciés* (6), *ciere* (21), *bouce* (24), *cose* (78); *ch* for *c*, as in *choie* (3), *deschovrir* (13), *chuer* (19); *k* for *ch*, as in *kiece* (81); free variation of *c, k, q(u)*, as in *quidoie* (43), *c'on* (65), *Kere* (67), *Kar* (75); *g* for *j*, as in *gugier* (16); *ir* for *ier*, as in *entire* RR (49); *poi* (44) for *peu*; *Boine* (49) for *bonne*; *jou* (35) for *je*; *mi* (47) for *moi*; *vo* (48) for *vostre*; *seïr* (69) for *seoir*; 2nd-pers. pl. verbs in *-(i)és*, as in *respondés* (2), *voliés* (12), *savés* (71); subj. in *-ce*, as in *kiece* (81).

TN: 71 The expression *.i. troie* belongs to dice game vocabulary. Margot is accused of not knowing a winning throw when she sees one. — 74 Långfors (1926) reads *dannoi* as a variant of *dosnoi*: "Celle-là est folle qui accorde ses faveurs pour de l'argent."

MC: Manuscript *a* transmits a different melody from the one in manuscript *A*. The existence of two unrelated melodies for this text suggests that even a poem in the voices of women was admired widely enough to have inspired different musical settings (see song no. 11).

2 LORETE & SUER
Jeu-parti

I Lorete, suer, par amor,   Lorete, sister, in the name of love,
    Ne me celler mie!   Do not conceal the truth from me!
    .ij. chivailliers de valor   Two knights, both worthy
    Et de cortoisie,   And refined,
    D'un pooir, d'une bontei,   Of equal power and equal kindness,
    Andui vos ont bien ameit.   Have both loved you dearly.
    Chascuns vos vuelt par mariaige [avoir].   Each one wants you in marriage.
    Li uns ver vous le celle a son pooir,   One hides it from you as best he can,
    Mais bien vous ait requis a vos amis,   But has sought you through your friends,
    Et fait ancor. De l'autre vos devis   And still does. The other, I tell you,
    Qu'il lou vos dit tot descovertement,   Lays bare his heart to you,
    Por ceu qu'il vuelt oïr vostre samblant. That he may hear your thoughts.
    L'un de ces .ij. vos covient retenir.   One of these two you must retain.
    Au queil vous plait il mieus a asantir?   To which one do you prefer to consent?

II — Suer, se Dieus me dont honor,
   N'an mantirai mie,
   Cil sant d'amor la savour
   Et la malaidie
   Qui n'ait lou cuer si osei
   K'il ot rekerre santei
   Lai ou il puet garison resevoir.
   Paors li fait relaixier son voloir
   Et fine amor, ki lou cuer li ait pris.

   A lui m'acort, k'il est de sans garnis,
   Cant par l'acort de mes amis me prant:
   Jai n'an serai blasmee de la gent.
   Qui ainme honor il la seit maintenir:
   Celui doit bien bone dame cherir.

III — Suer, vos preneis lou pïor
   An vostre partie.
   Amors met home an ardor
   Et an derverie.
   Je n'en i voi nul senei:
   Il i sont tuit anivrei,
   Li plus saiges n'i seit son point veoir.
   Dont ne doit nuns celui magrei savoir
   Se bone amor l'ait an ses lieins mis,
   C'il requiert ceu dont puet estre garis
   Vers celle cui il ainme loialment.
   Il li doit bien dire son errement:
   Puis [ke] lai vuelt a honor recuillir,
   Ne li doit pas sa pancee covrir.

IV — Suer, vos parleis de folor,
   Ne m'i acort mie.
   J'averoie de suor
   La color nercie,
   De honte et de flevetei,
   S'uns hons qui m'avroit amei
   Me requairoit; je vos di tot por voir,
   A mes amis an doit lou plait movoir.
   Mais .i. musars, .i. folz, .i. volantris

— Sister, by the honor God grants me,   15
I shall not lie;
He feels love's pleasures
And its sickness,
He whose heart is not so daring
As to seek well-being
In the very place he can find a cure.
Fear quiets his desire
And true love, which has taken hold of his
      heart.
To him do I consent, for he acts wisely
When he takes me with the assent of my friends:
Never will I be blamed for it.
He who loves honor knows how to sustain it:
He is the one a worthy lady should cherish.

— Sister, you defend the worse   29
By your choice.
Love kindles a man's desire
And drives him to insanity.
Not one of them is rational:
They are all intoxicated by it,
Even the wisest cannot discern his situation.
Therefore, no one should reproach him
If good love has bound him in its chains,
For he seeks what can cure him
In the presence of the one he loves faithfully.
He surely must disclose his desire to her;
Since it is there that he wants to reap honor,
He must not hide his feelings from her.

— Sister, you speak foolishly,   43
I simply do not agree.
I would be as black
As a cobbler
From shame and weakness
If a man who might love me
Solicited me; I tell you truthfully,
He should take up the matter with my friends.
But an idiot, an overzealous fool

Ne li chauroit ke por lui fut laidis,	Would not care who was dishonored for his sake,
Mais k'il peüst aconplir son talant.	As long as he could satisfy his desire.
Por ceu ne voil avoir acordement	For this reason, I refuse to consent
A home baut: nuns ne les doit joïr.	To bold men: no one should reward them with joy.
On n'an poroit a nul boin chief venir.	It can lead to no good end.

57 V — Suer, vous estes en errour,   — Sister, you are mistaken,

Je ne m'an dout mie.	I do not doubt it in the least.
Cant celui par sa dousor	When this one tenderly
Ver vous s'umelie	Humbles himself before you
Et vos requiert loialteit,	And requests your loyalty,
Vos lou teneis an vitei.	You feel contempt for him.
Je jugeroie et diroie por voir	I would judge and say truthfully
Qu'il doit trop muex an haute amor menoir	That he is far more deserving of lofty love
Ke li autres: s'est Renars li Werpis,	Than the other: he is Renart the Fox,
Ke quiert ses tors tant ke il soit saixis.	Who pursues his intrigue until he has seized his prey.
Et s'an panrai, par vostre loiement,	And so, with your permission, I will call on
De Linaige la contesse vaillant,	The worthy Countess of Linaige,
Mahau sa suer por lou droit departir.	And Mahaut, her sister, to render judgment.
Bien en sarait la veritei jehir.	The truth will be fully acknowledged.

RS 1962, L 172 and L 265-1100, MW 2287

Manuscript: *I* 182v-183r (190v-191r)

Editions: Steffens 1897a: 361; Lubinski 1908: 549; Långfors 1926, 2: 251; Kooijman 1974: 56 (French translation)

Text: Edited by ED-Q

RR: 7 avoir *missing (−2) (em. Lubinski)* — 16 mies — 34 anivreis — 37 ses] ces — 41 ke *missing (−1) (em. Lubinski)* — 44 mies — 46 De c. *(em. Lubinski)* — 65 s'est] seit *(em. Lubinski)* — 66 ses] ces.

DF: Lorraine, including *ai* for *a,* as in *mariaige* (7), *malaidie* (18); *a* for *al* or *au* before consonant, as in *magrei* (36); *an* for *en,* as in *an* (16), *sant* (17); *or, our* for *eur,* as in *ardor* (31), *savour* (17); *ei* for tonic *e,* as in *bontei* (5), *preneis* (29); *i* for countertonic *e,* as in *chivailliers* (3); *c* for *s,* as in RR (37, 66), *pancee* (42); *s* for *c,* as in *resevoir* (21); *x* for *ss,* as in *relaixier* (22); preservation of final *t,* as in *ameit* (6), *loialteit* (61); *w* for initial *g,* as in *Werpis* (65); *lou* (11) for *le; ceu* (12) for *ce; nuns* (36) for *nus;* rel. *ke* (66) for nom. *qui;* adverbs *lai* (21) for *la, jai* (26) for *ja;* 3rd-pers. sing. pres. ind. *ait* (19) for *a;* 3rd-pers. sing. fut. in *-ait,* as in *sarait* (70). Picard fut. *panrai* (67) for *prendrai;* cond. *chauroit* (52) for *chaudroit.*

TN: 65 Main protagonist of the episodic animal epic *Le Roman de Renart,* a comic satire of feudal society. Renart was reputed for the clever ruses he perpetrated against the other animals, especially the wolf Ysengrin, and was so renowned that *renart* replaced *golpil* as the common noun for *fox*. — 68-69 For identifications of the judges, see "Introduction to the Authors: What We Know, What We Can Surmise," in the introduction to this book.

3 SAINTE DES PREZ & DAME DE LA CHAUCIE
Jeu-parti

I   Que ferai je, dame de la Chaucie,
    S'il est ensi c'on me requiert m'amour?
    Conseilliez moi, par vostre courtoisie,
    El quel des deus j'avrai plus grant honnour:
    Ou ce que je lesse a celui tout dire
    Sa volenté, ou ançois l'escondire?
    Par fine amour, löez m'ent le meillour.

What shall I do, Lady of Chaucie,
If someone should seek my love?
Do advise me, most courteously,
In which of these I will reap greater honor:
Should I let him declare
His desire or instead refuse?
In the name of true love, recommend the better choice to me.

II   — Damoisele, de la moie partie
    Vous loe bien et pour vostre valor
    Que vous vueilliez souffrir que cil vous die
    Sa volenté, sans lui metre en errour;
    Qu'en lui oiant porrez vous bien eslire
    Se il vous plaist l'otroi ou le desdire,
    Et si savrez s'il dist sens ou folour.

— Maiden, my own choice   8
I recommend to you, for the sake of your worth:
Allow him to declare
His desire without causing him distress;
By listening to him you will be able to decide
If it pleases you to accept or refuse him,
And you will know if he speaks wisely or foolishly.

III   — Dame, c'est voirs, mes fame ne doit mie

    Home escouter, ains doit avoir paour
    Qu'ele ne soit a l'oïr engignie,
    Quar home sont trop grant losengeour
    Et leur raisons sevent tant bel descrire
    Qu'en eulz oiant puet a cele souffire

    Chose dont tost cherroit en deshonour.

— Lady, that is true, but a woman should really not   15
Listen to a man, rather, she should fear
Being seduced by the words she hears,
For men are consummate flatterers
And so skilled at couching their arguments
That simply by listening to them she could well agree
To something that would quickly dishonor her.

IV   — Damoisele, poi est de sens garnie
    Fame qui chiet pour parole en freour
    D'omme, s'il n'est cheüz en frenesie.

— Maiden, she has little sense,   22
The woman who fears the words
Of a man, unless he is mad.

Song no. 3, Rome, Biblioteca Apostolica Vaticana, Regina 1522, fol. 167r, Sainte des prez a la dame de la chaucie. Copyright © Biblioteca Apostolica Vaticana.

Bien escouter donne sens et vigour
De bel parler, ci a bel maestire.
Ja pour oïr homme n'iert fame pire

S'el ne se veult obeïr a folour.

V — Dame, bien voi tost seriez otroïe

A home oïr, se veniez a ce tour;

Mes, se Dieu plest, je n'iere ja moquie
D'omme vivant, ne de nuit ne de jour,
Quar de bien fait sevent il tost mesdire;
Pour ce, les vueil au premier desconfire,
Si que nulz n'ost a moi fere retour.

Careful listening yields wisdom and stimulates
Eloquence, a useful skill.
Never will a woman be the worse for listening to
    a man
If she does not succumb to foolishness.

— Lady, I can see that you would quickly
    consent
To listen to a man, if the occasion presented
    itself.
But I myself, God willing, will never be mocked
By any man alive, night or day,
For men are prompt to malign a good deed;
For this reason, I like to disarm them right away,
So that no man dare make a second advance.

29

RS 1112, L 246-1, MW 1986
Manuscript: *b* 167r (*Sainte des prez a la dame de la chaucie*)
Editions: Fiset 1906: 534; Schultz-Gora 1907: 500; Långfors 1926, 2: 169; Rosenberg
and Tischler 1981: 508; Rosenberg, Tischler, and Grossel 1995: 816 (French
translation)
Text: Rosenberg and Tischler 1981: 508
RR: 26 bele mestrie.
DF: Picard, including *ie* for *iee*, as in *Chaucie* (1) and *engignie* (17); *poi* (22) for *peu*;
e for *a*, as in *lesse* (5), *sevent* (19).

4 DAME DE GOSNAI & GILLEBERT DE BERNEVILLE
Jeu-parti

I   Dame de Gosnai, gardez
    Que soiez bien conseillie:
    A Robert Bosquet parlez
    Tant qu'il soit de vostre aïe.
    Je vous part, seignor avrez:
    S'a vo voloir le prenez,
    C'iert sans le gré vos amis
    — Ensi est le jeu partis —
    Ou vous l'avrez par leur gré
    Maugré vostre volenté.

Lady of Gosnai, be mindful
Of being well counseled;
Speak to Robert Bosquet
So that he can be of help to you.
I offer you the choice: you will take a husband;
If it is willingly that you accept him,
It will be against the wish of your friends—
Such is the dilemma—
Or you will have him with their consent,
But against your own will.

Song no. 4, Rome, Biblioteca Apostolica Vaticana, Regina 1522, fol. 168r, Gilebert de berneville a la dame de gosnai. Copyright © Biblioteca Apostolica Vaticana.

II — Gilebert, c'est grans vieutez
A dame d'user sa vie
Aveuc home qui amez
N'est de lui; mes ne doi mie
Contre tous mes foulz pensez,

S'aim mieux faire pis assez
Par leur los et par leur dis.
A ce me tenrai tout dis
Ne ja ne m'iert reprouvé
Qu'aie conseil refusé.

III — Dame, retenu avez
Le piour en vo partie.
De joie vous departez,
Si estes trop forvoïe.
Des ore mais soufferrez
Soulas trop malz savourez,
S'iert vos jugemens enquis
As vrais amans du païs
De ce qu'avez trespassé
Ce qu'Amours a commandé.

IV — Gilebert, vous mesprenez.
Amours veult bien et otrie
Que joie et ses biens doublez
Ait dame qui se marie;
Et je croi tant mes privez
Qu'a leur pooir m'iert donnez
Autieux ou mieudres maris
Que se je l'eüsse pris.
S'aim bien ce que m'ont greé
Et s'ai grant blasme eschivé.

V — Dame, bien sai que savez
Assez sens et cortoisie;
Tant iert vo cuers plus desvez
S'Amours est par vous traïe.
Pour Dieu, or vous repentez!
Jamais Robert ne creez!

— Gillebert, it is great vileness   11
For a lady to waste her life
With a man who is not loved
By her; but, I must not,
In opposition to everyone else, cling to my foolish
      thoughts.
Therefore, I would rather act disadvantageously
While heedful of their approbation and opinion.
To this I will always adhere;
Never shall I be reproached
For having refused advice.

— Lady, you have made   21
The worse choice.
You are parting with joy,
You stray from reason.
Henceforth, you will endure
Consolations that are most unsavory;
And the true lovers of the land
Will be asked to pass judgment on you
For having infringed
The commandments of Love.

— Gillebert, you are making an error.   31
Love permits and allows
Twice the joy and pleasure
To a lady who marries;
And I have such confidence in my family and friends
That by their power I shall be given
A husband who is as good as or even better
Than if I myself had chosen him.
In this way, I love the one they have approved
And have avoided great blame.

— Lady, I know you possess   41
Much sense and refinement;
Your heart will be all the more distraught
If Love is betrayed by you.
For God's sake, repent now!
Never believe Robert!

Bien sai qu'il a conseil mis	I know he was of counsel
A ce que vous avez pris.	In the choice you have made.
Portez Amours loiauté,	Give Love your loyalty,
Si vous iert tout pardonné.	And all will be forgiven.

51   VI   — Gilebert, vous me tenez   — Gillebert, you consider me
      A sage et a bien norrie;   Wise and well brought-up;
      Pour tant cuidier ne devez   You should not think on these grounds
      Que je face desverie.   That I commit a foolish act.
      Ains m'est li mieudres remez;   On the contrary, I was left with the better choice;
      . . . .
      Robert m'a bon conseil quis,   Robert put forward good advice,
      Mes vous vous estes partis   But you, you have strayed
      Du droit, s'avez mal ouvré,   From what is just; you have acted wrongly,
      S'avrez blasme et je bonté.   So you will incur blame, whereas I shall merit praise.

61   VII   — Hue d'Arras, soustenez   — Hue of Arras, uphold
      Le droit d'Amours et parlez   The right of Love and settle
      A teus drois de nos estris   Our dispute with due fairness—
      — En vous m'en sui du tout mis—   I have put myself entirely in your hands—
      Et, s'il vous plest, si chantez   And, if it pleases you, sing
      Ce chant quant apris l'arez.   This song when you have learned it.

RS 931, L 53 and L 84-31, MW 685

Manuscript: *b* 168r–v (*Gilebert de berneville a la dame de gosnai*)

Editions: Waitz 1899: 88; Långfors 1926, 2: 153; Rosenberg and Tischler 1981: 445; Fresco 1988: 207; Rosenberg, Tischler, and Grossel 1995: 746 (French translation)

Text: Fresco 1988: 207

RR: 56 *missing* — 63 deus.

DF: Picard, including *e* for *a(i)*, as in *plest* (65); *ie* for *iee*, as in *conseillie* (2), *forvoïe* (24); *vo* (6, 22, 43) for *vostre;* fut. *arez* (66) for *avrez, tenrai* (18) for *tendrai.*

TN: 1 Gosnay is a village approximately five kilometers southwest of Béthune. Nothing further is known regarding this woman. — 3 Robert Bosquet is not mentioned elsewhere, although his family name appears in Artesian charters. A certain Robert Boschet is named in the necrology of the *Confrérie des Ardents* for the year 1257 (Långfors 1926, 1: li; Petersen Dyggve 1934: 218; Berger 1981: 436). — 61 Hue (Huon) d'Arras was a trouvère who probably belonged to the family of the *châtelains* of Arras. He is named in documents dated 1268 and 1275. He is called upon by Jehan Bretel to judge a jeu-parti and is the addressee of a chanson by the Vilain d'Arras (Långfors 1926, 1: xl; Petersen Dyggve 1934: 133; Ungureanu 1955: 122; Berger 1981: 436). Only Hue d'Arras is formally called upon to judge the debate; Robert Bosquet, however, perhaps served as a second judge, in addition to advising the

Dame de Gosnai in her choice of debating position and argumentation. — 63
Rosenberg and Tischler (1981) adopt the emendation proposed by Långfors (1926):
Adés droit.

5 *DAME & ROLANT DE REIMS*
Jeu-parti

I   Concilliés moi, Rolan, je vous an pri.   Advise me, Rolant, I entreat you.
    Dui chivaillier me vont d'amor priant.   Two knights are seeking my love.
    Riches et prous est li uns, je vos di,   One is rich and worthy, I tell you,
    Et se n'ait pas faillit a hardement.   And has not lacked daring.
    L'autre, vos di, il est prous et hardis,   The other, I tell you, is worthy and courageous,
    Mais il n'ait pais tant d'avoir com ait cilz,   But does not possess as much wealth as the first,
    Mais cortois est et saiges et cellans,   Although he is refined and wise and discreet,
    Et bien se seit garder devant les gens.   And knows how to behave around others.
    S'ansi estoit ke je vosise amer,   If ever I should wish to love,
    A queil vos plait il miex a acorder?   Which one do you recommend I choose?

II   — Douce dame, et puis k'il est ansi   — Dear lady, since it is the case   11
    Ke bone Amor vos fait si bel presant,   That good Love offers you such a beautiful gift,
    S'ameir voleis, je vos conseil et pri   If you wish to love, I advise and beseech you
    Ke vostre cuer meteis au plus pairant.   To grant your heart to the more powerful one.
    Moins i avreis blasme s'il an saut cris.   Less blame will you incur if it were proclaimed.
    Riches hons prous doit bien estre saixis   A rich, worthy man deserves to possess
    De haute amor, au los de tous amans,   Lofty love, which all lovers would praise,
    Et bien afiert a dame soffisant   And surely it befits an important lady
    K'elle aint si haut c'on ne l'an puist   To love so highly that she cannot be blamed for it:
        blasmeir:
    Qui honor quiert a honor doit monter.   She who seeks honor should step up to honor.

III   — Certes, Rolan, je vos ai bien oï: — Truly, Rolant, I have heard you.   21
    Il me samble vos parleis faintement.   It seems to me that you speak deceitfully.
    Cant povres hons ait grant proësse an li   When a poor man possesses great prowess
    Et avuelz ceu sans et antandement,   Accompanied by wisdom and judgment,
    Et bien se seit celler, trop mués l'an pris.   And knows well how to be discreet, I esteem him
                                   much more.

    Dame n'i puet meffaire, ce m'est vis.   A lady cannot err in doing so, it seems to me.
    Mais vos estes un poc trop covoitans.   But you are a little too covetous.
    Ancontre sans ne valt ors ne argent,   Compared to good sense, gold and silver are
                                   worthless,

Et Amors vuelt c'on la saiche garder: And Love wants us to know how to guard it.
Por ceu m'acort au povre baicheleir.   For these reasons, I choose the poorer knight.

31 IV — Dame, saichiez, je croi j'aie chosit   — Lady, listen, I believe I have chosen
Trop lou millor, s'il vos vient a talant.   Much the better man, should he appeal to you.
Cant riches hons fait de son cuer otri   When a rich man bestows his heart
A bone Amor, et il se vait randant,   On good Love and does so ardently,
Amors l'aprant et anseigne toz dis: Love instructs him and teaches him every word:
Mieus valt li hons et plus se tient sougis   The man's worth increases, the more submissive he becomes

Ver sa dame; car li ris, li samblans,   Toward his lady; for smiles, appearance,
Li biaus parleirs et li acointemens   Sweet words, and amorous encounters
Li font lou cuers de joie remueir   Stir his heart with joy
Et tous orgoilz an sus de lui bouteir.   And fend off all pride.

41 V — Certes, Rolan, je vos voi trop merri,   — Surely, Rolant, you must have lost your mind
Cant vos parleis si desvoieement.   When you speak so insanely.
Dont l'averoit li povres mal partis.   That would not be fair to the poorer man.
Ke cuer et cors, avoir et tenement   For he who risks heart and body, riches and possessions

Met por avoir conkerre, los et pris,   To gain wealth, praise, and esteem
Aidier li doit bone dame de pris.   Deserves help from a lady of worth.
Et s'il avient car il soit requairans   And if ever he were seeking
Tres haute amor, et il i est venans,   A very lofty love, and he succeeded,
Tuit si panser ne sont c'ai bien celler   All his thoughts would go to keeping it secret
Et a servir sa dame et honorer.   And to serving and honoring his lady.

51 VI — Douce dame, laisons nos parlemens   — Dear lady, let us end our discussion,
Et s'an prenons juge por acorder   And let us call on a judge to settle it,
De Linaige la contesse vaillant;   The worthy Countess of Linaige;
Sor li an soit por lou droit raporter,   Let it be up to her to render judgment
Et sor sa suer Mahau de Commarsi.   And to her sister Mahaut of Commercy.
— Certes, Rolan, et je bien m'i otri: — Certainly, Rolant, I consent to it:
Sor elles soit, ja ne m'an kier oster.   Let it be up to them, I never object to this.

RS 1074, L 265-380, MW 2241
Manuscript: *I* 178r-v (186r-v)
Editions: Meyer 1868: 233; Steffens 1897a: 353; Lubinski 1908: 531; Långfors 1926, 2: 213; Kooijman 1974: 30 (French translation)
Text: Edited by JTG

RR: 12 si] ci — 15 s'il] c'il — 32 s'il] c'il; talant] plaixir *(em. Meyer)* — 42 si] ci — 47 s'il] c'il — 49 si] ci.

DF: Lorraine, including *ai* for *a,* as in *chivaillier* (2), *pais* (6), *saiges* (7); *an* for *en,* as in *an* (1, 15), *antandement* (24); *ei* for tonic *e,* as in *ameir* (13), *voleis* (13), *baicheleir* (30); *i* for countertonic *e,* as in *chivaillier* (2), *millor* (32); preservation of final *t,* as in *faillit* (4), *chosit* (31); *c* for *s,* as in RR; *x* for *s,* as in *saixis* (16), *plaixir* (32); *lou* (32, 39) for *le; ceu* (24, 30) for *ce; avuelz* (24) for *avuec;* adverbial *se* (4) for *si;* 3rd-pers. sing. pres. ind. *ait* (6, 23) for *a, vait* (34) for *va.* Picard, including *biaus* (38) for *beaus; k* for *qu,* as in *ke* (9), *conkerre* (45), *kier* (57); cond. *averoit* (43) for *avroit.*

TN: This song opens the jeux-partis section in manuscript *I,* under the rubric *vesci labecelaire des jeus partis.* It is introduced by a miniature portraying two men, one a merchant in secular garb, with an emblematic purse hanging from his belt, the other a clerk wearing a hooded tunic, illustrating the opposition between rich and poor that informs the debate. — 20 Related to Morawski 1925: no. 1959: "Qui honor chace honor ataint." — 51-57 This last stanza does not follow the rhyme scheme of the others and appears to be truncated (normally each partner is allotted the same number of lines). — 53-55 For identifications, see "Introduction to the Authors: What We Know, What We Can Surmise," in the introduction to this book.

6 *DAME & ROLANT DE REIMS*
Jeu-parti

I   Douce dame, respondez

Dear lady, do respond

A ceu ke je vos demant.

To what I ask you.

Dui chivaillier riche asseis

Two very rich knights

Sont an .i. païs menant.

Live in a prosperous region.

Li uns despant largement

One spends abundantly

A aleir par lou païs

On journeying across the land

Por conkerre los et pris;

To gain praise and honor.

Tot i met, aillors n'antant.

He spends everything on this, attentive to nothing else.

Li autres tient osteil grant,

The other has a lavish lifestyle,

Bien despandans, grant donor sans lasser,

Spending liberally, giving generously and tirelessly,

Et bien se fait a ses vexins douter.

And makes himself feared by his neighbors.

L'un de ces .ij. vos covient resevoir.

One of these two you must accept.

Lou keil prixiés vos muez? Dites me voir.

Which of them do you value more? Tell me truthfully.

II   — Rolan, de ceu ke m'avez

— Rolant, regarding the choice you have offered me   14

Parti dirai mon samblant.

I will give you my opinion.

Cilz doit bien estre honoreis
C'a honor lou sien despant

Et ke se vait travillant
Nut et jor; trop muez l'an prix.
Il doit bien estre saixis
De haute amor de jovant,
Cant por pluie ne por vant
N'est sejornans, s'afiert a bacheler;
Sai en arrier les soloit on amer.
A celui mes cuer et cors et voloir
Qui vait par tout por lui faire valoir.

The one who deserves to be honored
Is the one who spends his wealth in the pursuit of
    honor
And who toils
Night and day; I value him much more.
Well does he deserve to possess
The lofty love of youth,
When neither rain nor wind
Stay him, as suits an aspiring knight.
I know that in the past one used to admire such men.
I grant my heart and body and will
To the one who journeys widely to enhance his merit.

27   III   — Dame, li tans est remeis,
Li siecles ne valt niant.
Cant .i. jones bachelers
Vait par lou païs errant,
Dongier lou vait porxuant,
Sovant en est asaillis;
Destresse lou xeut toz dis,
Finance faut trop sovant,
Dont armes vont demorant.
Je pris celui, et on lou doit löer,
Boin otelier, large dou sien doner,
Ke bien se fait an son païs savoir
Et bien douter, cant il se vuelt movoir.

— Lady, times have changed for the worse,
The present is worthless.
When an aspiring knight
Goes seeking adventure through the land,
Danger stalks him,
Often assailing him;
Anguish trails him always;
His resources run short very often,
Wherefore his arms are idle.
I value—and everyone should praise—
The good host, who bestows his wealth with largesse
Who succeeds in being appreciated in his land
And greatly feared, when he wants to leave it.

40   IV   — Rolans, a tort astriveis,
Et si vos dirai comant:
N'est drois chivailliers nomeis
Qui vait armes esloignant,
Mais cilz qui les vait quairant
Est drois chivailiers gentis;
Avoirs i est bien assis,
Qu'il lou despant noblement.
Car vos saveis vraiement:
Nuns ne conquiert honor par sejorner,
Ne gentis hons ne doit aillors beer
C'a travillier son cors et main et soir,
Tant ke il put et los et pris avoir.

— Rolant, you debate wrongly,
And I will tell you why:
He who shuns arms
Cannot rightfully be called a knight,
But he who seeks them
Is a true noble knight;
Wealth is well placed there,
For he spends it nobly.
Now, this you know for a fact:
No one acquires honor by resting,
Nor should a noble man aspire to anything
Save to work his body both morning and night,
So that he may derive praise and merit.

V — Dame, je croi vos saveis
Mieux ke vos n'aleis disant.
Par Deu, j'an sai bien de teilz
Qui ont aleit grandement.
Asseis vait on tesmoignant
Qu'il sont prous, plus n'ont conquis,

Et s'i ont si lou tot mis
Qu'il ne püent en avant;
Et cant avoirs vait faillant,
Honors n'i valt, on les lait bien passer,
Li grant signors ne.s doignent esgarder.
Qui aikes ait, on lou seit bien veoir,

Et povres hons n'ait ne veux ne pooir.

VI — Rollans, mes cuers est müez
De vostre fol erremant.
Avoirs vait, mais li bonteis
Est a proudome durant
Ke l'ait aquis an soffrant
Et ait les travalz joïs,
Dont il est d'onor garnis.
Ne devez plus mettre avant
Chivaillier de remenant;
Mais prixiez ciaus qui font chevalz crever,

Lances brixier, banieres vanteler.
Cilz ke ceu fait paie bien son dovoir:
Il se doit bien an haute cort paroir.

VII — Dame, nos plais sont fineis:
Je vos don lou torniant,
Puis k'il vos vient a talant.

— Lady, I believe you grasp   53
More than you are letting on.
By God, I know of many such knights
Who have journeyed widely.
People often testify
That they are valiant, but they have gained nothing more,

And they have spent so much of their wealth
That they cannot go on;
And when wealth is wanting,
Honor becomes worthless; everyone lets them pass,
Great lords do not deign to look upon them.
When someone has little wealth, everyone is aware of it,

And a needy man has neither voice nor power.

— Rolant, my heart flutters   66
At your foolish behavior.
Wealth is fleeting, but goodness
Is forever lasting to the man of worth
Who has acquired it by suffering
And who has savored the toils,
Whence he is fortified with honor.
You should no longer prefer
The knight who stays on his land;
Rather, value those knights who fell horses,

Break lances, make banners fly.
He who acts thusly fulfills his obligation;
He fully deserves to appear in the royal court.

— Lady, our proceedings have ended.   79
I grant you the tourneying knight,
Since he appeals to you.

RS 944, L 242-2, MW 1765
Manuscript: *I* 183v–184r (191v–192r)
Editions: Steffens 1897a: 362; Lubinski 1908: 552; Långfors 1926, 2: 258
Text: Edited by WP

RR: 3 riches *(+1) (em. Lubinski)* — 11 ses] ces — 23 s'afiert bien *(+1) (em. Lubinski)* — 37 ocelier *(em. Lubinski).*

DF: Lorraine, including *an* for *en,* as in *an* (4), *antant* (8), *vant* (22), *comant* (41); *ei* for tonic *e,* as in *asseis* (3), *aleir* (6), *honoreis* (16); *i* for countertonic *e,* as in *chivaillier* (3), *signors* (63); *u* for *ui,* as in *nut* (19); *c* for *s,* as in RR (11); *s* for *c,* as in *resevoir* (12); *x* for *s,* as in *vexins* (11), *prixiés* (13), *saixis* (20), *porxuant* (31), *xeut* (33); preservation of final *t,* as in *aleit* (56); *aikes* (64) for *alques; veux* (65) for *voiz; Boin* (37) for *bon; lou* (6) for *le; dou* (37) for *del; ceu* (2) for *ce; nuns* (49) for *nus;* rel. *ke* (18) for nom. *qui;* 3rd-pers. sing. pres. ind. *ait* (64) for *a, vait* (18) for *va.* Picard, including *k* for *qu,* as in *ke* (2), *conkerre* (7); *li* (68) for *la* in nom. sing.; *ciaus* (75) for *cels, ceus.*

TN: 64-65 Långfors (1926) interprets *aikes* as a dialectal form of *aquest;* he glosses: "Celui qui possède, on le remarque bien, mais un homme pauvre n'a ni voix (c'est-à-dire on ne l'écoute pas) ni pouvoir" (He who has wealth is duly noticed, but a poor man has neither voice [that is, no one listens to him] nor power). — 75-76 Reminiscent of Bertran de Born's "Ar ven la coindeta sazos" (PC 80.5), ll. 22-24. — 79-81 In an unusual turn, that is, contrary to the conventions of the genre, Rolant concedes the match in his envoi. This last stanza appears to be truncated—it consists of only three lines—and it does not reproduce the rhyme scheme of the final portion of the preceding stanza.

7 *DAME & ROLANT DE REIMS*
Jeu-parti

I	Douce dame, volantiers	Dear lady, I would gladly
	Saroie, s'il vos plaixoit,	Learn, if it pleased you,
	Lou keil miex vos ameriés,	Which you would choose,
	Se estre lou covenoit:	If you had to:
	Ou chivaillier orguillous,	Either an arrogant knight,
	Qui a chascuns choseroit	Who would insult everyone
	Ne nul desdut ne vorroit,	And would not wish for any pleasure,
	Ou un autre, mesdixant,	Or another, a slanderer,
	Qui toz jors rioteroit	Who would quarrel always,
	Ne gracious ne seroit.	And would not be gracious.

11 II — Rolan, je n'an sai jugier, — Rolant, I do not know how to judge,
Ke bone dame n'ait droit For a worthy lady would not be in the right
K'elle se doie acointier If she were to have a relationship with
A chivaillier de teil ploit; A knight who acted thusly;
Et se panre l'un des .ij. But if one of these two
Me couvenoit orandroit, I had to choose now,
Li orguillous m'averoit. The arrogant knight would have me.

Ja n'amerai mon vivant	Never in my life will I love
Mesdisans, nuns ne les doit;	Slanderers; no one should.
Chascun fuïr les devroit.	Everyone should shun them.

III — Dame, j'an voil desrainier   — Lady, I want to plead   21
Contre vous, comant qu'il soit.   Against you, come what may.
Vous aveis pris lou mestier   You have chosen the attribute
Ke toz li mons haïr doit: That everyone should hate:
Orgoilz est pires de tous.   Arrogance is the worst vice of all.
Mesdisans bien s'aparsoit,   A slanderer could well amend,
Mais orguillous ne poroit.   But an arrogant man could not.
Toz jors li est au devant   Fear of humiliation is always before him,
Despis, qu'il ne sofferoit   Such that he would not tolerate
Qu'il paiast Amours nul droit.   Paying any tribute to Love.

IV — Rolan, j'ainme chivaillier   — Rolant, I like a knight   31
Que por riens ne mesdiroit.   Who under no circumstance would slander.
Je vuel l'orguilloz, lou fier,   I want the arrogant knight, the proud one,
Qui nul desdut n'averoit.   The one who would have no pleasure.
Orguillous doit estre prous.   An arrogant man must be valiant.
Amors, s'i ci ambatoit,   Love, if it penetrated his heart,
Toz malz laissier li feroit.   Would make him renounce all evil.
Mais langue de mesdisant   But a slanderer's tongue
Ocist proudome et dessoit,   Can kill a man of worth and deceive him,
Et fait de l'anver lou droit.   And turn everything topsy-turvy.

V — Dame, orguillous ne tient chier   — Lady, a proud man does not hold dear   41
Home qui antor lui soit: Anyone around him;
Choser vuelt et despitier.   He wants to insult and to scorn.
Sa nature lou desoit.   His nature betrays him.
Orguillous est covoitoz,   An arrogant man is covetous,
Li pires visces qui soit: Which is the worst vice of all:
Li uns de l'autre consoit.   One is engendered by the other.
Teilz mesdit qui s'an repant   Someone can slander, then regret it
Aprés, cant il s'aparsoit;   When he realizes what he has done,
Mais orgoilz ploier ne doit.   But pride must not yield.

VI — Rollans, ne poiez noier   — Rolant, you cannot deny   51
Mesdixans pires ne soit: That a slanderer is worse:
Mesdixans et losangiers   Slanderers and gossip-mongers
Ont mis lou monde a destroit.   Have subverted everything.

Coumant seroit amerous	How could a heart fall in love
Cuers que teil home vairoit,	Upon seeing such a man,
Qui toz jors rioteroit,	Who would always be quarreling,
Mal gracious, mal plaisant?	Ungracious, unpleasant?
Qui an jugeroit a droit,	To judge rightly,
Chascuns haïr les devroit.	Everyone should hate such men.

RS 1338, L 242-3, MW 1921
Manuscript: *I* 181v–182r (189v–190r)
Editions: Steffens 1897a: 360; Lubinski 1908: 546; Långfors 1926, 2: 245
Text: Edited by ED-Q
RR: 2 s'il] c'il — 25 empires *(em. Lubinski)* — 30 paaist *(em. Långfors)* — 34 Qu'il nul *(em. Lubinski)* — 41 orguillouse *(em. Lubinski)*.
DF: Lorraine, including *an* for *en*, as in *volantiers* (1), *an* (11), *comant* (22), *antor* (42); *ei* for tonic *e*, as in *keil* (3), *teil* (14), *aveis* (23); *i* for countertonic *e*, as in *chivaillier* (5); *ou* for *eu*, as in *gracious* (10); *u* for *ui*, as in *desdut* (7); *(s)s* for *c*, as in *dessoit* (39), *desoit* (44); *x* for *s*, as in *plaixoit* (2), *mesdixant* (8); *lou* (3) for *le*; *nuns* (19) for *nus*; rel. *que* (32) for nom. *qui*; 1st-pers. sing. pres. ind. *voil* (21) for *vueil*; inf. *panre* (15) for *prendre*. Picard cond. *averoit* (17) for *avroit*.

8 *DAME & ROLANT DE REIMS*
Jeu-parti

I	Douce dame, vos aveis prins marit,	Dear lady, you have taken a husband,
	Bel et vaillant et jone baicheleir.	A handsome and worthy young knight.
	Aucune gent qui ne vos ainme mi	Some people who do not like you
	Vos font savoir k'il ne fine d'aleir	Let you know that he frequents
	Deleiz femes. Je vos voil demandeir	Other women. I want to ask you
	Ke me dittes par amors, je vos prie,	To tell me please, in the name of love,
	Lou keil ariez plus chier, en vos partie,	Which choice you would prefer,
	Ou lou pooir de lui entierement	To possess him completely
	Et aillors fut sa volenteit menant,	While his desire was drawing him elsewhere,
	Ou li pooirs de lui fut mis aillours	Or to suffer others to possess him
	Et a vos fut sai volenteit tous jours?	While you were always the sole object of his desire?

12	II — Par Deu, Rollant, teil jeu m'aveis partit	— By God, Rolant, given the dilemma you have proposed,
	Ke je cuit bien au millour aseneir.	I am confident I can designate the better alternative.

Je pran lou poir mon marit, jou vos di,	I opt for possession of my husband, I tell you,
Que j'ai bien cors por teil fais a porteir.	For I have the body to bear such a burden.
An veude escuele fait trop mavais humeir.	It is unpleasant to drink from an empty bowl.
Sa volentei soit par tout otroïe,	Let his desire be allowed everywhere,
Mais ke j'aie de lui la druwerie.	But let me have sexual pleasure from him.
J'ai trop plus chier pooir que vient sovent	I prize frequent possession much more
Ke volenteit ou je ne pran niant.	Than desire, from which I gain nothing.
Feme ne vaut qui n'ait joie d'amors	Worthless is the woman who does not have love's joy
Et qui n'en sent nuit et jour lai dousour.	And who does not feel its sweetness night and day.

III — Dame, au pïour vos aveis asenti,	— Lady, you have consented to the worse choice,	23
Je lou vos voil bien par raison monstreir.	As I wish to demonstrate through reason.	
Leiz vos maris gixeis, or soit ansi,	Suppose you are lying near your husband,	
Et bien santeis qu'il ait boin poir d'ovreir,	And you feel sure he is fully capable of performing,	
Mais volenteiz ne s'i welt acordeir,	But his desire does not agree to it;	
Ainz lieve sus et lait vos compaignie,	Instead, he gets up and leaves your company	
Et si s'en vait ou volenteit li prie.	To go where his desire invites him.	
Vos demoreis marrie, a cuer dolant;	You are left distraught, with a lamenting heart;	
Jalozie vos court sus maintenant	Now jealousy assails you	
Et fait panceir qu'il ainme autre ke vos,	And makes you think he loves another,	
Dont vos aveis et mezaixe et corrous.	Which brings you sorrow as well as anger.	

RS 1054, L 242-4, MW 1883

Manuscript: *I* 193v-194r (201v-202r)

Editions: Steffens 1897a: 379; Lubinski 1908: 566; Långfors 1926, 2: 290

Text: Edited by JTG

RR: 5 vos *repeated* — 6 Lo ke *(+1)* — 17 otroiee *(em. Lubinski)*.

DF: Lorraine, including *a* for *al* or *au* before consonant, as in *mavais* (16); *ai* for *a*, as in *baicheleir* (2), *sai* (11); *an* for *en*, as in *pran* (14, 20); *ei* for tonic *e*, as in *aveis* (1), *aleir* (4), *Deleiz* (5), *keil* (7); *ie* for *iee*, as in *otroïe* (17); *our* for *eur*, as in *aillours* (10), *millour* (13), *dousour* (22); *x* and *z* for *s*, as in *gixeis* (25), *mezaixe* (33); preservation of final *t*, as in *marit* (1), *volenteit* (9, 11, 29), *partit* (12); *w* for *vu*, as in *welt* (27); intervocalic *w*, as in *druwerie* (18); *boin* (26) for *bon*; *lou* (7) for *le*; enclitic *jou* (14) for *je + lou*; 3rd-pers. sing. pres. ind. *ait* (26) for *a*, *vait* (29) for *va*; 1st-pers. pres. ind. *voil* (5) for *vueil*.

9. Douce dame, ce soit en vos nomer
T 51r-v

Dou - ce da - me, ce soit en vos no - mer:

Quels vo - lés vos que li vostres a - mis soit,

Buen che - va - lier, s'il li co - vient ar - mer,

Et de - sar - més n'i ait nul autre es - ploit

Ne nu - le rien de cour - toi - sie ait droit—

Tel le vos fas, c'en est l'u - ne par - ti - e—

U biaus et bons, de dou - ce com - pai - gni - e,

Sage et cour - tois et d'a - mou - rous sou - las,

Sans prou - e - ce, i - tel le vous re - fas.

9 *DAME & PERROT DE BEAUMARCHAIS*
Jeu-parti

I   Douce dame, ce soit en vos nomer: Dear lady, let this one be your call.
    Quels volés vos que li vostres amis soit,   Which of these do you wish your lover to be:
    Buen chevalier, s'il li covient armer,   A good knight, when he has to wage battle,
    Et desarmés n'i ait nul autre esploit   Whereas disarmed he has nothing to his credit
    Ne nule rien de courtoisie ait droit—   Nor frankly any refinement—
    Tel le vos fas, c'en est l'une partie—   Such I make him, that's one choice—
    U biaus et bons, de douce compaignie,   Or a handsome, good knight, of pleasing company,
    Sage et courtois et d'amourous soulas,   Wise and refined, and of loving cheer,
    Sans prouèce, itel le vous refas.   But lacking bravery, such I make the other.

II   — Par Dieu, Perrot, mout fait miex a amer   — By God, Perrot, of the two, it is preferable to love   10
    Li uns des deus ki proëce reçoit.   The one who is endowed with prowess.
    Boens chevaliers ne puet tant amasser   However many unfavorable attributes
    Males theches que tous jors preus ne soit;   A good knight may amass, he remains valiant forever;
    En lui blasmer n'a bone dame droit   A worthy lady does not have the right to blame him
    En sa mauté ne en sa vilonie.   For his maliciousness or his vileness.
    S'a l'un des .ij. me covient estre amie,   If I had to take one of these two as a lover,
    Au preu donrai mes guimples et mes las: To the brave one I would give my wimple and my laces:
    Tost le ferai cortois entre mes bras.   I would soon refine him in my arms.

III   — Ce n'en iert ja, douce dame vaillans,   — It will never come to pass, dear worthy lady,   19
    Que vers celui puissiés riens adrecier.   That you will ever redress him in the least.
    Sa proëce le doit mout metre avant,   His bravery must indeed make him preferable,
    Mais li sorplus vos doit mout anoier;   But the rest should really annoy you;
    Car li miens set d'amours le droit mestier,   For mine knows the ways of love:
    Si a larghece et sens et cortoisie,   He has generosity and wisdom and refinement,
    Et la bontés d'ami ne remaint mie.   And a lover's kindness never fails.
    Bien est honis ki a ces theches faut: Anyone lacking these traits is surely contemptible:
    N'est pas preudom ki desarmés ne vaut.   He who is meritless when disarmed is not a worthy man.

IV   — Par Dieu, Perrot, mout vaut miex .i. besans   — By God, Perrot, one bezant is worth much more   28
    Que troi tornois, qui a droit veut jugier.   Than three deniers, if one wants to judge rightly.

En chevalier ne vaut nule riens tant	Nothing is of as much value in a knight
Com proëce, c'est son milleur mestier.	As bravery; it's his best attribute.
Si s'en doit bien bele dame paier	A beautiful lady should indeed be satisfied with it
Et oublïer toute sa vilonie.	And forget all his vileness.
Pour tous mes mals prenc la chevalerie;	Despite all the grief I may encounter, I choose bravery;
Au preu me tieg, quel part que li jus aut:	I side with the brave knight, however the game should play out:
Mains en arai blasme, se blasme en saut.	Less blame will I incur, should blame come of it.

RS 876=878, L 203-2, MW 1802

Manuscripts: *T* 5lr-v♪ (base) (*Perros de bel Marçais*), *C* 50v-51r, *I* 193r (201r), *M* 173r (*pieros de bel marçais*), *U* 70v-71r

Editions: Dinaux 1843: 367; Brakelmann 1868a: 268; Steffens 1897a: 378; Långfors 1926, 2: 175; Tischler 1997, 6: no. 522♪.

Text: Edited by ED-Q

RR: 1 s. sans nul n. *(reading from CI)* — 5 de] ou *(reading from CI)* — 11 proëce] sa bonté *(reading from CIU)* — 18 Tout *(reading from C)* — 20 puissiens *(reading from CMU)* — 24 Et sa l. *(reading from CIMU)* — 29 .i. t. *(reading from CU)* — 34 mals] mes *(reading from U).*

TV: 1 ce] or *CIU;* vos] vo *U;* s. sanz nul n. *M* — 2 Q. vos *(added in a different hand)* voloiz *U;* Q. vollïés *I;* vostre *CIMU;* amin *I* — 3 Boens chevelliers *CU;* si lo *U;* li] le *CIM* — 4 autres *I* — 5 riens *CIM;* de] ou *M,* ne *U* — 6 ceu est *CM,* c'est *I;* l'une] li une *I,* une *M* — 7 Ou bel et blont (boin *I*) de bone (belle *I*) c. *CIU* — 8 courtois] riant *CIU;* r. d'amours et de s. *C* — 10 f. moins a blaimeir *CIU* — 11 cui p. *C;* sa bonté *M* — 12 Boin chivaillier *I;* ne seit *CIU* — 13 Mavaisse taiche *I;* t. c'adés proudons (prodom *U*) ne *CIU* — 14 bone] nulle *C* — 15 En son forfait ne *C,* Ne en son mal ne *M;* ne en] n'en en *U* — 17 *missing C; I inverts lines 17 and 18;* A lui d. *I* — 18 Tost] Tot *IMU* — 19 Se n'iere j. *C;* douce] bone *ICU;* vaillant *CI* — 20 K'envers *CIMU;* c. vos puissiés a. *C,* c. puisse droit a. *I;* rien *U* — 21 le puet bien m. *CIU* — 22 Et li *CIU;* mout] bien *CU;* s. doit mout bien a. *I* — 23 Et li *CIU* — 25 la biaulteis *(I ends here)* dame n'i r. *CIU;* bonté *M;* remaint] refaut *C* — 26 B. ait faillit *CU;* teil taiche *CU* — 27 Il n'est proudons *C;* pas *added in a different hand in U* — 29 uns t. *M;* s'a droit volou *(crossed out)* volez chaingier *U* — 30 A c. *CU* — 31 ces mueldres mestiers *CU* — 32 Si l'en *C;* bele] bone *U;* d. prisier *CU* — 33 toutes ces velonnies *C; M ends here* — 34 Sors *C,* Sor *U;* t. les biens *C* — 36 a. de blaime s'il en sault *CU.*

DF: Picard, including *e* for *a,* as in *theches* (13, 26); *u* for *eu,* as in *jus* (35); *gh* for *g,* as in *larghece* (24); *milleur* (31) for *meilleur;* 1st-pers. sing. pres. ind. in *-c,* as in *prenc* (34); 2nd-pers. pl. verbs in *-(i)és,* as in *volés* (2), *puissiés* (20); fut. *arai* (36) for *avrai.*

TN: 28 A bezant is a gold coin, the Byzantine solidus. — 29 A denier is a small silver coin of France and western Europe.

10. Amis, ki est li muelz vaillans
C 2v-3r (text)
O 13v (music)

A – mis, ki est li muelz vail - lans:

Ou cil ki gist tou - te la nuit

A – veuc s'a – mie a grant des - duit

Et sans fai - re tot son ta - lent,

Ou cil ki tost vient et tost prent

Et quant il ait fait, si s'en fuit,

Ne ju - e pais a re - me - nant,

Ains keut la flor et lait le fruit?

10 *DAME & AMI*
Jeu-parti

I   Amis, ki est li muelz vaillans: Friend, who is more worthy,
Ou cil ki gist toute la nuit   The man who lies all night
Aveuc s'amie a grant desduit   With his beloved in great delight,
Et sans faire tot son talent,   Yet without accomplishing his desire,
Ou cil ki tost vient et tost prent   Or the one who arrives quickly and takes quickly,
Et quant il ait fait, si s'en fuit,   And when he is done hastens off,
Ne jue pais a remenant,   For he does not play for keeps,
Ains keut la flor et lait le fruit?   But rather picks the flower and leaves the fruit?

9   II   — Dame, ceu ke mes cuers en sent   — Lady, what my heart feels about this
Vos dirai, maix ne vos anuit: I will tell you, if you do not mind:
Del faire viennent li desduit   Pleasure comes from doing it,
Et ki lou fait tan soulement   And he who does it until satiated
Partir s'en puet ligierement;   Can leave without regret,
Car tuit li autre fait sont vuit   For all other acts are vain
S'on ne.l fait aprés ou davant;   If one does not do it sooner or later.
Dont valt muelz li faires, je cuit.   Therefore, doing it is preferable, I think.

17   III   — Amis, muelz valt li acoleirs   — Friend, preferable are embracing
Et li jüers et li joïrs,   And playing and enjoying,
Li desduires et li sentirs,   Taking pleasure and caressing,
Li proiers et li esgardeirs   Imploring and gazing
Que li faires et puis aleirs,   To doing it and then leaving,
S'a faire n'est li grans loixirs;   If doing it is not leisurely;
Car trop est doulz li demorers   For lingering is so sweet,
Et trop est griés li departirs.   And parting is so dolorous.

25   IV   — Dame, moult est boens li jueirs   — Lady, it is very enjoyable to play
Et li baixiers et li gesirs,   And kiss and lie side by side,
Li desduires et li sentirs,   To take pleasure and caress,
Li proiers et li esgardeirs;   To implore and gaze;
Sans lou faire c'est li tueirs,   But to abstain from doing it is murder:
C'est la racine des sospirs   It is the root of all sighs
Et ceu k'en amors est ameirs;   And of all that is bitter in love.
Dont valt muelz faire et li foïrs.   Therefore, it is preferable to do it and flee.

33   V   — Amis, ne tieng pais a amor   — Friend, I do not regard it as love
Lou tost faire ne tost aleir: To do it hurriedly and hasten off:

Teille amor ne fait a amer,   Such love is not desirable,
Car elle n'ait poent de savor.   For it has no zest.
Maix cil n'ait pais moult grant dolor   But he who can embrace at leisure
Ke puet a loisir acolleir,   Does not feel much pain,
Et baissier ait joie grignor.   And kissing brings him even greater joy.
En teil amor fait sen entreir.   It makes sense to partake in such a love.

VI — Dame, onc ne vi guerir nul jor,   — Lady, I have never seen anyone heal   41
Por soi deleis s'amie esteir,   By staying near his beloved
Nullui ki fust navreis d'ameir,   When he has been wounded by love,
S'on ne li fist aucun boen tor.   Unless she granted him a good turn.
Teil amor semble feu en for   Such love resembles fire in an oven
Ke ne s'en ait par ou aleir,   That cannot find vent,
Mais enclos ait si grant chalor   But which contains such heat
C'on ne le puet desalumeir.   That one cannot extinguish it.

VII — Amis, or öeis ke je di: — Friend, heed my words: 49
Quant la bouche et li eul se paist   When the mouth and eyes feast
De la chose c'a cuer li plaist,   On the very thing that pleases the heart,
Dont n'en ist li feus par ici?   Is the fire not thereby vented?
— Dame, je ne di pais ensi,   — Lady, that is not what I am saying;
Maix quant li eulz plux se refait,   Rather, when the eye is most satisfied,
Dont trait Amors a cuer son vis   Then Love takes aim at the heart
Ke par loial cuer son dairt trait.   And shoots her arrow into the loyal heart.

VIII — Dame, por Deu, or escouteis: — Lady, for God's sake, listen to me: 57
Li jeus et li gais et li ris   Play and gaiety and smiles
Averont maint home mal mis   Have mistreated many a man
Ke li faires ait repaisseis;   Who would have been restored by doing it.
Dont valt muelz li faires aisseis,   It is therefore much preferable to do it;
Tesmoing de Gautier de Pontis,   Witness Gautier of Pontis,
C'an amor s'an est acordeis.   For he has come into accord with Love.
Or finons la kerelle ci.   Now let us end the dispute here.

RS 365, L 265-52, MW 2354
Manuscripts: *C* 2v-3r (base for the text), *I* 190v-191r (198v-199r), *O* 13v♪ (base for the music)
Editions: Sinner 1760-72, 3: 374; Brakelmann 1867: 347; Steffens 1897a: 374; Långfors 1926, 2: 202; Gennrich 1937: 47♪; van der Werf 1972: 91♪; Rosenberg and Tischler 1981: 165♪; Rosenberg, Tischler, and Grossel 1995: 344♪ (French translation); Tischler 1997, 3: no. 203♪

Text: Rosenberg and Tischler 1981: 165

RR: 6 si] et — 8 flor] foille — 14 s. ueut — 21 *missing (reading based on O, as in Långfors)* — 30 r. de son pis — 31 c. ke amors — 40 f. son sen e. *(+1)* — 41-43 Dame on kes ne vi guerir. nulluj ki damors fust naureis. por deleis samie seir. Ne por deleis samie esteir *(em. Långfors)* — 62-64 *missing (reading from I)*.

TV: Stanzas IV-VIII not included in *O.* — 1 ki] quelx *O* — 4 touz ses talanz *O* — 5 c. ke, et tot *I* — 7 Et naime p. au r. *I*, Ne bee p. au r. *O* — 8 flor] foille *I* — 9 Amie ce q. m. c. sent *O*, D. sonkes m. c. ot san *I* — 11 De f. uienne *I*, li geu tuit *O* — 12 Et quil ont f. *I*, Car cil qui tost vient et tost prent *O* — 14 autres *I*, fait] geu *O*, son veut *I* — 15 Sil *O* — 16 faire *IO*, ce c. *O* — 17 li deporters *O* — 18 Et li iuer *I*, Et li ueoirs et li sentirs *O* — 19 Li baisiers et li acolers *O* — 20 esgarder *I*, Et li parlers et li tenirs *O* — 21 *missing I*, Que li tost faire et p. aler *O* — 22 Sans *I*, Sau *O* — 23 est] iert *I*, *missing O* — 24 est] iert *I* — 26 baisier — 29 *missing* — 31 Et ceu camors iert li meris — 32 foir — 33 ting, amors — 34 ne] lou — 37 M. cilz en ait moult grant dosour — 38 Qui p. a l. escoler — 40 fait sans antrer — 41-43 Dame onkes ne vi garir. nelui qui damor fut naurez. ne por deleis samie oster — 44 f. an aucun t. — 45 Teile — 46 Ki — 47 en si] anci — 48 Qui — 50 b. o les eus s. — 53 di mies e. — 54 li oil — 55 amor an c. — 56 Qui, soudart t. — 61 dasseis.

DF: Lorraine, including *a* (7, 51) for *au; ai* for *a*, as in *pais* (7), *dairt* (56), *gais* (58); *ei* for tonic *e*, as in *acoleirs* (17), *aleir* (34), *Teille* (35), *deleis* (42); *poent* (36) for *point; boen* (44) for *bon; ceu* (9) for *ce; lou* (12) for *le;* 3rd-pers. sing. pres. ind. *ait* (6) for *a.* Epenthesized future *Averont* (59) suggests Picard origin of composition.

TN: Stanzas I-VI form a pattern of *coblas doblas,* broken by stanzas VII and VIII; one or both of these may be apocryphal. — 21 As in Långfors 1926, the manuscript *O* reading *li tost faire* is here emended to preserve the text's consistent use of nominative *-s* and because *tost* expresses an awkward anticipation of the next stanza. — 41-44 This passage is corrupt in both manuscripts. Rosenberg and Tischler (1981) have adopted Långfors' reconstruction. — 55-66 These lines are no doubt corrupt.

MC: Unlike the majority of melodies in *O,* this one is notated in nonmensural breves. This song is a contrafactum of Bernart de Ventadorn's "Can vei la lauzeta mover" (PC 70.43). Bernart's melody is the most widely disseminated of all troubadour songs, and it was borrowed for several French and Latin poems. Altogether the melody is extant for the original Old Occitan text in three manuscripts, for this text and that of song no. 17 in one manuscript each, for a third French text (RS 349) in two manuscripts, for a Latin poem attributed to Philip the Chancellor in four manuscripts, and for a late Occitan text in the manuscript of the mystery play of Saint Agnes. The consistency in transmission of all versions of the melody (which are given synoptically in van der Werf 1984: 62*-71*) is remarkable.

11. Dites, dame, li keilz s'aquitait muelz
 C 62v-63r (text)
 A 147r-v (music)

Di - tes, da - me, li keilz s'a - qui - tait muelz

En - vers a - mors: uns an - fes de ju - vant

De *quinze* ans fut en a - mors en - tan - tis,

Si a - mait tant ke il ot *cin* - *quante* ans,

Pués lait a - mors tous hai - tiez et tous sains,

Ou cil ki out *qua* - *rante* ans ou plu - sains

Con - qes a - maist, puis se prist a a - meir,

Et a - mait puis tant com il pout du - reir?

11 *DAME & SIRE*
Jeu-parti

I Dites, dame, li keilz s'aquitait muelz
Envers amors: uns anfes de juvant
De .xv. ans fut en amors entantis,
Si amait tant ke il ot .l. ans,
Pués lait amors tous haitiez et tous sains,
Ou cil ki out .xl. ans ou plusains
Conqes amaist, puis se prist a ameir,
Et amait puis tant com il pout dureir?

Tell me, lady, who has better discharged his debt
Toward love: a young man
Who at fifteen was heedful of love,
And loved until he was fifty,
Then forsook love while in full health and vigor;
Or someone who was forty or more before
He ever loved, then took to loving,
And loved henceforward till his dying day?

9 II — Biaus dous sire, il n'est mies soutis
Ki de ces .ij. ne seit lou jugemant.
Puis ke li hons atant tant k'il est vieus
Ainsois k'il aint, il ait mauvaisemant
Servit amors, de ce suis touz certains:
Car en amor doit li hons premerains
Metre son tens et jonece useir
Et, cant est vieus, a Deu merci crieir.

— Dear sweet lord, he is not very clever
Who cannot decide between these two.
Since one of them waits till he is old
Before loving, he has badly
Served love; of that I am quite certain.
For in loving one must first
Spend one's time and one's youth,
Then in old age ask God for his mercy.

17 III — Sachiez, dame, c'auteir mestier ait cil
De Deu servir ki vient novellemant
Com uns anneis, car tout prant a son chois;
Amors ausi an son chois chascun prant:
L'un prant anuit et l'autre au dariens,
Et cant aucuns s'est en amors enpoint;
Cil ke trait ne se puet ancuseir,
Mais cil ki sert jusc'a la fin est beirs.

— You should know, lady, that another office
Has he who comes to serve God newly
Like a lamb, for God takes all as He chooses;
Love likewise takes each of us as she chooses,
Taking one today and another later,
Whenever a person is ripe for love;
The one who defers cannot be blamed,
And he who serves love forever after is the
    worthy one.

25 IV — Biaus dous sire, mal estes antantis
Se vos creeis k'il soit si faitemant
C'on ne puet estre en amor trop tarris,
Puis c'on i soit jusc'au definemant.
Vous saveis bien ke li maus tient en rains,
Dont li vielars an sont ovriers dou moins;
Puis .xl. ans ne fait hons fors c'aleir,
Pou vaut on puis por deduit demeneir.

— Dear sweet lord, you are not shrewd
If you think it is thus,
That one cannot be too tardy in love,
Provided that one perseveres until death.
You know full well that back pain sets in,
Which keeps old men from laboring as long;
Beyond the age of forty one only declines:
One is then hardly suited to partake in pleasure.

V — Dame, meus vaut .i. lans ovriers tarris | — Lady, a slow, late worker is preferable
C'uns boins miaus ki d'ovreir se repant. | To one much superior who repents of having labored.

Li amors nait dou cuers, c'est ses drois leus; | Love is born in the heart: that is its proper seat;
Elle ne vient pas des rains tan ne quant, | It does not come from the loins to any extent,
Car d'un viel tor une vache meus prant | For a cow gets more from an old bull
Ke d'un jone vel ke houce et n'en chiet rans. | Than from a young calf that gets worked up for naught.
C'est geu d'anfant commanceir sans fineir: | It is child's play to start and not finish:
La bone fin fait l'ovraige loeir. | A good finish brings praise to the whole work.

RS 1354, L 133-55, MW 2084

Manuscripts: C 62v-63r (base for the text), A 147r-v♪ (base for the music), a 147r-148r♪, b 165v-166r, c 3r

Editions: Brakelmann 1868a: 283; Bertoni 1919: 56; Långfors 1926, 1: 274; Tischler 1997, 9: no. 765♪

Text: Edited by ED-Q

RR: 3 .vij. *(reading from Aab)* — 5 Puet — 7 Conquestes *(+1) (reading from Aab)* — 15 jonete — 22 s'est] c'est — 34 se] ce — 35 ses] ces.

TV: 1 Jehan Simon *Aab;* Biaux Grivelier *c;* le quel *bc;* s'acointa *c* — 2 amour *a;* u cil ki des (de *b*) j. *Aabc* — 3 seize *c;* a amer *Aa* — 4 Et *Aabc;* qu'il *Abc;* en ot *bc;* demie (demi *abc*) cent *Aabc* — 5 P. le laissa *Aabc;* tout h. *Ac;* tout s. *c* — 6 en ot .xl. ou *b* — 7 amait *Aab;* dont (quant *bc*) se (si *a*) *Aabc;* a l'amer *bc* — 8 a. tant com il pot puis d. *b* — 9 Sire Jehan (Jehans *a*) *Aabc;* chieus n'est mie s. *Aab,* cil est moult pou s. *c* — 11 li hom *ab* — 13 Paié *Aabc;* soiés c. *Aabc* — 14 amours *Aabc;* li hom *Aa* — 15 et sa j. *Aab,* t. sa j. et son cuer *c* — 17 *stanzas III–VIII missing c,* Chertes Jehan (Jehans *a*) autel *Aab* — 19 Que *b;* Mort p. *b* — 20 Et a. *Aa;* a s. *Aab* — 21 p. el ni *Aab;* a (aus *b*) d. *Aab* — 22 kascuns *Ab,* cascun *a;* s'est] est *b;* amour *Aa* — 23 ki recroit ne s'i p. aquiter *Aab* — 24 jusqu'en *b* — 25 Sire Jehan trop e. enfantix *Aab* — 26 Quant v. cuidiez *b* — 27 puist e. en amours (amour *a*) t. tardieus *Aab* — 28 Pour k'il *Aab;* sont *Aa;* jusque au *b* — 29 es r. *Aab* — 30 Et li viellart en s. esters au (del *ab*) mains *Aab* — 31-32 *occur as lines 47–48 in Aab* — 31 On ne doit pas sans amour meüürer *Aab* — 32 Mais jones (hom *added in b*) doit son deduit demener (mener *b*) *Aab* — 33 Jehan *Ab,* Jehans *a;* ouvries *A;* takieus *Aab* — 34 bien (biens *ab*) inniaus *Aab;* d'amer se reprent *Aa* — 35 cuer *Aa;* s'est s. *A,* cuer et nequedent *b* — 36 *missing b;* n'ist *A;* r. et *A;* nekedent *Aa* — 37 Fait uns vieus tors mieus une vake prains *Aab* — 38 C'uns (C'un *ab*) veelés *Aab;* grains *Aab* — 39 gus *Aa* — 40 Li *Aa;* fins *Aa* — 41-56 *Aab give one additional stanza and two envois:*

— Sire, sachiés k'entreus k'est biaus li geus
Le doit laissier ki tant a d'ensïent.
Ki puis .xvi. ans fu d'amer volentieus
.xxxiiij. ans il a fait paiement

Envers amours de ses jours souverains.
Ens el mort bos est lués li fus estains:
Puis .l. ans n'en fait on fors aler,
Poi vaut on puis pour amour demener.

49   — Ferri, son loier pert con faus et vains
Ki ne part sert, ne ja aveuc les sains
En paradis ne pora nus entrer
Se bone fin ne l'i met, ch'est tout cler.

53   — Felippot, on doit mengier a .ij. mains
Ki a bien fain et, qant ses cuers est plains,
Cesser; kar c'est anuis de tant limer.
Nus trop n'est preus; boin fait a droit siecler.

— 42 a escïent *b* — 43 d'amours *b* — 45 ses gieuz *b* — 46 mors *b;* et loez *b* — 48
deduit d. *b* — 50 parsert *b* — 53 cil d. *b* — 54 grant f. *b;* son cuer *b* — 55 C'est cler *b*
— 56 Nul t. n'est bon bon f. *b;* point s. *ab.*

DF: Lorraine, including *ai* for *a,* as in *ovraige* (40); *an* for *en,* as in *anfes* (2), *juvant*
(2), *prant* (20); *ei* for tonic *e,* as in *keilz* (1), *ameir* (7), *beir* (24); *c* for *s,* as in RR (22,
34, 35); *s* for *c,* as in *Ainsois* (12); preservation of final *t,* as in *Servit* (13); *ue, eu* for *ieu,*
as in *muelz* (1), *meus* (33), *leus* (35); *boins* (34) for *bons;* conj. *Pués* (5) for *puis; lou* (10)
for *le; dou* (30, 35) for *del;* 3rd-pers. sing. pres. ind. *ait* (17) for *a;* 3rd-pers. sing. pret.
in *-ait,* as in *aquitait* (1), *amait* (4); rel. *ke* (38) for nom. *qui.*

TN: We chose not to regularize the rhyme scheme of this song. Tyssens (1992)
eliminates this piece from her census of Old French jeux-partis and tensons authored
by women on the basis of inconsistent manuscript evidence: as transcribed in
manuscript *C,* the song opposes an anonymous Dame and an unnamed Sire, whereas
in three other manuscripts (*A, a,* and *b*) the participants in the exchange are given as
Jehan Bretel and Jehan Simon, and in a fourth (manuscript *c*) the latter is replaced
by Grivelier. In fact, this unstable attribution highlights the ease with which, in a
genre predicated on contradistinction, a given discourse can be appropriated by a
voice of a different gender. — 40 "La fin loe l'œuvre" (Morawski 1925: no. 1002).
"La fin couronne l'oevre" (Le Roux de Lincy 1859, 2: 493).

MC: Manuscript *a* transmits a different melody from the one in manuscript *A.* No
melody is extant for the text that has a female protagonist. The circulation of two
different melodies for the text with solely male voices suggests the possibility that
the instability of text authorship and attribution extended to the music as well.

12 BLANCHE DE CASTILLE & THIBAUT DE CHAMPAGNE
Tenson

Tensons, or lyric debates, are not regulated by the rigid conventions that gov-
ern jeux-partis: the questions argued need not be dilemmatic and the inter-

Song no. 12, Rome, Biblioteca Apostolica Vaticana, Regina 1522, fol. 169v, Le roi de navarre a la roine blanche. Copyright © Biblioteca Apostolica Vaticana.

12. Dame, merci, une riens vous demant
b 169v-170r (text)
K 33 (music)

-Da - me, mer - ci, u - ne riens vous de - mant:

Di - tes me voir, se Diex vous be - ne - i - e,

Quant vous mor - rez et je— mes c'iert a - vant,

Quar a - prez vous ne vi - ve - rai je mi - e—

Que de - ven - dra A - mours, cele es - ba - hi - e?

Qui tant a - vez sens, va - lour, et j'aim tant

Que je croi bien qu'a - prez nous iert fail - li - e.

locutors do not appeal to judges. In form, tensons may comprise fewer than
six stanzas, and they do not necessarily include envois.

I	Dame, merci, une riens vous demant:	Lady, I beg you, I ask you one thing:
	Dites me voir, se Diex vous beneïe,	Tell me truthfully, may God bless you,
	Quant vous morrez et je—mes c'iert avant,	When you and I die—but I shall die first,
	Quar aprez vous ne viverai je mie—	For after your death I could not survive—
	Que devendra Amours, cele esbahie?	What will become of Love, in such grief?
	Qui tant avez sens, valour, et j'aim tant	For you have so much good sense and worth, and I love you so
	Que je croi bien qu'aprez nous iert faillie.	That I do believe Love will end after we pass on.

II	— Par Dieu, Tiebaut, selonc mon escïant,	— By God, Thibaut, in my judgment, 8
	Amours n'iert ja pour nulle mort perie,	Love will never perish for anyone's death,
	Ne je ne sai se vous m'alez gabant,	Nor do I know if you are trying to dupe me,
	Que trop maigres n'estes encore mie.	For you are hardly scrawny yet.
	Quant nous morrons—Diex nous doint bone vie!—	When we die—God grant us long life!—
	Bien croi qu'Amours damage y avra grant,	I do believe Love will suffer great harm,
	Mes tous jors iert valours d'Amour emplie.	But Love's worth will always be consummate.

III	— Dame, certes, ne devez pas cuidier,	— Lady, surely, you must not think that; 15
	Mes bien savoir que moult vous ai amee.	Rather, know full well that I have loved you deeply.
	De la joie m'en aim miex et tieng chier	From this joy I love and esteem myself more
	Et pour ce ai ma grace recouvree;	And for this reason I have recovered my elegance;
	Onc Diex ne fist si tres bele riens nee	For never did God create anything as lovely
	Que vous, mes ce me fait trop esmaier,	As you, but it greatly troubles me that
	Quant nous morrons, qu'Amours sera finee.	When we die Love will cease to exist.

IV	— Tiebaut, taisiez! Ne devez commencier	— Thibaut, be silent! You should not utter 22
	Raison qui soit de tous biens desreee.	Words so devoid of sense.
	Vous le dites pour moi amoloier	You are saying that to soften me
	Encontre vous, que tant avez guilee.	Toward you, you who have beguiled me so.
	Je ne di pas, certes, que je vous hee,	I am not saying, of course, that I hate you;
	Mes se d'Amours me couvenoit jugier,	But, if I had to pass judgment on Love,
	Elle seroit servie et honnoree.	She would be served and honored.

V	— Dame, Diex doint que bien jugiez a droit	— Lady, God grant that you judge rightly 29
	Et connoissiez les maulz qui me font plaindre;	And know the pains that make me lament;

Mes je sai bien, quex le jugement soit,	But I know well, regardless of the judgment,
Se je y muir, Amours couvendra fraindre,	That if I die, Love will have to falter,
Se vous, Dame, ne le faites remaindre	Unless you, lady, make her remain
Dedens son leu arriere ou elle estoit;	Where she used to be in the past;
Quar vostre sens ne porroit nulz ataindre.	For no one could approach your wisdom.

36   VI — Tiebaut, s'Amours vous fait pour moi destraindre,

    — Thibaut, if Love makes you suffer for my sake,

Ne vous griet pas, quar s'amer m'estouvoit,

    Do not let it grieve you, for if I were obliged to love,

J'ai bien un cuer qui ne se saroit faindre.

    I have a heart that could not be false.

RS 335, L 240-58, MW 1279

Manuscripts: *b* 169v-170r (base for the text) (*Le roi de navarre a la roine blanche*), *A* 139r-v♪, *C* 51v-52r (*li rois thiebaus de naivaire*), *K* 33♪ (base for the music) (*Li rois de Navarre*), *M^t* 67v♪, *O* 37r♪, *S* 318v, *T* 15v-16r (*Li rois de Navare*), *V* 17r-v♪, *X* 37v-38r♪ (*Li rois de navarre*), *a* 137r-v♪

Editions: La Ravallière 1742, 2: 97; Tarbé 1851: 81; Brakelmann 1868a: 269; Wallensköld 1925: 163; Pauphilet 1952: 899; Woledge 1961: 153 (English translation); Mary 1967, 1: 358 (French translation); Anglès 1973: 67♪ (Spanish translation); Brahney 1989: 206 (English translation); Tischler 1997, 3: no. 195♪

Text: Edited by JTG

RR: 1 merci *missing (reading from ACKM^tOSTVXa)* — 3 mes jou qui ert avant *(reading from CM^tOTV)* — 24 amolier *(-1) (reading from CKM^tOTVXa)* — 32 fraindre] plaindre *(reading from KM^tX).*

TV: 2 m'en *M^tTX,* moy *CKSV;* beneine *A* — 3 morrez ou *S;* mais jou que c. *Aa;* serai vivant *(expunctuated)* mes *V;* c'ers *K* — 4 n'en *T;* vivroie *CKM^tOTVX,* morroie *S* — 5 devera *A,* devanrait *C;* d. cele amor e. *S* — 6 Que *CKM^tTVXa;* sen *O;* bialteis sens et cors gent *C,* sen biauté *M^t,* s. et valor *KVX;* et aim *X,* et je aim *M^t;* tent a vos sanz biauté et l'aim *S* — 7 nous] vos *CKM^tOSVX* — 8 ensient *ATa* — 10 guillant *AKM^tOTVXa* — 11 n'i estez e. *M^t,* n'estes vos e. *S;* Ke per mon greit ne lais e. *C* — 12 D. vos *OX* — 13 Je *ATa;* B. sai *S;* avrait *C* — 14 tout *Aa;* valour *ACTV;* j. s'est voloir *S;* d'amours complie *AKM^tOSTVXa,* d'amors joie *C* — 15 D. merci ne d. mais c. *S* — 16 savoir] croire *S;* moult] trop *ACKM^tOSTVXa* — 17 Et de la j. vos aig *S;* miex] plus *KOVX* — 18 p. ce ai (s'ai *C*) je *CM^t;* grace] joie *CV* — 19 Qu'ainz *CKM^tOSTVX,* Ains *Aa;* f. rien si tres bele n. *O* — 20 Com v. *AKM^tSTVXa,* Com v. estes ceu *C,* Con vos ma dame mout me *O;* trop *missing COS* — 21 vous morroiz *V,* n. norrons amors *S;* serait *C* — 22 Taixiés Thibaut *C;* nus (vos *SV*) ne doit c. *CKM^tSTVX* — 23 ke si est droit *C;* qui est de t. b. escontee *S;* tout *Aa;* biens] droiz *M^tOTVX;* desevree *ACKM^tOTVXa* — 25 que] ki *Aa* — 26 que] qui *X;* haice *C* — 27 se] s'il *Aa;* covient *X* — 28 Ele en s. *T* — 29 bien] vous *ACKM^tOSVXa,* nous *T* — 31 Que je s. *ACTa,* Que bien s. *KM^tOSVX;* quiex (quel *X,* quoi *T*) que *AKM^tOSTVXa;* le *missing ATa;* li jugierres *S;* j. en soit *M^t* — 32 je en (me *V*) m. *OS;* qu'A. *S;* couvanrait *C,* convient a *AKM^tOTVXa;* faindre *ACOTVa,* rendre *S* —

34 son leu] cele valour *S* — 35 Qu'a *AKM^{t}OTXa,* Que *V;* sen *M^t;* effaindre *C* — 36-38 *missing K* — 36 Thiebaus *C;* per m. destaindre *C* — 37 ke s'amer *ACSa;* que se a. n'estoit *M^{t}OTX,* que se ainz m'estoit *V* — 38 se] si *S;* qui] ke *C;* fraindre *M^t.*

DF: Picard, including *le* (33) for *la; jou* (3) for *je;* fut. *viverai* (4) for *vivrai;* cond. *saroit* (38) for *savroit.*

TN: The rubricator of manuscript *b* identifies Thibaut's interlocutor as *la roine blanche* in accordance with the legend linking Blanche de Castille and the King of Navarre. Wallensköld (1925) argues that Thibaut's partner is a fictitious character— that Thibaut is the sole author of this debate—on the grounds that the song has an odd number of stanzas and only one envoi. Thibaut de Champagne's latest editor (Brahney 1989) does not categorically deny Blanche's participation. For further details, see "Introduction to the Authors: What We Know, What We Can Surmise," in the introduction to this book.

ME: 6/5-6/6 *K* gives a separate note (a) over the word *et* between *sens* and *valour;* we have eliminated both the word and the note to avoid hypermetry.

MV: 1/3 ed *AOa;* eed *M^t* — 1/4 d *A* — 1/5-1/10 c-e-f-ge-fed-d *Aa* — 1/7 ggf *M^{t}X;* g *O* — 1/9 gfe *O* — 1/10 e *A;* fg *O;* d *a* — 2/1-2/2 a-b *O* — 2/4 c$_p$ *O* — 2/7 fe *M^t;* e *X* — 2/9-2/11 ga-aggf-g *O* — 2/10 e$_p$ed *a* — 2/11 f *AM^{t}a;* d *X* — 3/1 e *a* — 3/3 ed *AOa;* edd *X* — 3/4 d *A* — 3/5 c *A;* b *a* — 3/6 e *Aa* — 3/7 f *Aa;* g *O* — 3/7-3/9 gg-b-a *X* — 3/8 ge *Aa;* f *O;* f *M^t* — 4/1-4/2 a-b *O* — 4/4 cc$_p$ *O* — 4/7 fe *M^t* — 4/8 f *AM^{t}OXa* — 4/9 d *AM^t;* ga$_p$ *O;* fd *a* — 4/10 eed *AM^{t}Xa;* gf *O* — 4/11 g *O* — 5/1-5/4 aa$_p$-f-e-g *O* — 5/6 c *O;* b^b *a* — 5/7-5/11 b-c-bb$_p$-aga-f *O* — 5/9 ba *Aa* — 5/10 bc *AXa;* ba *M^t* — 5/11 c *Aa;* bc *M^t;* b *X* — 6/1-6/4 c-d-c-bc *O* — 6/5 a *Aa* — 6/7-6/10 d-d-b-c$_p$ *A;* g-a-b^b^{p}-ba *O* — 6/8-6/10 d-b-ccb *M^t* — 6/8-7/11 notes missing *a* — 7/1 a *AM^t;* bb$_p$ *O* — 7/3 a$_p$ *A;* ag *M^t* — 7/7 b^b *O* — 7/8-7/11 notes missing *M^t* — 7/10 abaf *O.*

MC: Manuscript *V* transmits a different melody from the one found in the other sources.

13 *DAME & SEIGNOR*
Tenson

I	Dites, seignor, que devroit on jugier	Tell me, my lord, how should one judge
	D'un traïtour qui faisoit a entendre	A traitor who claimed
	Que il avoit m'amour sanz destorber?	He had won my love without difficulty?
	Mais ce n'iert ja, Dex m'en puisse deffendre!	For this will never be, God forbid!
	Prenez le moi, sou me faites lier	Take him and tie him up for me,
	Et sor l'eschiele monter sanz lui descendre,	And have him climb the pillory; do not bring him down.
	Que nul avoir	No ransom
	N'en porroie je prendre,	Could I take for him;
	Ainz morra voir.	Rather, he will die, truly.

13. Dites, seignor, que devroit on jugier
O 43v-44r

Di - tes, sei - gnor, que de - vroit on ju - gier

D'un tra - i - tour qui fai - soit a en - ten - dre

Que il a - voit m'a - mour sanz des-tor - ber?

Mais ce n'iert ja, Dex m'en puis - se def - fen - dre!

Pre - nez le moi, sou me fai - tes li - er

Et sor l'es - chie - le mon - ter sanz lui des - cen - dre,

Que nul a - voir

N'en por - roi - e je pren - dre,

Ainz mor - ra voir.

II — Dame, merci: confession requier.
De mes pechiez me vuil corpaubles rendre
Vers vos, dame, cui cuidoie engignier.
Li deables le me fist entreprendre.
Cuidiiez vos que deüsse endurer
Les maus d'amer? Nenil, mie le moindre;
Por vos avoir
Je.l vos faisoie entendre
Por decevoir.

— Lady, have mercy, I need to confess.   10
I wish to plead guilty for my sins
Toward you, lady, whom I thought to seduce.
The devil made me do it.
Did you think I cared to endure
The pains of love? No, not in the least;
In order to have you
I conveyed this to you
So I could trick you.

III — Par Deu, ribauz, quant li autre savront,
Li tricheour, que tex est ma justice,
Que vos avroiz les ieuz sachiez dou front,

Ja mes par aux n'iert tel dame requise.
De la paour li autre s'en fuiront:
Lors verra l'en les lëaus sanz faintise
Apertement,
Quant la lengue iert jus mise
Qui d'amors ment.

— By God, you rake, when the others learn—   19
The cheats—what my verdict is:
That your eyes will be plucked from your
        forehead,
Never by them will such a lady be courted.
In fear those others will flee;
Then the loyal and guileless will be revealed
Openly,
When the tongue that lies about love
Is banished.

RS 1283, L 265-534, MW 923
Manuscript: *O* 43v-44r♪
Editions: Jeanroy 1889: 463; Gennrich 1956: 55♪; Tischler 1997, 8: no. 729♪
Text: Edited by WP
DF: Lorraine, including *a* velarized before *bl,* as in *corpaubles* (11); *dou* (21) for *del;*
aux (22) for *eus;* enclitic *sou* (5) for *si + lou;* fut. *avroiz* (21) for *avrez.* Burgundian *uil*
for *ueil,* as in *vuil* (11).
MC: The notation in manuscript *O* is mensural.

Voices in Monologue

Chansons

14
Chanson d'amour

The courtly chanson d'amour, labeled *grans chans* in manuscript *I* (from the first quarter of the fourteenth century), is lauded by Dante as the supreme poetic form (*De vulgari eloquentia* [ca. 1305] 2.8). Normally composed of five stanzas followed by an envoi, the genre treats a single subject, fin'amors—the true, perfect, refined love elaborated by the troubadours—using a set of fixed vocabulary and motifs (see "Fin'amors and the Women Trouvères," in the introduction to this book).

I La froidor ne la jalee	Neither cold nor frost
Ne puet mon cors refroidir,	Can chill my body,
Si m'ait s'amor eschaufee,	So much has his love enflamed me;
Dont plaing et plor et sospir;	So I lament and weep and sigh,
Car toute me seux donee	For I have devoted my whole being
A li servir.	To serving him.
Muels en deüsse estre amee	I should be better loved for it
. . . .	. . . .
De celui ke tant desir,	Of the one I so desire,
Ou j'ai mise ma pensee.	On whom I have fixed my thoughts.

II stanza with page number 11 in margin:

II Ne sai consoil de ma vie	I do not know how to lead my life
Se d'autrui consoil n'en ai,	Unless I obtain the counsel of another,
Car cil m'ait en sa baillie	For he has me in his sway
Cui fui et seux et serai.	Whose love I was, am, and will always be.
Por tant seux sa douce amie	I am so sweet on him
Ke bien sai	That I am certain,
Ke, por rien ke nuls m'en die,	Despite what anyone might tell me,
N'amerai	I will love
Fors lui, dont seux en esmai.	No one but him, who stirs me.
Quant li plaist, se m'ocie!	If he wants to, let him kill me!

III Amors, per moult grant outraige
    M'ocieis, ne sai por coi;
    Mis m'aveis en mon coraige
    D'ameir lai ou je ne doi.
    De ma folie seux saige
    Quant je.l voi.
    De porchaiscier mon damaige
    Ne recroi.
    D'ameir plux autrui ke moi
    Ne li doinst Deus couraige.

Love, through this great outrage 21
You are killing me, I do not know why.
You have incited me
To love where I should not.
In my madness I am clever
When I see him.
From pursuing my own harm
I do not retreat.
May God never move him
To love another more than me.

IV Ensi, laisse! k'en puis faire,
    Cui Amors justice et prant?
    Ne mon cuer n'en puis retraire,
    Ne d'autrui joie n'atent.
    Trop ont anuit et contraire
    Li amant:
    Amors est plux debonaire
    A l'autre gent
    K'a moi, ki les mals en sent,
    Ne nuls biens n'en puis traire.

So, alas! what can I do, 31
When Love rules and possesses me?
I cannot withdraw my heart,
Nor do I expect joy from another.
Too many torments and adversities
Do lovers endure:
Love is kinder
To others
Than to me, who feels its pain,
And can derive from it no good.

V Ma chanson isi define,
    Ke joie ait vers moi fineir;
    Car j'ai el cors la rasine
    Ke ne puis desrasineir,
    Ke m'est a cuer enterine,
    Sens fauceir.
    Amors m'ont pris en haïne
    Por ameir.
    J'ai beüt del boivre ameir
    K'Isoth but, la roïne.

My song ends here, 41
Since for me joy has ended;
For in my body grows a root
I cannot uproot,
It is planted deep in my heart,
Honestly.
Love hates me
For loving.
I have drunk of the bitter potion
That Yseut the queen drank.

RS 517, L 265-973, MW 801
Manuscript: *C* 136r–v (*une dame*)
Editions: Wackernagel 1846: 53; Bartsch 1920: 222; Bec 1978: 8; Rosenberg and
Tischler 1981: 84; Mölk 1989: 94 (German translation); Rosenberg, Tischler, and
Grossel 1995: 210 (French translation)
Text: Rosenberg and Tischler 1981: 84

RR: 2 refroidier — 8 *missing* — 26 j. uo — 30 douraige — 42 finei *(em. Bartsch).*
DF: Lorraine, including *ai* for *a,* as in *outraige* (21), *lai* (24), *porchaiscier* (27), *laisse*
(31); *ei* for tonic *e,* as in *ocieis* (22), *ameir* (29), *fineir* (42); *c* for *s(s)* and *s* for *c,* as in
justice (32), *fauceir* (46), *rasine* (43); preservation of final *t,* as in *beüt* (49); 3rd-pers.
sing. pres. ind. *ait* (3) for *a; seux* (14) for *sui.*
TN: 8 It is suggested in Bartsch 1920 that *Par desir* fill this lacuna. — 49-50 These
lines allude to the celebrated passage in Thomas de Bretagne's version of the legend
of Tristan and Yseut, where the couple speculates at length on the unsettling effects
of the love potion, which they have just drunk while on board the ship en route to
Cornwall. Both play on the polysemy of the Old French *(l')amer* which designates
love, bitterness, and the sea (Benskin, Hunt, and Short 1992-95: 301-3).

15 *MAROIE DE DIERGNAU*
Chanson d'amour

I Mout m'abelist quant je voi revenir
   Yver, gresill et gelee aparoir,
   Car en toz tans se doit bien resjoïr
   Bele pucele, et joli cuer avoir.
   Si chanterai d'amors por mieuz valoir,
   Car mes fins cuers plains d'amorous desir
7 Ne mi fait pas ma grant joie faillir.

Great is the pleasure I take upon the return
Of winter, when hail and frost appear,
For in every season a lovely maiden
Must indeed rejoice and have a cheerful heart.
So I will sing of love to increase my ardor,
For my true heart full of amorous desire
Will not let my great joy falter.

RS 1451, L 178-1, MW 964
Manuscripts: *M* 181r-v♪ (base) (*Maroie de dregnau de lille*), *T* 169r♪ (*Maroie de drignau*)
Editions: Laborde 1780, 2: 185 (French translation); Dinaux 1836: 39 (French
translation); Dinaux 1839: 318; Ulrix 1921: 79; Spanke 1929: 49; Coldwell 1986: 52♪
(English translation); Tischler 1997, 9: no. 820♪
Text: Edited by WP
TV: 4 et *missing.*
TN: The historical existence of this troveresse has long been accepted, most recently
by Tyssens (1992). See "The Case for the Women *Trouvères*" and "Introduction to the
Authors: What We Know, What We Can Surmise," in the introduction to this book.
This appears to be the initial stanza of a longer composition; in manuscript *M,* it is
followed by a blank space large enough to accommodate four more stanzas. Note the
inversion of the traditional springtime opening: she hails the advent of winter and
praises its harshness, for it gives her even more ardor to sing and love.
MV: 1/1-5/8 pitches a whole step higher — 5/9 d — 5/10-6/4 pitches a whole step
higher — 6/8-6/9 c-gf — 7/1-7/4 gᵖ-g-f-e.

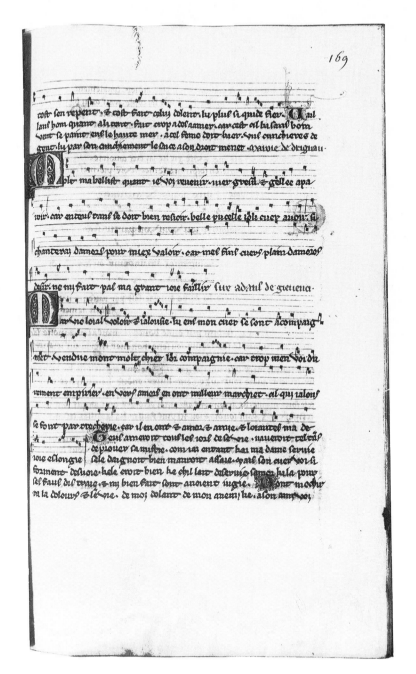

Song no. 15, Paris, Bibliothèque Nationale de France, fr. 12615, fol. 169r,
Maroie de drignau. Cliché Bibliothèque nationale de France, Paris.

15. Mout m'abelist quant je voi revenir
M 181r-v

Mout m'a - be - list quant je voi re - ve - nir

Y - ver, gre - sill et ge - lee a - pa - roir,

Car en toz tans se doit bien res - jo - ir

Be - le pu - cele, et jo - li cuer a - voir.

Si chan - te - rai d'a - mors por mieuz va - loir,

Car mes fins cuers plains d'a - mo - rous de - sir

Ne mi fait pas ma grant joi - e fail - lir.

16. Onqes n'amai tant que jou fui amee
a 68v

On - qes n'a - mai tant que jou fui a - me - e;

Or m'en re - pent, se ce pe - ust va - loir,

Q'a - mours m'a - voit au meil - lour as - se - ne - e,

Pour tou - te hou - nour et tou - te joie a - voir,

Et au plus bel de tou - te la con - tre - e;

Mais ore a il au - trui s'a - mour dou - ne - e,

Qi vo - len - tiers a soi l'a re - te - nu.

Las - se, pour koi fui je de me - re ne - e!

Par mon or - guel ai mon a - mi per - du.

16

Chanson d'amour

I *Onqes n'amai tant que jou fui amee;*	*Never did I love while I was loved.*
Or m'en repent, se ce peüst valoir,	Now I regret it, if only that mattered,
Q'amours m'avoit au meillour assenee,	For Love had allotted me the finest
Pour toute hounour et toute joie avoir,	And the most handsome man in all the land,
Et au plus bel de toute la contree;	To have all honor and all joy.
Mais ore a il autrui s'amour dounee,	But now he has given his love to another,
Qi volentiers a soi l'a retenu.	Who has gladly kept him for herself.
Lasse, pour koi fui je de mere nee!	Alas! Why was I ever born?
Par mon orguel ai mon ami perdu.	*By my pride I have lost my beloved.*

10 II Si me doint Dieus d'amours longe duree, May God grant me an enduring love,
Que je l'amai de cuer sans decevoir, For I loved him truly with all my heart
Qant me disoit k'iere de li amee, When he would tell me he loved me,
Mais n'en osai ains descouvrir le voir: But I never dared reveal the truth:
Des mesdisans doutoie la noumee. I feared the ignominy caused by slanderers.
Biau sire Dieus, baisie et acolee Dear Lord God, he would have kissed and embraced
M'eüst il or et aveuc moi geü; Me then, and lain with me,
Mais q'il m'eüst sans plus s'amour dounee, But had he done no more than give me his love,
Si m'eüst bien tous li siecles veü. Everyone would have noticed just the same.

19 III Or m'a amours malement assenee Now Love has dealt me a cruel blow
Qant çou que j'aim fait a une autre avoir, When it grants to another the one I love
Ne ne m'an laist retraire ma pensee, But does not let me stop thinking of him,
Ne si n'en puis soulas ne joie avoir. So that I can have neither comfort nor joy.
Lasse, l'amour que tant li ai veee Alas! The love I ardently refused to share with him
Li seroit ja otroiie et dounee; Will henceforth be conferred and bestowed on her;
Mais tart l'ai dit, car je l'ai ja perdu; But I have spoken too late, for I have already lost him.

Or me convient amer sans estre amee, Now I must love without being loved,
Car trop ai tart mon felon cuer vaincu. For I have vanquished my treacherous heart too late.

RS 498, L 223-11, MW 666, B 1427, Mot 820

Manuscripts: *a* 68v♪ (base) (*Maistre Richars*), *U* 137v–138r, *M* 205r♪, *T* 179r♪, *W2* 219ᵃv–220r♪, *Her* 2r♪

Editions: Raynaud 1883: 48; Jeanroy 1889: 501; Zarifopol 1904: 43; Gennrich 1926-27: 16♪; Gennrich 1956: 40♪; Mary 1967, 1: 260 (French translation); Tischler 1973: no. 13♪ (English translation); Bec 1978: 11; Rosenberg and Tischler 1981: 372♪;

Lepage 1981: 122; Alvar 1982: 286 (Spanish translation); Tischler 1982: 1019♪; Rosenberg, Tischler, and Grossel 1995: 618♪ (French translation); Tischler 1997, 4: no. 288♪

Text: Lepage 1981: 122

RR: 18 li] ti *(reading from U)* — 20 a .i. a. — 21 Ne le me l. *(reading from U)* — 23 vee *aU* — 24 sera *(reading from U).*

TV: In *U* stanza II consists of the first two lines of III (19-20), followed by the last seven lines of II (12-18), ending with the last two lines of I (8-9). Stanzas III and II then follow, in that order. — 1 que] com *UMTW2Her* — 2 se ce] si me *U,* s'il me *MW2;* ce] me *T* — 3 au] a *U* — 4 Pour] Por tout *(+1) W2,* Por tant por *(+2) Her;* toute hounour] tot deduit *MTW2Her,* tot desdut *U* — 5 au] le *THer;* au plus bel] a millour *U* — 7 Qi] Ke *U;* a soi] assoi *Her;* a soi l'a] l'a a soi *MW2;* l'a retenu] l'ait detenut *U* — 8 pour koi fui je] com mar sui (fui) ains *U* — 9 ami] amin *U* — 10 doint] doust *U* — 11 Que . . . cuer] Con je de cuer l'amai *U* — 12 Qant] On (Oni) *U;* k'iere de li] ke de lui (li) iere *U* — 13 Mais . . . descouvrir] Onkes (N'onkes) n'an pos (poi) reconoistre *U* — 14 noumee] crïee *U* — 16 geü] geïst *U* — 18 Si m'eüst bien] Et bien l'eüst *U* — 19 m'a] m'ont *U* — 20 fait a une autre] font ai atrui *U* — 22 si] se *U* — 25 l'ai] la *U* — 26 Or] Si *U.*

DF: Picard, including *ie* for *iee,* as in *baisie* (15), *otroiie* (24); *jou* (1) for *je; çou* (20) for *ce.*

TN: There is considerable disagreement regarding the authorship of this piece. Rosenberg and Tischler (1981) ascribe it to Richard de Fournival. Tyssens (1992) also expresses faith in this attribution. However, Lepage (1981) finds it dubious, as does Bec in his 1978 anthology, where he lists the author as "Richard de Fournival (?)." Yet a year later, in an article in which he seeks to prove that all chansons de femme were composed by men, Bec (1979: 258) cites the song as one of three examples of this lyric type whose authors are known to be male. Rosenberg, Tischler, and Grossel (1995) continue to ascribe the song to Richard, but they note Lepage's reservations. See Pfeffer 2001. — 1-9 Manuscripts *M, T, W2,* and *Her* preserve only this stanza, in a polyphonic context as the motetus (Mot 820) over the tenor "Sancte Germane." The two-line refrain—here divided (ll. 1 and 9)—is found as a lyric insertion in a number of narratives. — 2 Rosenberg reads *repenc,* which would be typical of Picard.

ME: 6/4 Manuscript *a* lacks a note for *il;* we have supplied an f as given in the other manuscripts.

MV: 1/2 a *MTW2Her* — 1/3-1/4 a-gfe *M* — 1/6 gfg *Her* — 2/1 cb *MTHer* — 2/3 a *W2* — 2/4 fef *MTHer* — 2/4-2/7 gfe-f-gag-ec *W2* — 2/9 f$_p$ *M;* fe *TW2Her* — 2/10 ed *MTW2Her* — 3/3 e$_p$ *W2Her* — 3/4 gfe *MT* — 3/6 gfg *Her* — 4/1 c$_p$ *MTHer* — 4/3 a$_p$ *T* — 4/4-4/7 gfe-f-g-ec *W2* — 4/9-4/10 fe-ed *MTW2Her* — 5/3-5/4 c$_p$-bag *W2* — 6/2-6/3 f$_p$-dc *T;* fe-dc *W2;* ff$_p$dc *Her* — 6/6-6/7 a-c$_p$ *TW2Her* — 6/9 a$_p$ *THer* — 6/9-6/10 a-gfed *W2* — 7/2-7/3 fe-d$_p$ *W2;* ff$_p$-d$_p$ *Her* — 7/5 g *TW2Her* — 7/6-7/7 a-gfe *T* — 7/6 aa$_p$ *W2Her* — 7/9-7/10 fe-d *THer* — 7/10 ed *W2* — 8/1 d *TW2Her* — 8/2 g *THer* — 8/2-8/10 ga-g$_p$-g-a-c-b-ag-a-gfed *W2* — 8/3 g *Her* — 8/6 b *T;* bcb *Her* — 9/2-9/6 fg-a$_p$-gf-g-aa$_p$ *T;* fef-g^p-gf-f^p-aa$_p$ *Her;* ff$_p$-d-f-g-aa$_p$ *W2* — 9/3-9/4 ga$_p$-gf *M* — 9/7 gfe *M* — 9/9 ff$_p$ *M;* fe *TW2;* f$_p$ *Her* — 9/10 ed *MTW2Her.*

17. Plaine d'ire et de desconfort
U 47v-48r

Plai – ne d'ire et de des – con – fort

Plor: en chan – tant m'en re – de – dui.

Sa – chiez de fi que j'ai grant tort,

Car as – sez trop har – di – e fui

Quant mon cuer ne ma boi – che mui

A rien qui te – nist a de – port,

Se por ceu non q'en – si re – cort

M'ire et mon duel et mon e – nui.

17
Chanson d'amour

I Plaine d'ire et de desconfort
   Plor: en chantant m'en rededui.
   Sachiez de fi que j'ai grant tort,
   Car assez trop hardie fui
   Quant mon cuer ne ma boiche mui
   A rien qui tenist a deport,
   Se por ceu non q'ensi recort
   M'ire et mon duel et mon enui.

   Full of anger and despair
   I weep: by singing I recover joy.
   You may be sure that I acted very wrongly,
   For I was much too bold
   When I made moan with heart and mouth
   At anything joyful,
   Were it not that in this way I express
   My anger and my grief and my sorrow.

II Dame cuidoie estre d'autrui,
    Mais bien sai que folie fis,
    Car conquise sui par celui
    Cui je cuidoie avoir conquis.
    Or en est devers moi li pis,
    Car il siens est et je si sui:
    Ensi somes sien ambedui,
    S'il est ensi com je devis.

    I thought I was another's lady,   9
    But I am sure I acted foolishly,
    For I am conquered by the one
    I thought I had conquered.
    Now the worst has devolved on me,
    For he is his and I too am his:
    Thus we are both his,
    If things are as I imagine.

III Trop ai vilainement mespris
     Cant malgré suen soie me faz,
     Qu'il n'a cure, ce m'est avis,
     Ne de moi ne de mon solaz;
     Desqu'il ne m'ainme, je me haz,
     Et s'amie serai toz dis,
     Encor soit il mes enemis:
     Ensi ma mort quier et porchaz.

     I made a terrible mistake   17
     When despite him I made myself his,
     For he shows no concern, it seems to me,
     Either for me or for my comfort;
     Since he does not love me, I hate myself,
     Yet I will always be his love,
     Though he be my enemy:
     So do I seek and pursue my death.

RS 1934, L 265-1326, MW 1087

Manuscripts: *U* 47v-48r♪ (base), *C* 191r-v

Editions: Brakelmann 1868b: 307; Gennrich 1924-25: 68♪; Gérold 1932: 163♪; Gennrich 1932: 237♪; Gennrich 1937: 47♪; van der Werf 1972: 91♪; Schutz 1976: 232; Mölk 1989: 98 (German translation); Tischler 1997, 3: no. 203♪

Text: Edited by ED-Q

RR: 14 siens *missing* (−1) *(reading from C).*

TV: 2 Plour et en chantant me desdui — 3 de voir — 5 c. et ma — 6 riens ke — 16 Si est — 18 Car.

DF: Lorraine, including *plor* (2) for *pleur; boiche* (5) for *boche; ceu* (7) for *ce.*

MC: Contrafactum of "Can vei la lauzeta mover" by Bernart de Ventadorn (PC 70.43). See MC to song no. 10.

18 *DUCHESSE DE LORRAINE*
Plainte

The lyric plainte celebrates the memory of a public figure, bewails the passing of a patron, or grieves the loss of a beloved. The four surviving Old French laments occasioned by the death of a lover lack a clear generic outline; compared to their Occitan counterparts, from which they diverge considerably, the French plaintes are disparate compositions, heterogeneous in form and expression, combining elements of the courtly chanson as well as the elegy, to voice a private mourning (Rosenberg 1983).

I   Par maintes fois avrai esteit requise   Many a time I have been asked
    C'ains ne chantai ansi con je soloie;   Why I no longer sing as I used to;
    Car je suix si aloingnie de joie   In truth, I am so removed from joy
    Que j'en devroie estre plus antreprise,   That I ought to be deterred from it even further,
    Et a mien voil moroie an iteil guise   And if I could have my wish I would die in the same way

    Con celle fist cui je sanbler voroie: As the woman I would like to emulate:
    Didol, qui fut por Eneas ocise.   Dido, who for Aeneas was slain.

8   II   Ahi, amins! tout a vostre devise   Oh, my love! Why did I not comply fully
    Que ne fis jeu tant con je vos veoie?   With your wishes while I could still see you?
    Jant vilainne cui je tant redotoie   Vile people, whom I greatly feared,
    M'ont si greveit et si ariere mise   So tormented and restrained me
    C'ains ne vos pou merir vostre servise.   That I could never reward your service.
    S'estre poioit, plus m'an repantiroie   If it were possible, I would repent more
    C'Adans ne fist de la pome c'ot prise.   Than Adam did for taking the apple.

15   III   Ains por Forcon ne fist tant Afelisse   Never for Fouque did Anfelise do as much
    Con je por vos, amins, s'or vos ravoie;   As I would for you, my love, if I had you back.
    Mais ce n'iert jai, se premiers ne moroie.   But that will never be, unless first I die.
    Mais je [ne] puis morir an iteil guise,   But I cannot die in this way,
    C'ancor me rait Amors joie promise.   For Love has again promised me joy.
    Si vuel doloir an leu de mener joie: Yet I wish to grieve rather than act joyful:
    Poinne et travail, ceu est ma rante assise.   Pain and torment, such is the penalty imposed on me.

182

·lxviij·

si desconsillier ke ma dame ne me gient de prixon· Douce dame
en droit moustre z raixon ke uos ameis uostre loiaul amin· ali
gies moi sil uos plaist mes dolors· car ie seux cil ki muels uos ai ser
uir· de uos atent gueridon z merci· ke ma ioie ne puet uenir dail
lors· z se grian mors seux z mar uos ni· iai dit ke fols amis me tieg
agueri· maix trop uient lens dame uostre secors· Del teneir pais
douce dame afoler· se ie uos aim z ser z doui z pri· tant seruirai ure
en serait lonor· quit uos manueil mon seruixe merir· de uos amer
me dout z fais hardir· ken amors ait herdement z paour· ne tout
ne soil mon cuer ne tot· nel di· maix se ie uiens per pace i obli
uanke pitei douce dame z amors· e fins amans destrois z angoi
xous dont ioie auoir por seruir loiaulment· dont doi ie bien per droit
estre ioious· car ie seux cil ki plux en ait torment· car tant uos aim
dame z pri bonement· ne por autre ne puis estre amerous· z mes chan
sons fais por uos soulement· nonkes un ior ne chantai faintement·
si me doinst deus dame ior de uos· Ma dame aim plux ke rien ke
soit el mont· maix losengier ne men laissent ioir· ki tout ades ali
muenent z uont· z dist del tout chascuns a son plaisir· maix per rai
xon ne me pueent nuisir· se deus ioie men doinst ne gueridon· quit a

li seux si solpir de prront z
quit men pant mat ke del
Per maintes fois aurai estei requise· mort· si doucement me
deshait
z confot

ke ne chantai ensi com ie soloie· ke tant per seux aloignie

de ioie· ke ie uodroie estre aruels entreprise· a mien ueul moroie

le duchaise de lorainne

Song no. 18, Bern, Burgerbibliothek, cod. 389, fol. 182r, le duchaise de lorainne.
Courtesy of Burgerbibliothek Bern.

22 IV Par Deu, amins, en grant dolour m'a   By God, my love, into deep sorrow I have been
        mise   plunged
      Mors vilainne, qui tout lou mont gerroie.   By vile death, which wars against everyone.
      Vos m'at tolut, la riens que tant amoie!   It has robbed me of you, the one I loved so much!
      Or seu Fenis, lasse, soule et eschise,   Now I am a Phoenix—weary, alone, and bereft—
      Dont il n'est c'uns, si con an le devise.   Although only one exists, so people say.
      Mais a poinnes m'en reconfortiroie   But with difficulty I might yet find comfort
      Se por ceu non, c'Amors m'at an justice.   Were it not for this, that Love has me in its power.

RS 1640, L 57-1, MW 2344

Manuscripts: *U* 97r–v (base), *C* 182r–v (*le duchaise de lorainne*)

Editions: Jubinal 1838: 54; Tarbé 1850: 25; Hofmann 1867: 516; Brakelmann 1868b: 293; Kooijman 1974: 82 (French translation); Rosenberg and Tischler 1981: 503; Mölk 1989: 100 (German translation); Rosenberg, Tischler, and Grossel 1995: 808 (French translation); Rosenberg, Switten, and Le Vot 1998: 355 (English translation)

Text: Rosenberg and Tischler 1981: 503

RR: 18 *(–1)* — 25 eschiue — 26 le] la — 28 Ce.

TV: 2 Ke ne — 3 Ke tant per seux a. de j. — 4 Ke ie uodroie e. muels entr. — 5 Et *missing* — 6 C. fist celle c. resembleir v. — 7 Dido ke f. p. eneam o. — 8 Biaus douls am. — 9 tandis com uos auoie — 10 Gens — 14 Cadam ne fust — 15-19 *occur as lines 22-26* — 15 tant ne fist anfelixe — 16 s'or] se — 17 se aincois ne m. — 18 Ne j. — 20 Or v. — 21 t. iert maix ma r. a. — 22-26 *occur as lines 15-19* — 22 P. d. amors — 23 qui] ke — 24 Tolut maueis la r. ke plux a. — 25 eschiue — 27 M. a mien ueul se men repentiroie — 28 Se p. tant niert c.

DF: Lorraine, including *ai* for *a* in *jai* (17); *ei* for tonic *e,* as in *esteit* (1), *iteil* (5); *poinne* (21) for *peine; an* for *en,* as in *antreprise* (4), *Jant* (10) for *gent, rante* (21); progressive nasalization in *amins* (8); *ss* or *c* for *s,* as in *Afelisse* (15), *justice* (28); preservation of final *t,* as in *esteit* (1), *at* (24), *tolut* (24); *jeu* (9) for *je; ceu* (21) for *ce; lou* (23) for *le; seu* (25) for *sui;* 3rd-pers. sing. pres. ind. *rait* (19) for *ra.*

TN: For possible identifications of the Duchesse de Lorraine, see "Introduction to the Authors: What We Know, What We Can Surmise," in the introduction to this book. Jeanroy (1889: 96) was extremely skeptical regarding the attribution in manuscript *C.* Tyssens (1992: 380) advances three arguments to counter his disbelief: first, the song is a veritable woman's lament; second, the fact that the rubricator of *C* ascribed another song (song no. 34) to the Duchesse at a healthy interval from this one indicates that he gave credence to the existence of a poet by this name; third, the woman who is the subject of the lament claims that she is recognized as the author of other songs. Kooijman (1974: 80) does not question the historical existence of this troveresse; on chronological grounds, he leans toward identifying the Duchesse as Marguerite de Champagne. Rosenberg also accepts the attribution in the Bern chansonnier. He includes the song in all three of his anthologies (Rosenberg and Tischler 1981; Rosenberg, Tischler, and Grossel 1995; Rosenberg, Switten, and Le Vot

1998); it is also featured in his examination of the lyric death-lament in the Old French lyric (Rosenberg 1983). We gratefully acknowledge our debt to the translation in Rosenberg, Switten, and Le Vot 1998. — 15 Fouque and Anfelise are the hero and heroine of Herbert le Duc de Dammartin's epic poem, *Fouque de Candie*. The characters appear in Old French romance literature as well.

19
Chanson d'ami
Ballette

We define the chanson d'ami as a lyric monologue, in the form of a chanson à refrain or chanson avec des refrains, in which an apparently unmarried woman yearns for a lover—present or past. She either feels the urge to love—in keeping with the season, her youth, and her charm—or expresses her sorrow and despair over her sweetheart's absence, sometimes blaming herself for having rebuffed him. She cannot be dissuaded from loving, despite the opposition of her parents and the threat posed by detractors: gossip-mongers, flatterers, and slanderers.

Under the rubric *balletes,* manuscript *I* groups monodic songs, most often composed of three stanzas, generally three to four lines each, rhyming *aa(a)b.* The meter of each line varies from seven to twelve syllables. A one- to three-line refrain, which may also precede the first stanza, is repeated at the end of each strophe. The metrical and rhyme structure of the refrain need not correspond to that of the stanzas, although a typical two-line refrain (*AB* or *BB* or *CB*) is usually linked, through its rhyme scheme, to the last line of each strophe. As its name implies, the ballette was originally meant to accompany dancing (Bec 1977: 228-33).

Deduxans suis et joliette, s'amerai.	*I am charming and pretty, so I will love.*

I	Ier matin me levai droit au point dou jour,	Yesterday morning I rose right at the break of day, 2
	On vergier mon peire antrai ki iert plains de flours;	Entered my father's orchard which was all abloom;
	Mon amin plus de cent fois i souhaidai.	My sweetheart I wished for a hundred times and more.
	[Deduxans suis et joliette, s'amerai.]	*I am charming and pretty, so I will love.*
II	J'amerai mon amin, ke proiét m'an ait;	I will love my sweetheart, who has asked for my love; 6

Il est biaus et cortois, bien deservit l'ait;	He is handsome and refined and has well deserved it;
Mon fin cuer mal greit peire et meire li donrai.	I will grant him my true heart despite my father and mother.
[Deduxans suis et joliette, s'amerai.]	*I am charming and pretty, so I will love.*

10 III Chanson, je t'anvoi a toz fins loialz amans,   Song, I send you to all true, faithful lovers,

Qu'il se gaircent bien des felz mavais mesdisans,   So they may guard against mean, wicked slanderers,

Car j'ain tant bien sai ke covrir ne m'an porai.   For my love is so strong I know I could not conceal it.

[Deduxans suis et joliette, s'amerai.]   *I am charming and pretty, so I will love.*

RS 59a=983, L 265-455, MW 502, B 469
Manuscript: *I* 223r (234r)
Editions: Jeanroy 1889: 495; Stengel 1896: 103; Steffens 1897b: 363; Gennrich 1921: 185; Bec 1978: 166; Rosenberg and Tischler 1981: 4; Mölk 1989: 106 (German translation); Rosenberg, Tischler, and Grossel 1995: 82 (French translation)
Text: Rosenberg and Tischler 1981: 4
RR: 11 se] ce.
DF: Lorraine, including *ai* for *a*, as in *gaircent* (11); *ei* for tonic *e*, as in *peire* (3), *greit* (8); *amin* (4) for *ami*; preservation of final *t*, as in *proiét* (6), *deservit* (7), *greit* (8); 3rd-pers. sing. pres. ind. *ait* (6, 7) for *a*.

20

Chanson d'ami
Ballette

Dues, Dues, Dues, Dues,	*Lord, Lord, Lord, Lord,*
Dues, donneis honor a seus	*Lord, grant honor to those*
Ki amor maintiennent mues!	*Who keep love secret!*

4 I Cant je fu petite garce,   When I was a little girl,

Si me norit ma mairaistre.   My stepmother raised me.

El me fist garder les vaiches   She made me tend the cows

Tote soule a .i. pastour.   All alone with a shepherd.

[Dues, Dues, Dues, Dues,   *Lord, Lord, Lord, Lord,*

Dues, donneis honor a seus   *Lord, grant honor to those*

Ki amor maintiennent mues!]   *Who keep love secret!*

II	Je m'an antrai on boucaige	As I entered a grove	11
	Aprés une de mes vaiches,	After one of my cows,
	Si trovai Robin lou saige,	I found Robin, the sly one,
	Lou veirelit me fist puez.	Then he played me a *virelai*.
	[Dues, Dues, Dues, Dues,	*Lord, Lord, Lord, Lord,*
	Dues, donneis honor a seus	*Lord, grant honor to those*
	Ki amor maintiennent mues!]	*Who keep love secret!*

RS 1013, L 265-498, MW 382, B 507

Manuscript: *I* 224r–v (235r–v)

Editions: Steffens 1897b: 366; Gennrich 1921: 193; Mölk 1989: 108 (German translation)

Text: Edited by ED-Q

RR: 6 Elle *(+1) (em. Gennrich).*

DF: Lorraine, including *ai* for *a*, as in *mairaistre* (5), *vaiches* (6), *boucaige* (11), *saige* (13); *an* for *en*, as in *an antrai* (11); *ei* for tonic *e*, as in *donneis* (2); preservation of final *t*, as in *veirelit* (14); *s* for *c*, as in *seus* (2); *Dues* (1) for *Dieus*; *puez* (14) for *puis*; *lou* (13) for *le*; enclitic *on* (11) for *en + le*; 1st-pers. sing. pret. *fu* (1) for *fui*. Picard *c* for *ch*, as in *boucaige* (11).

TN: 14 A type of dance song (from the verb *virer*, "to turn") closely related to the ballette.

21

Chanson d'ami
Ballette

	E, bone amourette,	*Hey, pleasing love song,*
	Tres saverouzette,	*So delectable,*
	Plaisans,	*So charming,*
	N'oblïeiz nuns fins amant.	*Do not forget any true lover.*

I	Amors m'aprent a ameir,	Love is teaching me to love,	5
	C'est mout bone vie!	What a great life!
	J'en oz tant de gens lower	I hear so many praise it
	Qu'il me prent anvie	That I have the urge
	D'estre amerouzette;	To be in love;
	Plus suis jolïette	I am more cheerful,
	.C. tans	A hundredfold,
	Ke n'estoie devant.	Than I was before.

[E bone amourette,	*Hey, pleasing love song,*
Tres saverouzette,	*So delectable,*
Plaisans,	*So charming,*
N'oblïeiz nuns fins amant.]	*Do not forget any true lover.*

17 II J'ain loialment sans fauceir,   I love faithfully, that's no lie,

J'ain loialment sans fauceir,	I love faithfully, that's no lie,
C'est grant melodie!	What a lovely melody!
Se ne m'an doit nuns blameir,	So no one should blame me for it,
Ce seroit folie:	That would be crazy:
Car je suis jonette,	For I am young,
Plaisans et doucette,	Charming and sweet,
Rians:	Full of laughter:
S'amerai tout mon vivant.	So I will love my whole life long.
[E bone amourette,	*Hey, pleasing love song,*
Tres saverouzette,	*So delectable,*
Plaisans,	*So charming,*
N'oblïeiz nuns fins amant.]	*Do not forget any true lover.*

29 III

Amins, cui je n'oz nomeir,	Sweetheart, whom I dare not name,
Ne me fauceir mie.	Do not betray me.
Je vos ain, nou pux celleir,	I love you, I cannot hide it,
Et, sans vilonie,	And, not wishing to deceive,
Ceste chansonette	With this little song
Voix de ma bouchette	On my lips I go along
Chantant,	Singing,
An despit des mesdixant:	In spite of the slanderers:
[E bone amourette,	*Hey, pleasing love song,*
Tres saverouzette,	*So delectable,*
Plaisans,	*So charming,*
N'oblïeiz nuns fins amant.]	*Do not forget any true lover.*

RS 970, L 265-578, MW 2210, B 802

Manuscript: *I* 222r-v (233*bis*r-v)

Editions: Steffens 1897b: 362; Jeanroy 1889: 492; Bec 1978: 172

Text: Edited by ED-Q

RR: 11 stans *(em. Jeanroy)* — 20 Ce] se — 23 Et r. *(+1) (em. Bec).*

DF: Lorraine, including *an* for *en,* as in *anvie* (8), *an* (19); *ei* for tonic *e,* as in *ameir* (5), *fauceir* (17), *nomeir* (29); *u* for *ui,* as in *pux* (31); intervocalic *w,* as in *lower* (7); *c* for *s(s),* as in *fauceir* (17); *x* for *s,* as in *mesdixant* (36), *pux* (31), *Voix* (34); *nuns* (4) for nus; *amins* (29) for *amis;* enclitic *nou* (31) for *ne + lou;* adverbial *se* (19) for *si;* 1st-pers. sing. pres. ind. *pux* (31) for *puis.*

22
Chanson d'ami

<table>
<tr><td>I</td><td>Lasse, pour quoi refusai</td><td>Alas, why did I refuse</td><td></td></tr>
<tr><td></td><td>Celui qui tant m'a amee?</td><td>The one who loved me so?</td><td></td></tr>
<tr><td></td><td>Lonc tens a a moi musé</td><td>He whiled away much time with me</td><td></td></tr>
<tr><td></td><td>Et n'i a merci trouvee.</td><td>And found no mercy there.</td><td></td></tr>
<tr><td></td><td>Lasse, si tres dur cuer ai!</td><td>Alas, what a cold heart I have!</td><td></td></tr>
<tr><td></td><td>Qu'en dirai?</td><td>What can I say?</td><td></td></tr>
<tr><td></td><td>Forssenee</td><td>Insane</td><td></td></tr>
<tr><td></td><td>Fui, plus que desvee,</td><td>Was I, more than mad,</td><td></td></tr>
<tr><td></td><td>Quant le refusai.</td><td>To rebuff him.</td><td></td></tr>
<tr><td></td><td>*G'en ferai*</td><td>*I will do*</td><td></td></tr>
<tr><td></td><td>*Droit a son plesir,*</td><td>*Justice to his wishes*</td><td></td></tr>
<tr><td></td><td>*S'il m'en daigne oïr.*</td><td>*If he should deign to hear me.*</td><td></td></tr>
</table>

<table>
<tr><td>II</td><td>Certes, bien me doi clamer</td><td>In truth, I should proclaim myself</td><td>13</td></tr>
<tr><td></td><td>Et lasse et maleüree</td><td>Both wretched and unfortunate</td><td></td></tr>
<tr><td></td><td>Quant cil ou n'a point d'amer,</td><td>When he who knows no bitterness,</td><td></td></tr>
<tr><td></td><td>Fors grant douçor et rousee,</td><td>Only great sweetness and warmth,</td><td></td></tr>
<tr><td></td><td>Tant doucement me pria</td><td>Courted me so sweetly,</td><td></td></tr>
<tr><td></td><td>Et n'i a</td><td>Yet in me</td><td></td></tr>
<tr><td></td><td>Recouvree</td><td>Found</td><td></td></tr>
<tr><td></td><td>Merci; forssenee</td><td>No mercy; insane</td><td></td></tr>
<tr><td></td><td>Fui quant ne l'amai.</td><td>Was I not to love him.</td><td></td></tr>
<tr><td></td><td>*G'en ferai*</td><td>*I will do*</td><td></td></tr>
<tr><td></td><td>*[Droit a son plesir,*</td><td>*Justice to his wishes*</td><td></td></tr>
<tr><td></td><td>*S'il m'en daigne oïr].*</td><td>*If he should deign to hear me.*</td><td></td></tr>
</table>

<table>
<tr><td>III</td><td>Bien deüst avoir trouvé</td><td>He should have found</td><td>25</td></tr>
<tr><td></td><td>Merci quant l'a demandee;</td><td>Mercy when he sought it;</td><td></td></tr>
<tr><td></td><td>Certes, mal en ai ouvré</td><td>Surely, I acted wrongly</td><td></td></tr>
<tr><td></td><td>Quant je la li ai vëee;</td><td>When I deprived him of it;</td><td></td></tr>
<tr><td></td><td>Mult m'a mis en grant esmai.</td><td>This has thrown me into such distress</td><td></td></tr>
<tr><td></td><td>G'en morrai,</td><td>That I will die</td><td></td></tr>
</table>

22. Lasse, pour quoi refusai
K 343-344

Las - se,   pour quoi re - fu - sai

Ce - lui   qui   tant   m'a   a - me - e?

Lonc   tens   a   a   moi   mu - sé

Et   n'i   a   mer - ci   trou - ve -   e.

Las - se,   si   tres   dur   cuer   ai!

Qu'en di - rai?

Fors - se - ne - e

Fui,   plus   que   des - ve -   e,

Quant le   re - fu - sai.

G'en fe - rai

Droit   a   son   ple - sir,

S'il   m'en   daigne   o - ir.

S'acordee	If I am not reconciled
Sanz grant demoree	Soon
A lui ne serai.	With him.
G'en ferai	*I will do*
Droit [a son plesir,	*Justice to his wishes*
S'il m'en daigne oïr].	*If he should deign to hear me.*

IV
A touz ceus qui l'ont grevé	To all those who have tormented him	37
Dont Deus si fort destinee	May God give this harsh fate:	
Q'il aient les euz crevez	Let their eyes be plucked out	
Et les orilles coupees!	And their ears cut off!	
Ensi ma dolor perdrai.	In this way I will ease my sorrow.	
Lors dirai:	Then will I say:	
Genz desvee,	Lunatics,	
Ma joie est doublee,	My joy is doubled,	
Et se mesfet ai,	And if I have done wrong,	
G'en ferai	*I will do*	
[Droit a son plesir,	*Justice to his wishes*	
S'il m'en daigne oïr].	*If he should deign to hear me.*	

V
Chançon, va sanz delaier	Song, go without tarrying	49
A celui qui tant m'agree.	To the one so dear to me.	
Pour Dieu li pri et reqier	In God's name, beg and entreat him	
Viengne a moi sanz demoree.	To come to me without delay.	
En sa merci me metrai,	I will throw myself at his mercy;	
Tost avrai	Quickly will I find	
Pes trouvee,	Peace of mind,	
Se il li agree,	If he consents,	
Car je trop mal trai.	For I endure such pain.	
G'en ferai	*I will do*	
[Droit a son plesir,	*Justice to his wishes*	
S'il m'en daigne oïr].	*If he should deign to hear me.*	

RS 100, L 265-990, MW 2024, B 1040

Manuscripts: *K* 343-44♪ (base), *N* 166r-v♪, *P* 177r-v♪, *X* 224r-v♪

Editions: Jeanroy 1889: 499; Noack 1898: 40; Spanke 1925: 114, 431♪; Gennrich 1956: 37♪; Gennrich 1958c: 34♪; Bec 1978: 7; Rosenberg and Tischler 1981: 102♪; Kasten 1990: 186 (German translation); Rosenberg, Tischler, and Grossel 1995: 244♪

(French translation); Tischler 1997, 7: no. 556♪; Rosenberg, Switten, and Le Vot 1998: 213♪ (English translation)

Text: Rosenberg and Tischler 1981: 102

RR: 28 ai uee.

TV: 8 que riens nee *P* — 13 men *X* — 14 Lasse et male e. *N* — 16 pitie et r. *P* — 20 forsee *N* — 25 trouuee *P* — 39 leur eus *P* — 40 estoupees *X* — 45 meffait *X* — 47 droit *added in N* — 49 ua ten s. *P* — 55 P. recouuree *N* — 56 sil *P* — 57 Que *NX*; maus *P* — 59-60 droit a son plaisir sil men deigne oir *added in X*.

TN: Rosenberg regards this text as the Francien transcription of a Lorraine poem (Rosenberg and Tischler 1981; Rosenberg, Tischler, and Grossel 1995; Rosenberg, Switten, and Le Vot 1998). With the exception of the last two lines of the refrain, there is essentially only one rhyme in this song: *a* (represented by *-ai, -é, -er, -ez*, and even *-ier*) and its feminine equivalent, *b* (represented by *-ee*); the rhyme words *pria* and *a* (17-18) would have occurred as *priait* and *ait* in Lorraine, and thus would have conformed to the *a* rhyme. We gratefully acknowledge our debt to the translation in Rosenberg, Switten, and Le Vot 1998.

MV: 1/6 aga *X* — 2/8 a^p *NX* — 3/6 ag^p *N* — 4/5 a *PX* — 4/8 a^p *NX* — 5/7 ga^p *NX*; gab *P* — 12/3-12/4 cba-aga *X*.

MC: Contrafactum of "Helas! je sui refusez" (RS 939) by Gillebert de Berneville (Fresco 1988: 124).

23

Chanson d'ami

I   L'on dit q'amors est dolce chose,
Mais je n'en conois la dolçor;
Tote joie m'en est enclose,
N'ainz ne senti nul bien d'amor.
Lasse! mes mals ne se repose,
Si m'en deplaing et faz clamor.
Mar est batuz qui plorer n'ose,
N'en plorant dire sa dolor.
Ses duels li part qui s'ose plaindre;
Plus tost en puet son mal estaindre.

They say that love is a sweet thing,
But I do not know its sweetness;
All its joy is barred to me,
Nor have I ever felt any of its pleasures.
Alas, my pain never ceases,
So I lament and cry out.
She is woefully defeated who dares not weep
And in weeping express her grief.
She who dares lament chases her sorrow away;
She can sooner extinguish her pain.

11 II   De ce me plaing qu'il m'a traïe;
S'en ai trop grant duel acoilli,
Quant je qui sui leals amie
Ne truis amor en mon ami.
Je fui ainçois de lui baisie,

My complaint is that he betrayed me;
And I have reaped such great sorrow,
For I who am a faithful lover
Find no love in my beloved.
Time was when I was kissed by him,

23. L'on dit q'amors est dolce chose
U 47v

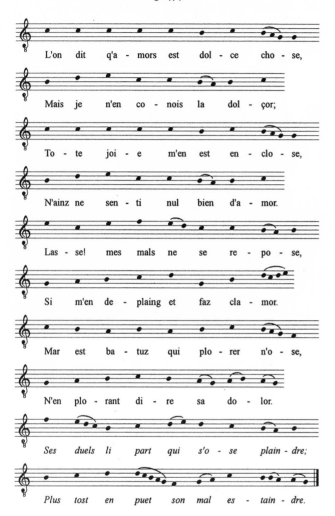

L'on dit q'a - mors est dol - ce cho - se,

Mais je n'en co - nois la dol - çor;

To - te joi - e m'en est en - clo - se,

N'ainz ne sen - ti nul bien d'a - mor.

Las - se! mes mals ne se re - po - se,

Si m'en de - plaing et faz cla - mor.

Mar est ba - tuz qui plo - rer n'o - se,

N'en plo - rant di - re sa do - lor.

Ses duels li part qui s'o - se plain - dre;

Plus tost en puet son mal es - tain - dre.

Si lo fis de m'amor saisi;	So I gave him possession of my love;
Mais tels baise qui n'aime mie:	Yet there are those who kiss but do not love:
Baisier ont maint amant traï.	Kisses have led many a lover astray.
[Ses duels li part qui s'ose plaindre;	*She who dares lament chases her sorrow away;*
Plus tost en puet son mal estaindre.]	*She can sooner extinguish her pain.*

21 III Estre cuidai de lui amee   I thought I was loved by him

Quant entre ses braz me tenoit;	When he held me in his arms;
Cum plus iere d'amors grevee,	When I was most tormented by love,
A son parler me refaisoit;	He restored me with his words;
A sa voiz iere si sanee	By his voice I was revived
Cum Piramus quant il moroit:	Like Pyramus when he lay dying:
Navrez en son flanc de s'espee,	Pierced in the side by his own sword,
Au nom Tisbé les iauz ovroit.	On hearing Thisbe's name he opened his eyes.
[Ses duels li part qui s'ose plaindre;	*She who dares lament chases her sorrow away;*
Plus tost en puet son mal estaindre.]	*She can sooner extinguish her pain.*

RS 1937, L 265-1235, MW 827, B 1716

Manuscripts: *U* 47v♪ (base), *C* 168v-169r

Editions: Wackernagel 1846: 12; Paris 1856: 813; Schutz 1976: 202; Rosenberg and Tischler 1981: 82♪; Rosenberg, Tischler, and Grossel 1995: 208♪ (French translation); Tischler 1997, 12: no. 1104♪; Rosenberg, Switten, and Le Vot 1998: 211♪ (English translation)

Text: Rosenberg and Tischler 1981: 82

RR: 6 deplaig — 10 Plust — 11 qui.

TV: 3 j. ait en li e. — 4 nuls biens damors — 13 loiaul — 25 Asauoir.

TN: 26-28 The reference is to the fate of Pyramus, lover of Thisbe, recounted in Ovid's *Metamorphoses* 4: 142-46 and the anonymous twelfth-century French adaptation (Boer 1921: ll. 892-97; trans. Rosenberg, Switten, and Le Vot 1998: 210):

"Piramus, ves ci vostre amie.	"Pyramus, this is your belovèd.
Car l'esgardez, si ert garie."	Look at her, and she will be healed."
Li jovenciaus, la ou moroit,	The youth, as he was dying,
Entr'oevre les iex et si voit	Half-opened his eyes and saw
Que ce iere Tisbé s'amie	That it was Thisbe his belovèd
Qui l'apeloit toute esmarie.	Who in distress was addressing him.

Note that the female speaker compares herself to the *male* figure. In the story, Pyramus' glance at Thisbe is immediately followed by his death.

24
Chanson d'ami
Ballette

I Osteis ma kenoille! Je ne pux fileir	Take away my distaff! I cannot spin
Cant il me sovient	Whenever I recall
D'amors ki me tient,	The love that so grips me
Si ke je ne puis dureir;	That I cannot survive;
Et ciz que me doit ameir	And the man who should love me
Ne vait ne ne vient.	Neither comes nor goes.
Bien voi k'il ne m'ainme nient,	I see clearly that he loves me not in the least,
Et je ne puis mie sans amor dureir:	And I cannot survive without love.
Je voix kerre amors, Deus me.s dent troveir.	*I go looking for love; God grant that I find it.*

II — Sote ribaudelle, ou welz tu alleir?	— Foolish wench, where would you go?	10
Tu lou dis por nient,	You're wasting your breath,	
Tu n'an irais nient,	You'll not leave,	
Car je t'irai l'ux fermeir.	For I'll lock the door on you.	
Or welz tu trop ahonteir	Now you really want to heap shame	
Sous qui t'apartient.	On the one who is related to you.	
Mais se tes peires revient,	But if your father comes back,	
Par tai pute estrainne te ferait chanteir:	For your debauched straying he'll make you sing:	
Je voix kerre amors, Dex me.s dent troveir.	*I go looking for love; God grant that I find it.*	

III — Par Deu, belle meire, vos ne dites riens.	— By God, dear mother, those are idle words.	19
Por tout vostre avoir	For all your wealth	
Sans amin n'ier jen,	I'll not be without a lover,	
Car je l'ai biaul et jolit,	For mine is handsome and cheerful,	
Si lou voil ameir,	And I want to love him,	
Qui ke m'an doie blamer.	No matter who blames me.	
Ne peire ne meire ne m'an puet torneir	No father or mother can make me change my mind	
N'aille kerre amors, Dex me.s dent troveir.	*Nor keep me from looking for love; God grant that I find it.*	

RS 856, L 265-1290, MW 2364, B 1152

Manuscript: *I* 229r (240r)

Editions: Steffens 1897b: 373; Mölk 1989: 102 (German translation)

Text: Edited by ED-Q

RR: 9 dent] dont *(em. Mölk) (lectio difficilior)*.

DF: Lorraine, including *an* (12) for *en*; *ei* for tonic *e*, as in *Osteis* (1), *fileir* (1), *peires* (16); *oil* for *ueil*, as in *voil* (23); *u* for *ui*, as in *pux* (1), *ux* (13); preservation of final *t*, as in *jolit* (22); *w* for *vu*, as in *welz* (10, 14); *x* for *s*, as in *pux* (1), *voix* (9), *ux* (13); *amin* (21) for *ami; lou* (11) for *le; tai* (17) for *ta; Sous* (15) for *cil; biaul* (22) for *bel;* rel. *que* (5) for nom. *qui;* 3rd-pers. sing. pres. ind. *vait* (6) for *va;* 3rd-pers. sing. fut. in *-ait*, as in *ferait* (17). Picard, including *ciz* (5) for *cil;* enclitic *me.s* for *les + me*.

TN: 19–26 Mölk (1989) rejects the third stanza as corrupt. Its irregular rhyme scheme and number of lines would indicate a later addition.

25

Chanson d'ami

Qui de .ii. biens le millour	*A woman facing two choices*
Laist, encontre sa pensee,	*Who sets aside the better one, against her judgment,*
Et prent pour li le pïour,	*Choosing for herself the worse,*
Bien croi que c'est esp[ro]vee	*Demonstrates, I do believe,*
Tres haute folour.	*Extreme folly.*

6   I

Cause ai d'avoir mon penser	I have reason to consider
A ce que serve ai esté,	That I have served—
Ai! et sui de vrai ami,	Alas!—and still do, a faithful lover,
Sage, courtois, bien secré,	Wise, refined, highly discreet,
G[ou]vrené par meureté,	Of mature conduct,
Et gentil, preu et hardi,	And noble, worthy, and bold,
Et qui sur tous a m'amour.	And who over all others has my love.
Dont sui souvent eno[ree]	I am often favored with
D'autrui amer, sans secour.	The love of another, but in vain.
Mais pour mon mieuls sui donnee,	Yet I am bestowed to my advantage,
S'en ferai demour.	So I will remain with him.
[Qui de .ii. biens le millour	*A woman facing two choices*
Laist, encontre sa pensee,	*Who sets aside the better one, against her judgment,*
Et prent pour li le pïour,	*Choosing for herself the worse,*
Bien croi que c'est esprovee	*Demonstrates, I do believe,*
Tres haute folour.]	*Extreme folly.*

22   II

Lasse! il m'est trop mal tourné	Alas, it turned so badly
A dolour et a grieté	Into pain and suffering
Quant je ai si mal parti	When I chose so poorly
Qu'il me faut cont[re] mon gré,	That I must, against my will,
Par droite necessité,	By rightful necessity,
De corps eslongier cheli	Distance myself from the one

A qui m'otroi sans folour,   To whom I give myself without folly,
Et sans estre au[trui] voee   And without being committed to another
De coer; mais c'est vains labours,   From the heart; but it is a vain endeavor,
Car tant ne doit estre amee   For a leaf should not be prized
Foelle con la flours.   As much as a flower.
[Qui de .ii. biens le millour   *A woman facing two choices*
Laist, encontre sa pensee,   *Who sets aside the better one, against her judgment,*
Et prent pour li le pïour,   *Choosing for herself the worse,*
Bien croi que c'est esprovee   *Demonstrates, I do believe,*
Tres haute folour.]   *Extreme folly.*

III   Or m'ont amours assenee;   Now love has dealt me a blow;   38
Mais, si c'a leur volenté,   But, since such is its will,
Est mieuls qu'il n'affier a mi.   It is better that it not concern me.
Tous jours doi av[oir] fondé   I should always have based
Mon desir sur loiaulté,   My desire on loyalty,
En espoir d'amour qu'ai ui,   Putting my hope in the love I now have,
Car tout passe de valour   For the one I love
Chus dont s[ui en]amouree;   Exceeds everything in value;
D'un si gracieus retour   Of such a fortunate turn of events
Saige doi estre avisee,   I should be considered wise,
Se j'ai chier m'onnour.   If I cherish the honor that has come to me.
[Qui de .ii. biens le millour   *A woman facing two choices*
Laist, encontre sa pensee,   *Who sets aside the better one, against her judgment,*
Et prent pour li le pïour,   *Choosing for herself the worse,*
Bien croi que c'est esprovee   *Demonstrates, I do believe,*
Tres haute folour.]   *Extreme folly.*

RS 1999a, L 265-1528, MW 489, B 1593
Manuscript: ƒ 123r
Edition: Boucherie 1872: 321
Text: Edited by ED-Q
RR: With the exception of refrain lines, square brackets indicate conjectures
necessitated by mutilation of the manuscript. Aside from line 29, the conjectured
readings are the same as those found in Boucherie 1872. — 38 assene.
DF: Picard, including *ai* for *a,* as in *saige* (47); *ch* for *c,* as in *cheli* (27), *Chus* (45);
millour (1) for *meilleur;* demonstrative pronouns *cheli* (27), *Chus* (45). Lorraine,
including *loiaulté* (42) for *loialté; our* for *eur,* as in *demour* (16), *labours* (30).
TN: 29 Boucherie 1872 reads *a . . . voee.*

26

Chanson d'ami
Ballette

Trop me repent, mais tairt mi suis parsue	*Greatly do I repent, but I was late to realize*
Ke je suis jai laide, vielle, pessue.	*That I am already ugly, old, and decrepit.*

3 I Je ne trus mais qui me voille esgardeir,
  Ains dit chascuns: "Por Deu, vos an
    gardeis!
  Ne veeiz vos coment elle est ridee?"
  Et cant je l'oï, j'an suis desesperee,
  C'on me souloit tenir a cortoise et anette;
  Si soit malditte l'oure ke je fus nee,
  Kant je n'amai jonette.
  [Trop me repent, mais tairt mi suis parsue
  Ke je suis jai laide, vielle, pessue.]

I no longer find anyone who wants to look at me,
Rather, everyone says: "For God's sake, stay clear
  of her!
Don't you see how wrinkled she is?"
And when I hear this I despair,
For I was once considered refined and honorable;
Cursed be the hour I was born,
Since I did not love in my youth.
Greatly do I repent, but I was late to realize
That I am already ugly, old, and decrepit.

12 II *Vos lou me deffendreis l'ameir,*
  Mais vos gaisteis vostre fransois,
  Car, par Deu, vos areis ansois
  Faite iawe douce de la meir.
  Mes cuers est durs a antameir,
  Por ceu d'ameir ne partirai,
  Car on ne trueve point d'ameir,
  Et par Deu je l'amerai.
  [Trop me repent, mais tairt mi suis parsue
  Ke je suis jai laide, vielle, pessue.]

You could forbid me to love,
But you are wasting your words,
For, by God, you would have sooner
Made fresh water from the sea.
My heart is hard to wound,
So I will not forsake love,
For it holds no bitterness,
And by God I will love him.
Greatly do I repent, but I was late to realize
That I am already ugly, old, and decrepit.

RS 2069, L 265-1703, MW 542, B 1809/1859
Manuscript: *I* 229v (240v)
Edition: Steffens 1897b: 374
Text: Edited by ED-Q
RR: 3 Ne — 19 je] ce.
DF: Lorraine, including *ai* for *a*, as in *tairt* (1), *jai* (2), *gaisteis* (13); *an* for *en*, as in *an* (4), *antameir* (16); *ei* for tonic *e*, as in *esgardeir* (3), *gardeis* (4), *meir* (15); *our* for *eur*, as in *oure* (8); *u* for *ui*, as in *trus* (3); intervocalic *w*, as in *iawe* (15); *s* for *c*, as in *parsue* (1), *fransois* (13); *lou* (12) for *le; ceu* (17) for *ce.* Champenois *an* for *on*, as in *anette* (7). Picard fut. *areis* (14) for *avrez.*
TN: Stanza II is grafted (*enté*) on a widely circulating refrain: *"Vous le me défendés*

l'amer, / Mes, par Dieu, je l'amerai" (B 1859). Note that Boogaard (1969) did not detect the occurrence of this refrain in RS 2069. — 12-18 See TN to song no. 14, ll. 49-50.

27
Chanson de croisade
Rotrouenge

As its name implies, a crusade song is a lyric composition occasioned by the call to liberate the Holy Land from the Saracens. The earliest Old French example of the genre (also the first extant Old French lyric) dates from 1146 and is contemporary with the Second Crusade. Crusade songs are either exhortations to take the cross—which may be read as propaganda—or love songs that exploit the separation motif, offering would-be crusaders the means of reconciling fin'amors and religious fervor by assimilating service to the lady with service to God. A few songs express the pain of separation from the woman's perspective. Some pieces include political criticism, moral complaints, and satirical attacks against the management of the Crusades (Dijkstra 1995).

   Little is known regarding the Old French rotrouenge. Medieval poet-musicians sometimes refer to their own compositions using the designation *rotrouenge*—a designation that appears in a song's final stanza or envoi—yet the term does not seem to correspond to a poetic or musical form. The few extant examples differ from one another in versification; further, those preserved with melodies have no structural or stylistic musical characteristics in common. The text of a rotrouenge consists of an indeterminate number of stanzas (normally three or more), each consisting of two to eight monorhymed isometric lines, followed by a one- to two-line poststrophic refrain, which has a different rhyme. The refrain could be linked to the stanza by rhyming the last line of the stanza with a line of the refrain. The most representative rhyme scheme is *aaa . . . (b) + (A)B* or *(B)B* (Bec 1977: 183-89).

I	Chanterai por mon corage	I will sing for the sake of my heart,
	Que je vueill reconforter,	Which I wish to comfort;
	Car avec mon grant damage	In the face of my great suffering
	Ne vueill morir n'afoler,	I wish to neither die nor go mad,
	Quant de la terre sauvage	When I see no one return
	Ne voi nului retorner	From that barbarian land
	Ou cil est qui m'assoage	Where he is, the one who calms
	Le cuer quant j'en oi parler.	My heart whenever I hear his name spoken.
	Deus, quant crïeront "Outree,"	*God, when they shout "Charge!"*

27. Chanterai por mon corage
M 174v

Chan - te - rai   por   mon   co - ra - ge

Que   je   vueill   re - con - for - ter,

Car   a - vec   mon   grant   da - ma - ge

Ne   vueill   mo - rir   n'a - fo - ler,

Quant   de   la   ter - re   sau - va - ge

Ne   voi   nu - lui   re - tor - ner

Ou   cil   est   qui   m'as - so - a - ge

Le   cuer   quant   j'en   oi   par - ler.

Deus,   quant   cri - e - ront   "Ou - tre - e,"

Sire,   ai - diez   au   pe - le - rin

Por   qui   sui   es - po - en - te - e,

Car   fe - lon   sunt   Sar - ra - zin.

Sire, aidiez au pelerin   *Lord, please help the pilgrim:*
Por qui sui espöentee,   *I am terrified for him,*
Car felon sunt Sarrazin.   *For ruthless are the Saracens.*

II   Souffrerai en tel estage   I will suffer in this state   13
     Tant que.l voie rapasser.   Until I see him come back.
     Il est en pelerinage,   He is on a pilgrimage,
     Dont Deus le lait retorner.   God grant that he return.
     Et maugré tot mon lignage   Despite my whole family
     Ne quier ochoison trover   I do not wish to have grounds
     D'autre face mariage;   To marry another man;
     Folz est qui j'en oi parler.   Anyone I hear suggest it is a fool.
     Deus, [quant crïeront "Outree,"   *God, when they shout "Charge!"*
     Sire, aidiez au pelerin   *Lord, please help the pilgrim:*
     Por qui sui espöentee,   *I am terrified for him,*
     Car felon sunt Sarrazin].   *For ruthless are the Saracens.*

III De ce sui au cuer dolente   What pains my heart   25
     Que cil n'est en cest païs   Is that he is not in this land,
     Qui si sovent me tormente;   The one for whom I am in anguish;
     Je n'en ai ne gieu ne ris.   I have neither pleasure nor mirth.
     Il est biaus et je sui gente.   He is handsome and I am lovely.
     Sire Deus, por que.l feïs?   Lord God, why have you done this?
     Quant l'une a l'autre atalente,   When we desire each other,
     Por coi nos as departis?   Why have you parted us?
     Deus, [quant crïeront "Outree,"   *God, when they shout "Charge!"*
     Sire, aidiez au pelerin   *Lord, please help the pilgrim:*
     Por qui sui espöentee,   *I am terrified for him,*
     Car felon sunt Sarrazin].   *For ruthless are the Saracens.*

IV   De ce sui en bone atente   What gives me hope   37
     Que je son homage pris;   Is that I received his homage;
     Et quant la douce ore vente   And when the sweet breeze blows
     Qui vient de cel douz païs   From that sweet land
     Ou cil est qui m'atalente,   Where he is, the one I desire,
     Volentiers i tor mon vis;   Gladly do I turn my face to it;
     Adont m'est vis que je.l sente   Then I seem to feel him
     Par desoz mon mantel gris.   Under my gray cloak.
     Deus, [quant crïeront "Outree,"   *God, when they shout "Charge!"*

Sire, aidiez au pelerin   Lord, please help the pilgrim:
Por qui sui espöentee,   I am terrified for him,
Car felon sunt Sarrazin].   For ruthless are the Saracens.

49   V   De ce fui mout deceüe   What disappointed me greatly
         Que ne fui au convoier.   Was that I was not present to escort him out.
         Sa chemise qu'ot vestue   The tunic he had worn
         M'envoia por embracier.   He sent for me to embrace.
         La nuit, quant s'amor m'argüe,   At night, when his love spurs me,
         La met delez moi couchier,   I lay it down beside me,
         Toute nuit a ma char nue,   All night, against my naked skin,
         Por mes malz assoagier.   To soothe my pain.
         Deus, [quant crïeront "Outree,"   God, when they shout "Charge!"
         Sire, aidiez au pelerin   Lord, please help the pilgrim:
         Por qui sui espöentee,   I am terrified for him,
         Car felon sunt Sarrazin].   For ruthless are the Saracens.

RS 21, L 106-4, MW 861, B 552

Manuscripts: *M* 174v♪ (base) (*Guios de digon*), *C* 86v-87r (*lai dame dou fael*), *E*ⁿ 91-92, *K* 385-86♪, *O* 28r♪, *T* 128v-129r♪, *X* 248r-v♪

Editions: Crapelet 1829: xvii (French translation); Michel 1830: 95; Le Roux de Lincy 1841: 105 (French translation); Paris 1856: 556; Crépet 1861: 188 (French translation); Brakelmann 1868a: 315; Meyer 1877: 368; Bédier and Aubry 1909: 107♪, 308♪ (French translation); Gennrich 1925: 44♪; Spanke 1925: 188; Nissen 1928: 1; Pauphilet 1952: 907; Gelzer 1953: 3; Woledge 1961: 111 (English translation); Henry 1967, 1: 227; Mary 1967, 1: 226 (French translation); Picot 1975, 2: 10 (French translation); Bec 1978: 92; Contini 1978: 50; Rosenberg and Tischler 1981: 293♪; Collins, Cook, and Harmon 1982: 39 (English translation); Lea 1982: 76 (German translation); Baumgartner and Ferrand 1983: 248 (French translation); Dufournet 1989: 196 (French translation); Guida 1992: 86 (Italian translation); Rosenberg, Tischler, and Grossel 1995: 504♪ (French translation); Tischler 1997, 1: no. 16♪; Rosenberg, Switten, and Le Vot 1998: 290♪ (English translation)

Text: Rosenberg and Tischler 1981: 293

RR: 13-14 Ie souferrai mon damage / Tant que lan verrai passer — 49 deceüe] engignie — 50 Quant.

TV: Stanzas:

TC   *I*   *II*   *III*   *IV*   *V*
XKO   *I*   *III*   *II*   *V*   *IV*

1 Ge ch. *C* — 2 resconforteir *C* — 3 Quauecques *XKO* — 4 vueill] quier *XKO;* ne foler *X* — 6 nului] mes nul *XKO* — 7 rassoage *XKO* — 8 Le cuer] Mes maus *XKO;* ai *K* — 9

crierons *XKO;* entree *O* — 10 apalerin *C* — 11 qui *missing in X;* enpoentee *C* — 13 Ie sofferrai mon damaige (outraige *C*) *TC* — 14 Tant qou uoie repasser *O*, Tant ke lans iert trespasses *TC* — 16 laist *TC;* Mult atent son retorner *XKO* — 17 Et] Ne *C;* Car autre (augre *O*) de mon l. *XKO* — 19 Dautrui *XO*, Autrui *K;* faites *C* — 20 oi] os *C;* Mult est fox qui en ueut parler *XKO* — 21 quant crieront outree *added in C* — 25 ceu seux a cuer *C* — 26 Q. c. n. en biau uoisin *XKO* — 27 En qui iai (cui ia *O*) mise mentente *XKO* — 28 Je] Or *XKO*, Ke ie nai *C* — 29 Il] Sil *XKO* — 30 S. por quoi le f. *XKO;* Sires *C;* (coi *C*) fesis *TC* — 31 lun *O* — 32 que *O;* as] en *XKO* — 33 quant *added in O;* quant crieront outree *added in C* — 37 fui *O*, seux *C;* entente *XKO* — 38 Quant *XO* — 39 Quant lalaine douce uente *XKO* — 40 Ke *C;* de cel] dou (du *K*) tres *XKO* — 43 Adont m. v.] dex m. v. *K*, et lors mestuet *O*, *missing in X;* je.l] ie le *XK*, ie la *O*, ie *T* — 45 quant crierons *added in O;* quant crieront outree *added in C* — 49 sui *T*, seux *C;* mout] ie *O;* deceüe] engignie *TC* — 50 Quant *XO;* au] a *C* — 53 samors *OT* — 54 delez] auec *XKO* — 55 Toute n.] mult estroit *XKO* — 56 rassouaigier *TC* — 57 quant *added in T.*

TN: We can reject the fanciful attribution in manuscript *C:* the Dame de Fayel, legendary lover of the Chastelain de Couci, was the fictitious heroine of Jakemes' *Roman du Chastelain de Couci.* As Tyssens (1992: 379-80) notes, because Jakemes' romance was inspired by the work of the trouvère, the rubricator has by implication transformed the romance into a razo of this song. Regarding the attribution to Guiot de Dijon found in manuscript *M*, there is a measure of disagreement. Some scholars, such as Zink (1996: 143 and 147), express little doubt that Guiot composed this piece, but Tyssens (1992) voices skepticism, and although Rosenberg and Tischler (1981) accept the attribution, they refer the reader to Hans Spanke's review of Nissen 1928 for doubts regarding his authorship. This attribution is maintained in Rosenberg, Tischler, and Grossel 1995, whereas Rosenberg, Switten, and Le Vot (1998) admit that the song cannot be ascribed with certainty to Guiot de Dijon, as he "is not known to have composed any other songs touching on a crusade or voicing the sentiments of a woman" (289). Bec (1978: 92-94) credits Guiot in his anthology but concedes in a note that this attribution is uncertain, whereas in an article published the following year, in which he claims that all chansons de femme were composed by men, he cites it among three examples of this lyric type whose authors are known to be men (Bec 1979: 258). — 9 The exhortation *Outree* is attested in several pilgrims' songs, introduced by either the verb *crier* or *chanter* (Paris 1880: 44-45). — 39 The invocation of the breeze that blows from the land of the beloved is a well-documented motif in Occitan, Galician-Portuguese, and Old French texts. These lines are reminiscent of the first stanza of Bernart de Ventadorn's "Quan la douss'aura venta" (PC 70.37). — 51 According to Bédier and Aubry (1909: 116-17): "The *chemise* was a tunic layered over other clothing. Crusaders would equip themselves as pilgrims when they started out, take the *escharpe*, that is, a beggar's pouch, and a pilgrim's staff, and set off to the next destination accompanied by family and friends; they usually 'walked, barefoot and dressed in a woolen tunic.' That was the 'convoy' or procession. At the next destination, this quasi ceremony would end; the crusader donned his shoes and normal clothing. What our pilgrim has sent his lady is in all likelihood the *chemise* . . . symbolizing the pilgrim's oath taken at the time of departure."

MV: 1/2 ga *K* — 1/6-1/8 cd-cb-a *K* — 1/8 ba *T* — 2/1 gf *O* — 2/2 ga *T* — 2/5-2/7 b-cd-cba *K* — 2/6 c^p *O* — 2/7 cba *T* — 3/1-3/8 ga-bc-a-g-e-f-e-d *K* — 3/2 ab *O;* ga *T* — 3/6-3/7 f^p-fe *O* — 3/8 ba *T* — 4/2-4/4 gf-g-ga *K* — 4/2 ga *T* — 4/6 b *T* — 4/7 ba *KT* — 5/1-5/8 bc-b-a-g-ef-f-f-ed *K* — 5/1-5/2 a-bc *O* — 5/2 ba *T* — 5/5-5/8 e-f^p-fe-d *O* — 5/7-6/1 c-cbab-ga *T* — 6/2-6/4 f-gb-ga *K* — 6/2 ga *T* — 6/3 g *O* — 6/7 cba *K;* ba *O;* cba^p *T* — 7/1 abc *T* — 7/1-7/2 a-bc *K* — 7/5-7/8 e-f-e-ed *K* — 7/6-7/8 f^p-fe-d *O* — 7/7-7/8 eaef-fe *T* — 8/2 ga *T* — 8/2-8/7 f-g-ga-c-bagab-ag *K* — 8/6 bb$_p$ *O* — 8/6-8/7 gf-gagf *T* — 9/5-9/8 b-c^p-a *O* — 9/6-9/8 cd-cb-ba *K* — 9/7-9/8 c-bab *T* — 10/2 ga *XO* — 10/6-11/2 cd-cba-a-bc *K* — 11/1 abc *T* — 11/2 bcb *O* — 11/5-12/7 e-f-e-ed-a-gf-g-ga-c-bagab-ag *K* — 11/5-11/8 f-f-gagf-e *T* — 11/6-11/7 f^p-fe *O* — 12/2-12/7 ga-c-b-ag-f-abag *T* — 12/6 b-b$_p$ *O.*

28

Chanson de croisade

I   Jherusalem, grant damage me fais,
    Qui m'as tolu ce que je pluz amoie.
    Sachiez de voir ne vos amerai maiz,
    Quar c'est la rienz dont j'ai pluz male joie;
    Et bien sovent en souspir et pantais
    Si qu'a bien pou que vers Deu ne m'irais,
    Qui m'a osté de grant joie ou j'estoie.

Jerusalem, you cause me great harm,
Taking from me what I loved most.
Know in truth that I will no longer love you,
For that is what brings me the most doleful joy;
Often I sigh and am so short of breath
That I am on the verge of turning against God,
Who has deprived me of the great joy I had.

8   II   Biauz dous amis, com porroiz endurer
    La grant painne por moi en mer salee,
    Quant rienz qui soit ne porroit deviser
    La grant dolor qui m'est el cuer entree?
    Quant me remembre del douz viaire cler
    Que je soloie baisier et acoler,
    Grant merveille est que je ne sui dervee.

Dear sweet beloved, how can you endure
Such great pain for my sake on the salty sea,
When nothing in this world could ever express
The great sorrow that has entered my heart?
When I recall the sweet, radiant face
I used to kiss and caress,
It is truly a wonder I do not go mad.

15   III   Si m'aït Deus, ne puis pas eschaper:
    Morir m'estuet, teus est ma destinee;
    Si sai de voir que qui muert por amer
    Trusques a Deu n'a pas c'une jornee.
    Lasse! mieuz vueil en tel jornee entrer

So help me God, I cannot escape:
Die I must, such is my fate;
Yet I know truly that whoever dies for love
Has more than one day's journey to God.
Alas! I would rather embark on such a journey

Que je puisse mon douz ami trover
Que je ne vueill ci remaindre esguaree.

To find my dear beloved
Than remain here forsaken.

RS 191, L 265-939, MW 596

Manuscript: *M* 180r-v (*Gautiers d'espinau,* in rubric; *Jehans de nuevile,* in table of contents)

Editions: Du Méril 1850: 334; Brakelmann 1870-91: 19; Jeanroy 1889: 498; Schultz 1891: 237; Lindelöf and Wallensköld 1901: 98; Bédier and Aubry 1909: 275 (French translation); Woledge 1961: 116 (English translation); Bec 1978: 10; Rosenberg and Tischler 1981: 107; Dufournet 1989: 48 (French translation); Mölk 1989: 92 (German translation); Kasten 1990: 190 (German translation); Rosenberg, Tischler, and Grossel 1995: 250 (French translation); Rosenberg, Switten, and Le Vot 1998: 214 (English translation)

Text: Rosenberg and Tischler 1981: 107

TN: Most modern scholars would agree with Rosenberg and Tischler (1981: 108) that this song is "best regarded as anonymous," given that the editors of both Gautier d'Epinal (Lindelöf and Wallensköld 1901: 230) and Jehan de Nuevile (Richter 1904: 15) reject the attributions that appear in the manuscript rubric and in the manuscript table of contents, respectively. Dronke (1996: 106) agrees that the attributions are improbable and adds: "I think it quite possible that the author was a woman." The song appears to be a fragment. The identical rhymes in stanzas II and III suggest that it was composed in coblas doblas and should therefore consist of at least four stanzas (normally six) of which the present stanza I would have been either the first or second; after the last stanza, the scribe leaves a blank space large enough to accommodate two more stanzas. — 18 As noted by Rosenberg (Rosenberg and Tischler 1981: 108; Rosenberg, Tischler, and Grossel 1995: 941; Rosenberg, Switten, and Le Vot 1998: 211), the construction *n'a pas c'une* is ambiguous in Old French; it could also be interpreted to mean "has only one." Our translation follows that of Bédier and Aubry 1909; Dufournet 1989; Rosenberg, Switten, and Le Vot 1998; and others.

29
Aube
Rotrouenge

The erotic dawn song, or aube, is a lyric monologue on the pain of separation. It is so named because the arrival of dawn brings an end to a couple's night of pleasure. The lament is most often voiced by the lady, who deplores the lark's singing and reluctantly begs her beloved to be on his way, but the farewell can also be uttered by the male lover. The song sometimes includes a third figure, a watchman who warns the lovers of the advent of day. There are but five extant Old French examples of the genre, only two of which are complete; the genre found more resonance among the Occitan troubadours and German minnesingers. The reference to daybreak within the song's refrain is its most distinctive formal trait. See also motet no. 72, whose motetus has the same theme.

I	Cant voi l'aube dou jor venir, Nulle rien ne doi tant haïr, K'elle fait de moi departir Mon amin, cui j'ain per amors. *Or ne hais riens tant com le jour,* *Amins, ke me depait de vos.*	When I see the dawn of day appear, There is nothing I am bound to hate as much, For it takes away My beloved, whom I love with all my heart. *Now I hate nothing so much as day,* *Beloved, for it parts me from you.*

7 II Je ne vos puis de jor veoir,
Car trop redout l'apercevoir,
Et se vos di trestout por voir
K'en agait sont li enuious.
Or ne hais riens [tant com le jour,
Amins, ke me depait de vos].

I cannot see you in the daytime,
For I greatly fear being discovered,
And this I tell you in truth:
The envious lie in ambush.
Now I hate nothing so much as day,
Beloved, for it parts me from you.

13 III Quant je me gix dedens mon lit
Et je resgairde encoste mi,
Je n'i truis poent de mon amin,
Se m'en plaing a fins amerous.
Or ne hais riens [tant com le jour,
Amins, ke me depait de vos].

When I am lying in my bed
And, looking beside me,
Find not my beloved,
I lament to all true lovers.
Now I hate nothing so much as day,
Beloved, for it parts me from you.

19 IV Biaus dous amis, vos en ireis;
A Deu soit vos cors comandeis.
Por Deu vos pri, ne m'oblieis!
Je n'ain nulle rien tant com vos.
Or ne hais riens [tant com le jour,
Amins, ke me depait de vos].

Dear sweet love, be on your way;
May God protect you.
In God's name, I beg you, do not forget me!
I love nothing so much as you.
Now I hate nothing so much as day,
Beloved, for it parts me from you.

25 V Or pri a tous les vrais amans
Ceste chanson voixent chantant
Ens en despit des mesdixans
Et des mavais maris jalous.
Or ne hais riens tant com lou jor,
Amins, ke me depait de vos.

Now I beg all true lovers
To go singing this song
Quite in spite of slanderers
And mean, jealous husbands.
Now I hate nothing so much as day,
Beloved, for it parts me from you.

RS 1481, L 65-12, MW 369, B 1453

Manuscript: *C* 44v-45r (Gace Brulé)

Editions: Wackernagel 1846: 9; Tarbé 1850: 134; Paris 1856: 566; Bartsch 1920: 190; Petersen Dyggve 1951: 441; Pauphilet 1952: 880; Woledge 1961: 89 (English translation); Hatto 1965: 371 (English translation); Toja 1966: 181; Goldin 1973: 402 (English translation); Picot 1975, 1: 74 (French translation); Bec 1978: 26; Rosenberg and Tischler 1981: 240; Lea 1982: 98 (German translation); Baumgartner and Ferrand 1983: 276 (French translation); Bergner et al. 1983: 424 (German translation); Rosenberg, Danon, and van der Werf 1985: 266 (English translation); Mölk 1989: 90 (German translation); Rosenberg, Tischler, and Grossel 1995: 120 (French translation); Rosenberg, Switten, and Le Vot 1998: 194 (English translation)

Text: Rosenberg, Danon, and van der Werf 1985: 266

RR: 15 *followed by supernumerary line* medixant men ont fait partir.

DF: Lorraine, including *a* for *al* or *au* before consonant, as in *mavais* (28); *ai* for *a*, as in *depait* (6); *ei* for tonic *e*, as in *ireis* (19); *poent* (15) for *point*; *amin* (4) for *ami*; adverbial *se* (9, 16) for *si*; *lou* (29) for *le*.

TN: The attribution to Gace Brulé is rejected in Petersen Dyggve 1951: 156; Rosenberg and Tischler (1981) admit that this authorship is not certain; moreover, in Rosenberg, Tischler, and Grossel 1995 and in Rosenberg, Switten, and Le Vot 1998 the song is judiciously classified as anonymous. Two arguments speak against ascribing the song to Gace: the attributions of manuscript *C* are at times unreliable, and this composition differs markedly from any others ascribed to Gace, whose corpus consists almost exclusively of courtly chansons d'amour. Gale Sigal (1996: 8) regards the *alba* lady as a literary creation and views her song as a "purposeful fiction presented in the guise of autobiography." Although she cannot rule out the possibility that the author of anonymous dawn songs was a woman, she presumes nonetheless that the alba lady's voice is "man-made" (18), that it represents a male-constructed ideal rather than a real woman (75). — 6 Note that *ke* may be either the causal conjunction *que* or the relative pronoun *qui*. — 10 The manuscript reading *enuious* is ambiguous. The form may be understood—as in Petersen Dyggve 1951—to represent *ennuyeux* (in the medieval sense of "wrongdoers," "those who harm"); taking the first *u* as a *v*, it can also be understood to represent *envieux*—as in Bartsch 1920; Woledge 1961; Rosenberg, Danon, and van der Werf 1985; and others.

30
Aube

I   Entre moi et mon amin,
      En un boix k'est leis Betune,
      Alainmes juwant mairdi
      Toute lai nuit a la lune,
      Tant k'il ajornait

           My love and I,
           In a wood near Bethune,
           Spent all night Tuesday
           Playing in the moonlight,
           Till day dawned

<table>
<tr><td>Et ke l'alowe chantait</td><td>And the lark sang,</td></tr>
<tr><td>Ke dit: "Amins, alons an."</td><td>Saying: "My love, let us go."</td></tr>
<tr><td>Et il respont doucement:</td><td>And my love answered softly:</td></tr>
<tr><td>*Il n'est mie jours,*</td><td>*It is not nearly day,*</td></tr>
<tr><td>*Saverouze au cors gent;*</td><td>*My delightful, fair one;*</td></tr>
<tr><td>*Si m'aït Amors,*</td><td>*So help me Love,*</td></tr>
<tr><td>*L'alowette nos mant.*</td><td>*The lark deceives us.*</td></tr>
</table>

13   II   Adont se trait pres de mi,   Then he drew close to me,

Adont se trait pres de mi,	Then he drew close to me,
Et je ne fu pas anfruine;	And I did not draw back;
Bien trois fois me baixait il,	A good three times he kissed me,
Ausi fix je lui plus d'une,	And I him more than once,
K'ainz ne m'anoiait.	For it certainly did not displease me.
Adonc vocexiens nous lai	How we would have wished
Ke celle neut durest sant,	That night to last a hundred,
Mais ke plus n'alest dixant:	With no further need to say:
Il n'est mie jours,	*It is not nearly day,*
[Saverouze au cors gent;	*My delightful, fair one;*
Si m'aït Amors,	*So help me Love,*
L'alowette nos mant].	*The lark deceives us.*

RS 1029, L 265-665, MW 2240, B 892

Manuscript: *I* 207v (216v)

Editions: La Villemarqué 1856: 100; Bartsch 1870: 27; Steffens 1897b: 95; Brittain 1951: 150; Woledge 1961: 88 (English translation); Hatto 1965: 370 (English translation); Bec 1978: 25; Rosenberg and Tischler 1981: 28; Lea 1982: 94 (German translation); Baumgartner and Ferrand 1983: 278 (French translation); Bergner et al. 1983: 420 (German translation); Kasten 1990: 192 (German translation); Rosenberg, Tischler, and Grossel 1995: 118 (French translation); Rosenberg, Switten, and Le Vot 1998: 193 (English translation)

Text: Rosenberg and Tischler 1981: 28

RR: 11 Si meut *(em. Bartsch)* — 13 se] ce — 15 Il me b. bien iii fois *(em. Bartsch).*

DF: Lorraine, including *ai* for *a,* as in *mairdi* (3) and *lai* (4); *leis* (2) for *les; anfruine* (14) for *enfrune; amin* (1) for *ami; neut* (19) for *nuit;* intervocalic *w,* as in *juwant* (3); *x* for *s(s),* as in *vocexiens* (18), *dixant* (20); confusion of *s* and *c,* as in *vocexiens* (18) and *sant* (19); 3rd-pers. sing. pret. in *-ait,* as in *ajornait* (5), *chantait* (6); 3rd-pers. sing. imp. subj. in *-est,* as in *durest* (19); rel. *ke (k')* (2, 7) for nom. *qui.*

TN: Classified in manuscript *I* among the pastourelles.

31
Chanson de malmariée
Ballette

The unhappy, frustrated wife heard in a chanson de malmariée bewails her fate at the hands of a husband (whom she calls a *vilain*, or boorish lout) who often holds her captive and who is old, ugly, jealous, sometimes impotent, and even brutal. She either longs for compensation or has already exacted satisfaction by taking a lover who possesses all the attributes lacking in the husband she despises: her ami is young, handsome, refined, cheerful, and ardent in love. The genre reflects the reality that in the thirteenth century women were generally obliged to marry men chosen by their families for purely socioeconomic reasons. See also song nos. 47, 50, and 52 (all rondeaux) and motet nos. 64–65, 69, and 73–74.

A variant of the chanson de malmariée, the chanson de nonne, gives voice to a young nun cloistered against her will, who laments her confinement—pointing an accusatory finger at those who have sentenced her to the convent—and yearns for a lover who will liberate her. Young women of noble birth were often forced to take the habit when their families could not secure the dowry needed to arrange a marriage. For examples of these motifs, see motet nos. 67 and 71.

Au cuer les ai, les jolis malz.	*In my heart I feel them, the sweet pains.*
Coment an guariroie?	*How could I be cured of them?*

I Kant li vilains vait a marchiet,　　When the boor goes to market,　　3
　Il n'i vait pais por berguignier,　　He does not go there to bargain,
　Mais por sa feme a esgaitier　　But to spy on his wife
　Que nuns ne li forvoie.　　Lest someone seduce her.
　Au cuer les ai, les jolis malz.　　*In my heart I feel them, the sweet pains.*
　Coment an guariroie?　　*How could I be cured of them?*

II Vilains, car vos traites an lai,　　Boor, get away from me,　　9
　Car vostre alainne m'ocidrait.　　For your breath will kill me.
　Bien sai c'ancor departirait　　I am certain that your love and mine
　Vostre amor et la moie.　　Will yet separate.
　[Dieus,] j'ai a cuer [les jolis malz.　　*In my heart I feel them, the sweet pains.*
　Coment en guariroie?]　　*How could I be cured of them?*

15   III   Vilains, cuidiez vos tout avoir,   Boor, do you think you can have it all,
            Et belle dame et grant avoir?   Both a lovely lady and great wealth?
            Vos avereiz lai hairt on col,   You'll have a noose around your neck,
            Et mes amins lai joie.   And my lover will have joy.
            Dieus, j'ai a cuer [les jolis malz.   *In my heart I feel them, the sweet pains.*
            Coment en guariroie?]   *How could I be cured of them?*

RS 386, L 265-154, MW 410, B 193
Manuscript: *I* 198v-199r (208v-209r)
Editions: Bartsch 1870: 21; Steffens 1897b: 82; Gennrich 1921: 104; Bec 1978: 169;
Rosenberg and Tischler 1981: 3; Rosenberg, Tischler, and Grossel 1995: 82 (French
translation)
Text: Rosenberg and Tischler 1981: 3
RR: 15 O vilains *(+1)*.
DF: Lorraine, including *a* (13) for *au; ai* for *a,* as in *pais* (4), adverb *lai* (9), article *lai*
(17), *hairt* (17); *nuns* (6) for *nus* and *amins* (18) for *amis;* preservation of final *t,* as in
vait (3), *marchiet* (3); 3rd-pers. sing. fut. in *-ait,* as in *ocidrait* (10), *departirait* (11).
TN: Classified in manuscript *I* among the pastourelles.

32

Chanson de malmariée
Ballette

            Mesdixant, c'an tient a vos   *Slanderers, why should you care*
            Se je voil ameir par amours?   *If I want to love faithfully?*

3   I   Ains ke fuxe marïee   Before I was married
          Fu je par amors amee.   I was loved faithfully.
          A tort m'an ont escuzee   Wrongly did they deter me,
          Li mavais lozangeours.   The wicked scandalmongers.
          [Mesdixant, c'an tient a vos   *Slanderers, why should you care*
          Se je voil ameir par amours?]   *If I want to love faithfully?*

9   II   Cant j'o amors premerainnes,   When I experienced my first love,
          Je les o si tres certainnes   I felt it so strongly
          K'ains por travail ne por poinne   That never for torment or suffering
          Je ne po panceir aillors.   Could I think of anything else.
          [Mesdixant, c'an tient a vos   *Slanderers, why should you care*
          Se je voil ameir par amours?]   *If I want to love faithfully?*

III	Or suis je bien asenee	Now I am destined	15
	D'estre par amors amee;	To be loved faithfully;
	A boin qui fiert de l'espee	To the good man who wields the sword
	Ai je doneit mon cuer dous.	I have given my tender heart.
	[Mesdixant, c'an tient a vos	*Slanderers, why should you care*
	Se je voil ameir par amours?]	*If I want to love faithfully?*

IV	Dame qui est bien amee	A lady who is well loved	21
	Ne doit pais estre blamee;	Should not be reproached;
	Qui bien ainme a recellee	She who loves sincerely and discreetly
	Haïr doit les anvïous.	Should disdain the envious.
	[Mesdixant, c'an tient a vos	*Slanderers, why should you care*
	Se je voil ameir par amours?]	*If I want to love faithfully?*

V	Prions Deu qu'i nos anvoie	Let us pray God to send us	27
	De nos amouretes joie,	Love's pleasure,
	Et a la fin totevoie	And in the end, all things considered,
	Ain je bien lou gueridon.	I like the reward.
	[Mesdixant, c'an tient a vos	*Slanderers, why should you care*
	Se je voil ameir par amours?]	*If I want to love faithfully?*

RS 2048, L 265-1154, MW 384, B 1325

Manuscript: *I* 224r (235r)

Editions: Steffens 1897b: 366; Gennrich 1921: 192

Text: Edited by JTG

RR: 2 Se] Ce.

DF: Lorraine, including *a* for *al* or *au,* as in *mavais* (6), *A* (17); *ai* for *a,* as in *pais* (22); *an* for *en,* as in *an* (1), *anvïous* (24), *anvoie* (27); *ei* for tonic *e,* as in *ameir* (2), *panceir* (12); *oil* for *ueil,* as in *voil* (2); *c* for *s,* as in RR, *panceir* (12); *x* or *z* for *s(s),* as in *Mesdixant* (1), *fuxe* (3), *escuzee* (5); preservation of final *t,* as in *doneit* (18); *poinne* (11) for *peine; boin* (17) for *bon; lou* (30) for *le;* 1st-pers. sing. pret. *fu* (4) for *fui, o* (9, 10) for *oi, po* (12) for *poi;* 1st-pers. sing. imp. subj. *fuxe* (3) for *fusse.*

33

Chanson de malmariée
Ballette

Por coi me bait mes maris?	*Why does my husband beat me?*
Laisette!	*Poor wretch!*

3	I	Je ne li de rienz meffis,	I've done him no wrong,
		Ne riens ne li ai mesdit	Said nothing against him,
		Fors c'acolleir mon amin	Just embraced my lover
		Soulete.	All alone.
		[Por coi me bait mes maris?	*Why does my husband beat me?*
		Laisette!]	*Poor wretch!*
9	II	Et s'il ne mi lait dureir	And if he won't let me be
		Ne bone vie meneir,	Or lead the good life,
		Je lou ferai cous clameir	I'll have him called a cuckold
		A certes.	For sure.
		[Por coi me bait mes maris?	*Why does my husband beat me?*
		Laisette!]	*Poor wretch!*
15	III	Or sai bien que je ferai	Now I know what I'll do,
		Et coment m'an vangerai:	How I'll get my revenge:
		Avec mon amin geirai	I'll lie with my lover
		Nüete.	All naked.
		Por coi me bait mes maris?	*Why does my husband beat me?*
		[Laisette!]	*Poor wretch!*

RS 1564, L 265-1346, MW 417, B 1515

Manuscript: *I* 197r (207r)

Editions: Meyer 1868: 237; Bartsch 1870: 20; Steffens 1897b: 79; Gennrich 1921–27, 1: 102♪ and 2: 104♪; Pauphilet 1952: 866; Gennrich 1955: 54♪; Gennrich 1958c: 35♪; Chastel 1959: 774; Toja 1966: 129; Mary 1967, 1: 298 (French translation); Goldin 1973: 410 (English translation); Bec 1978: 166; Rosenberg and Tischler 1981: 2♪; Lea 1982: 70, 167♪ (German translation); Baumgartner and Ferrand 1983: 364 (French translation); Bergner et al. 1983: 418 (German translation); Mölk 1989: 104 (German translation); Kasten 1990: 196 (German translation); Rosenberg, Tischler, and Grossel 1995: 80♪ (French translation); Tischler 1997, 10: no. 901♪; Rosenberg, Switten, and Le Vot 1998: 181 (English translation)

Text: Rosenberg and Tischler 1981: 2

RR: 3 Je ne li ai rienz meffait *(em. Bartsch)* — 9 s'il] cil.

DF: Lorraine, including *ai* for *a,* as in *bait* (1), *Laisette* (2); *ei* for tonic *e,* as in *acolleir* (5), *dureir* (9); *amin* (5) for *ami; lou* (11) for *le.*

TN: Classified in manuscript *I* among the pastourelles. A version of the text appears as the tenor in a fourteenth-century motet by Guillaume de Machaut, "Lasse, comment oublieray / Se j'aim mon loyal ami / POUR QUOY ME BAT MES MARIS?"; all three of these texts are in the female voice. The music of the tenor is roughly in the form of a virelai.

34 *DUCHESSE DE LORRAINE*
Chanson de malmariée
Aube
Chanson avec des refrains

Unlike the chanson à refrain, where a single refrain reappears at regular, pre-established intervals, the roughly one hundred extant chansons avec des re-frains (songs with multiple or variable refrains) consist of an indeterminate number of stanzas—ranging from two to eight—each followed by a different refrain, presumably borrowed or cited (intertextual repetition). Although such refrains do not recur within the song, they can be recognized by their place-ment. The appearance of each refrain entails a metrical and melodic break, because all stanzas are sung to the same melody and have the same meter and rhyme scheme, while each refrain has its own melodic phrase and versifica-tion. Nonetheless, a variable refrain is often integrated into the stanza through a transitional line announcing it (Doss-Quinby 1984: 96–111).

I	Un petit davant lou jor	Just before daybreak
	Me levai l'autrier,	I rose the other day,
	Sospris de novelle amor	Smitten by a new love
	Ke me fait vellier.	That has kept me awake.
	Por oblïeir mes dolors	To forget my sorrows
	Et por aligier,	And soothe them,
	M'en alai coillir la flor	I went off to gather flowers
	Dejoste un vergier.	Near an orchard.
	Lai dedans, en un destor,	There, in a secluded spot,
	Oï un chevalier,	I heard a knight,
	Desor lui, en haute tour,	And above him, in a high tower,
	Dame ke moult l'ot chier.	A lady who cherished him dearly.
	Elle ot frexe la color	She had a fresh complexion
	Et chantoit per grant dousor	And was singing so sweetly
	Uns douls chans pitous melleit en plor.	A sweet, poignant song mingled with tears.
	Pués ait dit, com loiauls drue:	Then she said, as a loyal lover:
	"Amins, vos m'aveis perdue,	*"Beloved, you have lost me,*
	Li jalous m'ait mis en mue."	*The jealous one has imprisoned me."*
II	Quant li chevaliers entent	When the knight heard
	La dame a vis cleir,	The lady with the radiant face,
	De la grant dolor k'il sent	From the great anguish he felt
	Comance a ploreir.	He began to weep.

19

34. Un petit davant lou jor
C 247v-248r (text)
a 109r-v (music)

Un pe - tit da - vant lou jor

Me le - vai l'au - trier,

Sos - pris de no - velle a - mor

Ke me fait vel - lier.

Por o - bli - eir mes do - lors

Et por a - li - gier,

M'en a - lai coil - lir la flor

De - joste un ver - gier.

Lai de - dans, en un des - tor,

O - i un che - va - lier,

De - sor lui, en hau - te tour,

Da - me ke moult l'ot chier.

Elle ot fre - xe la co - lor

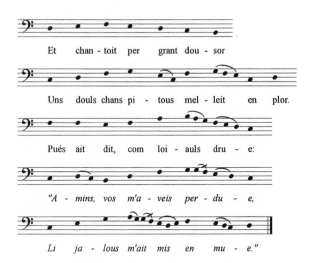

Et chan - toit per grant dou - sor

Uns douls chans pi - tous mel - leit en plor.

Pués ait dit, com loi - auls dru - e:

"A - mins, vos m'a - veis per - du - e,

Li ja - lous m'ait mis en mu - e."

Refrain II (music from *T* 182r, originally a fifth higher)

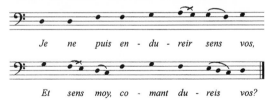

Je ne puis en - du - reir sens vos,

Et sens moy, co - mant du - reis vos?

Refrain VI (music from *T* 195r)

A Deu co - mans je mes a - mors

Ki les me gairt.

se de samor puis esploitier· ne iamais ior senf ioie ne seroie· celle la me
neuilt otroier· Le desir tant li embraissier· z li ueoir z li ou· se de li ai un
douls baixier· ne me porroit nuls mals uenir· ne me porroient foruigier ma
naire genf per lor mentir· coi b·il men doie auenir· ie latandrai tout alorsir·
car fine amor me fait cuidier· boenf seruixes ne puet perir·

la duchai-
se de lou-
rainne

Un petit dauant lou ior me leuai lautrier· sospris de nouelle amor

be me fait ueiller· por oblier mes dolor z por abgier· men alai coilliir flors

de ioste un uergier· lai dedans en un destor· oi un cheualier· desor lui en hau

te tour· dame be nist lot chier· elle or freye color· z chantoit per grant dou

lor· uns douls chanf pitous· meller en plor· puis air dit com loiauls drue·
Qant li chai-
toit la dame a
amins uof maueis perdue· li ialous mait· ais en mue· iuf cleur de la
grant dolor b·il ot comance aplorer· puis air dit en sospirant mar ui enser
reir· dame ufe corf lou genf be doie tant amer· or men couuenir durestit
lef douf biens z·pareir· be uolentierf z souent me solies doneir· lais or me
uair malement· trop air si aypre torment· sil nof dure longuement· trof
doul deuf be deuanirons nof ie ne puis durer senf uof· z uof senf moy

Song no. 34, Bern, Burgerbibliothek, cod. 389, fol. 247v, le duchase de lourainne.
Courtesy of Burgerbibliothek Bern.

Pués ait dit en sospirant: Then he said with a sigh:
"Mar vi enserreir,   "Woe, lady, that I ever saw confined
Dame, vostre cors lou gent   Your gracious body,
Ke doie tant ameir!   Which I cannot help loving!
Or m'en covient durement   Now I must pay dearly
Les dous biens compaireir   For the sweet favors
Ke volentiers et sovent   You so willingly and often
Me soliés doneir.   Used to grant me.
Lais! or me vait malement: Alas! Now I do not fare well:
Trop ait si aipre torment!   It is such bitter torment!
Et se ceu nos dure longuement,   If we must endure it for long,
Tres dous Deus, ke devanrons nos? Dear God, what will become of us?
Je ne puis endureir sens vos,   *I cannot survive without you,*
Et sens moy, comant dureis vos?"   *And you without me, how can you survive?"*

III Dist la belle: "Boens amis,   The lovely lady replied: "Dear friend,   37
    Amor me maintient;   Love sustains me;
    Aisseis est plux mors ke vis   Whoever suffers anguish
    Ki dolor soustient.   Is far more dead than alive.
    Leis moi geist mes anemis,   Beside me lies my enemy,
    Faire le covient;   I have to comply;
    Et se n'ai joie ne ris   And yet, I have no joy or pleasure
    Se de vos ne vient.   Unless it comes from you.
    J'ai si mon cuer en vos mis   I have my heart so placed in you
    Tout adés m'en sovient.   That you are always on my mind.
    Se li cors vos est eschis,   Even if my body is denied you,
    Li cuers a vos se tient,   My heart remains bound to you,
    Si faitement l'ai empris.   That is the commitment I have made.
    Et de ceu soiiés tous fis,   You can be certain
    Ke sens repentir serai toudis   That with no regret I will forever be
    Vostre loiaul amie.   Your loyal lover.
    Por ceu se je ne vos voi,   *And so even if I do not see you,*
    Ne vos oblierai mie."   *I will certainly not forget you."*

IV "Dame, je.l cuit bien savoir,   "Lady, I know full well,   55
    Tant l'ai esprovei,   So much have I seen proof of it,
    K'en vos ne poroit avoir   That in you there could not be
    Cuer de fauceteit.   A deceitful heart.
    Maix ceu me fait moult doloir   But it fills me with anguish

Ke j'ai tant estei.	That I have lingered so long.
Dame de si grant voloir,	My very worthy lady,
Or ai tout pansei:	Now I have thought it through:
Deus m'ait mis en nonchailoir	God has become indifferent to me
Et de tout oblïeit	And has forgotten me so completely
Ke je ne puisse cheoir	That I could not fall
En gringnor povreteit!	Into greater misery!
Maix jeu ai moult boen espoir	Still I have a fond hope
K'encor me puet bien valoir,	That He can yet help me:
Et Deus le me doinst encore avoir;	God grant that I may have you again.
Drois est ke je lou die:	Rightly do I say:
Se Deu plaist, li jalous morait,	*God willing, the jealous one will die,*
Si raverai m'amie."	*And I will have my lover back."*

73   V

"Amins, se vos desireis	"Beloved, if you desire
La mort a jalous,	The death of the jealous one,
Si faic jeu, si m'aït Dés,	Even more do I desire it, so help me God,
Cent tens plux de vos!	A hundred times more than you!
Il est viels et rasoteis	He is old and besotted,
Et glous comme lous,	Gluttonous as a wolf,
Si est maigres et pailés,	And scrawny and bald,
Et si ait la tous.	And he has a cough.
Putes taiches ait aisseis,	He has so many foul traits,
Li deloiaus, li rous;	The perfidious redhead;
Tote la graindre bonteis	The greatest merit he has
C'est de ceu k'il est cous.	Is to be a cuckold.
Amins, mar fu mes cors neis	Friend, alas that I was ever born,
Quant por vos est ensereis,	When my body is captive because of you
Et aitres en ait ses volenteis;	And another has his will;
Drois est ke je m'en plaing:	Rightfully do I complain:
Comant guerirait dame sens amin	*How can a lady without her lover heal*
Cui amors mehaigne."	*When love torments her."*

91   VI

"Biaus amins, vos en ireis,	"Fair friend, be on your way,
Car je voi le jor.	For I see daylight.
Des ore maix i pöeis	From now on you could
Faire lonc sejor.	Be lingering too long.
Vostre fin cuer me laireis;	Leave me your true heart;
N'aiés pais paour,	Have no fear,

C'aveuc vos enportereis	Since you will be taking with you
La plux fine amor.	The most perfect love.
Des ke vos ne me pöeis	Since you cannot
Geteir de ceste tor,	Free me from this tower,
Plux sovant la resgairdeis,	Gaze at it all the more often,
Por moi, per grant dousor."	For my sake, with much tenderness."
Et cil s'en part toz iriés	And so he departs full of ire
Et dist: "Lais! tant mar fu neiz,	Saying: "Alas that I was ever born!
Quant mes cuers est ci sens moi remeis.	Since my heart stays here without me.
Dolans m'en pairt.	Doleful I depart.
A Deu comans je mes amors	*I commend my love to God,*
K'i les me gairt."	*May He protect it for me."*

RS 1995, L 34-2, MW 785, B 134/1009/1497/1666/377/13

Manuscripts: *C* 247v-248r (base for the text) (*le duchase de lourainne*), *H* 218r-v, *K* 320-21♩, *N* 153r-v♪, *P* 168r-169r♪, *T* 79v-80r♪ (*Capelains de loon*), *U* 67v-68v♪, *a* 109r-v♪ (base for the music)

Editions: Keller 1844: 308; Tarbé 1850: 26; Mätzner 1853: 70; Dinaux 1863: 155; Baret 1867: 268; Hofmann 1867: 524; Brakelmann 1868b: 388; Bartsch 1870: 35; Bertoni 1917: 322, 354; Bartsch 1920: 218; Spanke 1925: 35, 444♪; Mary 1967, 1: 246 (French translation); Kooijman 1974: 84 (French translation); Baumgartner and Ferrand 1983: 160 (French translation); Tischler 1997, 13: no. 1137♪

Text: Edited by JTG, ED-Q, and WP

RR: 7 la *missing (–1) (reading from HKNPUa)*; flors — 13 la *missing (–1) (reading from HKNPTUa)* — 19 oit *(reading from HTUa)* — 21 ot *(reading from Ta)* — 33 S'il *(–2) (reading from KPTUa)* — 35 dureir *(–1) (reading from a)* — 36 Et vos *(+1) (reading from KNPTUa)* — 50 *missing (reading from a)* — 51 Ke je serai sens repentir *(–1) (reading from a)* — 61 valor *(reading from HTa)* — 68 moult b. *(+1) (reading from KNPT)* — 69 *missing (reading from T)* — 75 Aincor la desire jeu *(reading from TUa)* — 79 Et *(+1)*; maiges *(em. Hofmann) (reading from TUa)* — 80 est lais *(–1) (reading from Ua)* — 81 Tant *(+1) (reading from TUa)* — 83 La gringnor bonteit k'il ait *(reading from T)* — 85 Et dist lais tant mar fu neis *(reading from a)* — 86 *missing (reading from a)* — 87 C'a. *(–1) (reading from a)*; ses] ces — 90 *missing (reading from U)* — 93 Desormaix *(–1) (reading from Ta)* — 94 trop l. *(+1) (reading from NTUa)* — 103 cil] sil — 105 *missing (reading from Ta)*.

TV: 2 sorpris *H* — 3 *missing KNP* — 4 *missing KNP*; Qui *HTUa* — 5 conforter *Ta*; ma dolor *HKNPTUa* — 6 eslagier *U* — 7 ala *T*; la flor *missing T* — 8 Dedenz *KNP* — 9 destroit *T* — 11 Desus *KNPTUa*; en une t. *U*; haure t. *H* — 12 Fu cele *U*; qui *HKNPTUa* — 14 Si *N*; chanta *KNP*; per grant dousor *missing U* — 15 Un *HKNTUa*; douls *missing U*; chant *HKNPTU,* tans *a*; pitous *missing H*; a plor *HTa* — 16 Et (E *H*) dist (disoit *U*) *HKNPTUa* — 17-18 *replaced in KNP by three-line refrain:* Li jalos m'a mise (mis *P*) en mue / Et perdue et retrouvee / Li jalos m'a enmuree — 19 oï *KNP* — 20 au v. *KPTUa*

— 21 pitié *KNP;* k'il ot *KNPU, missing H* — 23 Et *KNP,* Lors *Ta;* li dist *U;* d. a cuer
dolant *H* — 24 enserré *KN* — 25 biau cors g. *HTUa* — 26 Cui *HU;* tant doi *HTUa;*
tant ai amé *KNP* — 27 me c. *HKNP;* m'estovra *Ta,* me faites *U;* chierement *HUa,*
longement *T* — 28 dous] granz *HTUa;* bien *K,* maus *P;* endurer *a* — 31 *missing U;*
nous vet *KNP* — 32 *missing KNP;* Las ci a a. *U* — 33 Et *missing N;* S'ensi *H;* dire *Ta* —
34 Sire Deux *HKNPTUa* — 35 Ja (Je *HP*) ne puis je durer *HKNPU;* Coment durés
vous coment puis je durer sans vous *T* — 36 *missing H;* durer *P* — 37 belle] dame
HKNPTa; Boens] doz *HTa,* biax *KNP;* Biax a. ceu d. la dame *U* — 38 Amors (*repeated
U*) *HTUa;* Qu'amors *KNP;* sotient *HKNPTa* — 40 tel d. *U;* dolors *Ta;* meintient
HKNPTa — 41 moi] mois *T,* mors *a;* mes *missing U* — 43 Mes (Ne *HPTa*) je *HKNPTa;*
n'ai] ne *P;* Ja n'avrai *U;* joie] ne jeu *a* — 44 ne me *H* — 45-54 *missing H, with a blank
space large enough to accommodate the rest of the stanza* — 45 Mon c. ai si *KNPa,* Ens vos
ai mon penser m. *T* — 46 Que t. *N,* K'adés *U* — 47 li] mes *a* — 50 *missing KNPTU* —
51 Que sui et (*missing N*) serai toz dis *KNP,* Ke je serai a t. *T;* Or soiez loials amis *U* —
52 loiaus *a;* Je sui leals a. *U* — 53 ne *repeated N* — 54 oubli je *KNPTUa* — 55 je.l] je
HTU; sai b. (tot *Ha*) de voir *HKNPTa* — 56 Bien *HKNPa,* Si *T;* l'] j' *N* — 57 Que vos
(*missing HKNP*) ne poroiez *HKNPTUa* — 59 moult] si *Ta;* M. j'ai mult le cuer dolent
KNP — 60 je ai e. *Ha* — 61 Sires *HKNPTUa;* si] mon *T;* haut *KNP;* povoir *KNPU* — 62
ai] rai *KN,* est *U;* passé *HKNPTUa* — 63-64 *inverted with lines 65–66 in HKNPa* — 64
de] du *KNPTa;* toz *H;* t. en vilté *U* — 65 Ke *missing HKNPTUa;* peüsse *KNPTa;* je] Ja
H; p. je *H,* p. pas *U* — 66 plus grant *H* — 67-90 *missing H* — 67-68 *occur as lines 68-
69 in a, preceded by* De vous ne me kier mouvoir — 67 je sui em b. *T;* J'ai el (u *P*) cuer
un tel e. *KNP;* Car j'ai .i. si b. *a* — 68 bien] moult *U;* Qui bien (encore *a*) mi porra
(porroit *N*) v. *KNPTa* — 69 *missing KNPU* — 70 Si est (S'est *TUa*) droiz que g'en (je.l
U, jou *a*) d. *KNPTUa* — 71 Dex *NUa* — 73-90 *missing N* — 73-108 *missing KP* — 74 a]
au *T,* del *a* — 76 mil *a* — 77 K'il *Ta;* radotés *a* — 78 *T inverts lines 78 and 80* — 79 Lais
et m. *T,* Fel et m. *a* — 80 le t. *a* — 81 Males *Ta* — 83 la] sa *T;* Toutes ses meillours
bontés *a;* La greignor b. qu'il at *U* — 84 Est de *T,* Sont de *a* — 85 Diex fait il com sui
irés *T;* Et dist las tant mar fui nez *U* — 86 *missing TU* — 87 K'il en *T,* Quant a. en fait
U — 88 S'est d. ke m'en p. *T;* je *missing U;* Mes cuers a vous s'en claime *a* — 89 a tel
mari *Ta* — 90 Coment garira s'ele n'aime *Ta* — 91 Doz a. *HN;* Amis or *Ta;* alés *Ta* —
93 Des or mes *NU;* i] n'i *NTa,* ne ci *U;* porrés *Ta;* Plus demorer ne p. *H* — 94 Ne faire
s. *H* — 95-96 *inverted with lines 97-98 in U* — 95 Et le vostre me l. *U* — 96 Et n'aiez
paor *HNTa;* Je n'en ai pas paor *U* — 97 C' *missing U;* Qe (Car *a*) vos avez (aurez *N*) et
avroiz (avez *N*) *HNTa* — 98 loal *HNT;* Mon cuer et m'amor *U* — 99 Puis *N;* Se vos ne
m'en p. *H;* Et et se v. *a* — 100 c. haute t. *H;* De ceste tor geter *N* — 101 volentier le a
gardez *H;* la] le *Ta* — 102 De voz eiauz *HTa,* Por la moie amor *N,* Amis *U;* grant
missing Ta; por amor *H* — 103 Lors s'en (s'em *T*) part cil *HTa;* Et li chevalier fu i. *N* —
104 Et si s'en va corociez *N;* si mar *a* — 105 *missing U;* me c. *H;* ci *missing H* — 106-8
missing a — 105-6 *replaced in N with lines 107-8* — 107 je *missing N* — 108 Q'il les *H;*
me] mes *T* — 107-8 Et li vilains soit penduz / A une hart *N.*

DF: Lorraine, including *a* for countertonic *e,* as in *davant* (1); *ai* for *a,* as in *lai* (9),
Lais (31), *aipre* (32), *taiches* (81); *an* for *en,* as in *anemis* (41); *auls* for *aux,* as in *loiauls*
(16); *ei* for tonic *e,* as in *oblïeir* (5), *melleit* (15), *aveis* (17), *cleir* (20), *neis* (85); *en* for *an,*

as in *sens* (36); *ou, o* for *eu,* as in *pitous* (15), *plor* (15); loss of *l* before consonant, as in *a vis* (20), *a jalous* (74), *aitres* (87); *c* for *s* and *s* for *c,* as in RR (87, 103); *x* for *s,* as in *plux* (39), *maix* (67); preservation of final *t,* as in *fauceteit* (58), *oblïeit* (64); *amins* (17) for *amis; frexe* (13) for *fraische; Boens* (37) for *bons; gringnor* (66) for *graignor; coillir* (7) for *cueillir; vellier* (4) for *veillier; jeu* (67) for *je; lou* (1) for *le; ceu* (53) for *ce;* adverbial *se* (43) for *si;* conj. *Pués* (16) for *puis;* rel. *ke* (4) for nom. *ki;* 1st-pers. sing. pres. ind. *faic* (75) for *faz;* 3rd-pers. sing. pres. ind. *ait* (16) for *a, vait* (31) for *va;* 3rd-pers. sing. fut. in *-ait,* as in *morait* (71), *guerirait* (89). Picard fut. *devanrons* (24) for *devendrons.*

TN: For possible identifications of the Duchesse de Lorraine, see "Introduction to the Authors: What We Know, What We Can Surmise," in the introduction to this book. Jeanroy was extremely skeptical regarding the attribution in the Bern chansonnier. He also found this chanson "fort immodeste" (highly immodest) (Jeanroy 1889: 96). Tyssens (1992: 380) also discounts the manuscript evidence, owing to the presence of a male narrator; she clearly cannot conceive of a female trouvère who could compose in the male voice, even though male trouvères were known to compose in the female voice. Kooijman (1974: 80) does not question the attribution; on chronological grounds, he leans toward identifying the Duchesse as Marguerite de Champagne. — In our edition of this song, we have used a more interventionist approach than is our norm. Because our base manuscript does not contain music, we have adapted its text to the structure of the first stanza in manuscript *a* (our base for the music). In order to regularize the meter and the rhyme scheme, we drew on the variants of the seven other manuscripts, clothing the readings in Lorraine, the dominant dialect of our base text. It should be noted that Bartsch (1870 and 1920) was the first to adopt many of these readings, although he included others that we did not deem necessary. Moreover, our edited text differs from his in that he chose the Francien graphy of manuscript *N,* thus eliminating all traces of the Lorraine dialect. Our translation does not respect the alternation of tenses in parts of this song, such as stanza II. — 35-36 We have emended the text of the refrain both to adapt its meter to the music transmitted in *T* (see the MC section below) and to align the meter of the second verse of the refrain with that of the transitional line that precedes it, as is typical of a chanson avec des refrains. This refrain is reminiscent of the famous line in Marie de France's *Chievrefoil* (l. 78) where Tristan encapsulates the love he shares with Yseut: "Ne vus sanz mei, ne jeo sanz vus" (Rychner 1966: 153).

ME: 3/1-5/7 raised a step, after *TU* — 7/1-8/1 raised a step, after *TU.*

MC: The melody of *a* differs significantly from all other readings of this song, and we decided that listing all of the variants would be hopelessly complicated; the reader may consult Tischler 1997: no. 1137 for a synoptic transcription of all versions. The most striking difference is the pitch level, which generally is a fourth lower than that of *KNPT,* a fifth lower than in *U.* Even transposed to a common pitch level (as Tischler does in his edition), the reading in *a* often differs by one or more steps from at least one of the other versions. The version in *a* is more elaborate on the whole than the others, which tend to be syllabic in texture. The divergences in *a* become more numerous in verse 11, and they continue to increase from there to the end. —

13 *T* lacks music from here to the end. — 35-36 The refrain at the end of stanza II occurs as a divided refrain in the motetus (Mot 523) of a motet that survives in several manuscripts (a3 in *T* 182r, *Cl* 380r-v, and *Her* 1r-v, and a4 in *W2* 209v-211r and *Mo* 49v-52r) over the tenor "Justus germinabit" (M53). The version from *T* (fol. 182r) presented here is transposed a fifth lower than in the motet to place it in the same range as the chanson. — 53-54 There is no music extant for the refrains at the ends of stanzas III, IV, and V. — 107-8 The refrain at the end of stanza VI forms the last two lines of the motetus (Mot 673) of a two-voice motet in *T* (fol. 195r), "Quant de ma dame part / Eius" (tenor O16).

35
Chanson pieuse
Rotrouenge

The nonliturgical devotional songs of the trouvères are closely modeled on the secular repertoire, sharing its vocabulary, metaphors, and motifs, as well as its forms. It is possible to distinguish various types of religious verse. Those in the masculine voice are often Marian songs (chansons à la Vierge), combining praise, supplication, and offers to serve the Virgin. Pious transpositions of the courtly chanson d'amour assimilate the lady to the Virgin, thereby converting sexual desire into spiritual longing. Chansons pieuses in the feminine voice that substitute Christ for the lover are akin to the chanson d'ami, while complaints of the Virgin can be viewed as religious paraphrases of women's laments. Some chansons pieuses may be contrafacta of secular songs (Epstein 1997).

		Amis, amis,	*My love, my love,*
		Trop me laissie[z en] estrange païs.	*You leave me too long in an alien land.*

3   I   L'ame qui quiert Dieu de [veraie en]tente   The soul that seeks God with true intent
       Souvent se plaint [et] forment se demente   Often complains and bitterly laments,
       Et [s]on ami, cui venue est trop len[te],   And grieves that she does not appeal
       Va regretant que ne li atalente.   To her beloved, who is long in coming.
       Amis, amis,   *My love, my love,*
       [Trop me laissiez en estrange païs].   *You leave me too long in an alien land.*

9   II   [T]rop me laissiez [ci] vous longue[m]ent querre.   Too long you leave me here seeking you.

       En [ci]el regnés et en [m]er et en terre;   You reign in heaven and on land and sea;
       [E]nclose sui en cest cors qui me serre,   I am confined in this body that constrains me,

35. Amis, amis

i 264r-v

A - mis, a - mis,

Trop me lais - sie[z en] es - tran - ge pa - is.

L'a - me qui quiert Dieu de [ve - raie en -] ten - te

Sou - vent se plaint [et] for - ment se de - men - te

Et [s]on a - mi, cui ve - nue est trop len - [te],

Va re - gre - tant que ne li a - ta - len - te.

A - mis, a - mis,

Trop me lais - siez en es - tran - ge pa - is.

[D]e ceste char qui souvent me fait guerre. In this flesh that often wars with me.
[A]mis, amis, *My love, my love,*
[Trop me laissiez en estrange païs]. *You leave me too long in an alien land.*

15 III [D]ieus, donnez moy ce que mes cuers God, grant me what my heart desires,
     desirre,
   [P]our cui languis, pour cui sui a martire. What I yearn for, what martyrs me.
   [J]hesucrist est mes amis et mon sire, Jesus Christ is my beloved and my lord,
   [L]i biaus, li bons, plus que nul ne scet dire. More beautiful, more kind than anyone can say.
   [A]mis, amis, *My love, my love,*
   [Trop me laissiez en estrange païs]. *You leave me too long in an alien land.*

21 IV [M]on createur, quar je sui sa faiture, My creator—for I am His creature—,
   [Q]ui me nourrit et de tout me procure, Who nurtures me and tends to my every need,
   [M]es amis est, quar en moy mist tel cure Is my beloved, for He has shown me such care
   [Que] par amour se joint a ma nature. That through His love He is now part of my nature.
   [A]mis, amis, *My love, my love,*
   [Trop me laissiez en estrange païs]. *You leave me too long in an alien land.*

27 V [I]l m'apela ains que je l'apelasse, He called for me before I could call Him,
   [S]i me requist ainz qu'aprez lui alasse. And summoned me before I could go to Him.
   [O]r est bien drois qu'en lui querre me lasse Now it is right that I should toil to seek Him
   [S]i que cest mont pour lui trouver And leave this world in search of Him.
     trespasse.
   [A]mis, amis, *My love, my love,*
   [Trop me laissiez en estrange païs]. *You leave me too long in an alien land.*

33 VI [E]t quant j'avray passé ceste bruïne And once I have passed beyond this mist,
   [O]u li jour faut et le vespre decline, Where day fails and evening wanes,
   [Ci]lz qui les cuers alume et enlumine He who lights up and illuminates our hearts
   [Se] moustrera; lors avray joie fine. Will appear; then I will know true joy.
   [A]mis, amis, *My love, my love,*
   [Trop me laissiez en estrange païs]. *You leave me too long in an alien land.*

RS 747, L 265-978, MW 78, B 123

Manuscript: *i* 264r-v♪

Editions: Bartsch 1884: 582; Jeanroy 1889: 480; Schläger 1911: 371♪; Järnström and Långfors 1927: 195; Picot 1975, 1: 114 (French translation); Bec 1978: 66; Rosenberg and Tischler 1981: 9♪; Dufournet 1989: 68 (French translation); Rosenberg, Tischler, and Grossel 1995: 90♪ (French translation); Tischler 1997, 5: no. 438♪; Rosenberg, Switten, and Le Vot 1998: 182♪ (English translation)

Text: Rosenberg and Tischler 1981: 9

RR: With the exception of lines 8, 14, 20, 26, 32, and 38, square brackets indicate conjectures necessitated by mutilation of the manuscript.

TN: We gratefully acknowledge our debt to the translation in Rosenberg, Switten, and Le Vot 1998. — 3 The conjectured reading given here, as in Bartsch 1884 and Järnström and Långfors 1927, differs from that proposed in Jeanroy 1889: *de [toute s'en]tente.*

MC: The jagged marginal trimming of this manuscript resulted in the loss of some notes and the clefs from 3/6 through 6/11. Some pitches can be reconstructed by comparison with internally repeated phrases (3/7-3/8 = 4/7-4/8; 4/5 = 3/5). Most problematic is the section from 5/2 to 6/11, which is not repeated music. Our reconstruction—which differs from those in Rosenberg and Tischler 1981; Rosenberg, Tischler, and Grossel 1995; Tischler 1997; and Rosenberg, Switten, and Le Vot 1998— assumes that the clef placement on the two staves in question is the same as on all other staves (where it is on the second line from the top). We were also guided by faint flat signs between 5/4 and 5/5 and before 6/6 (not indicated in previous editions), which could only mean b♭ on 5/6 and 6/6 respectively.

36 *BLANCHE DE CASTILLE*
Chanson à la Vierge
Rotrouenge

I	Amours, u trop tart me sui pris,	Love, to which I have been drawn so late,	
	M'a par sa signourie apris,	Has instructed me by its nobility,	
	Douce dame de paradys,	Dear lady of paradise,	
	Ke de vous voeill un cant canter:	To wish to sing a song of you:	
	Pour la joie ki puet durer	*For everlasting joy*	
	Vous doit on servir et amer.	*It is you one should serve and love.*	
II	Et pour çou ke nus n'a mespris	For there is no one who has erred	7
	Tant vers vo fill n'en fais n'en dis,	Toward your son, however greatly, in word or deed—	
	S'il s'est en vo service mis,	Provided he has turned to serving you—	
	Ke vous ne.l faciés racorder:	Whom you would not reconcile with Him:	
	Pour la joie ki puet durer	*For everlasting joy*	
	Vous doit on servir et amer.	*It is you one should serve and love.*	
III	Virge roïne, flours de lis,	Virgin queen, lily flower,	13
	Com li hom a de ses delis	The great delight one feels	

Song no. 36, Paris, Bibliothèque Nationale de France, n. a. fr. 21677, fol. 2r, Li roine blanche. Cliché Bibliothèque nationale de France, Paris.

36. Amours, u trop tart me sui pris
j 2r

A - mours, u trop tart me sui pris,

M'a par sa si - gnou - rie a - pris;

Dou - ce da - me de pa - ra - dys,

Ke de vous voeill un cant can - ter:

Pour la joi - e ki puet du - rer

Vous doit on ser - vir et a - mer.

Ki de vous amer est espris,
Nus hom ne.l saroit reconter:
Pour le joie ki puet durer
[Vous doit on servir et amer].

When enflamed with love for you,
No one could recount:
For everlasting joy
It is you one should serve and love.

19 IV Mout fu li vaissiaus bien eslis,
Douce damë, u Sains Espris
Fu .ix. mois tous entiers nouris:
Ce fu vos cuers, dame sans per;
Pour la joie ki puet durer
Vous doit on servir et amer.

The vessel was indeed well chosen,
Dear lady, in which the Holy Spirit
Was nourished for nine full months:
It was your heart, peerless lady;
For everlasting joy
It is you one should serve and love.

RS 1604a, L 265-117, MW 371, B 1508
Manuscript: *j* 2r♪ (*Li roine blance*)
Editions: Bédier 1910: 912; Gennrich 1927: 125♪; Järnström and Långfors 1927: 56; Maillard 1967a: 63♪; Maillard 1967b: 67♪; Coldwell 1986: 53♪ (English translation); Tischler 1997, 10: no. 924♪
Text: Edited by WP
RR: 2 apres.
DF: Picard, including *c* for *ch*, as in *cant canter* (4); final *s* for *z*, as in *Sains* (20); *vaissiaus* (19) for *vaisseaus; signourie* (2) for *seigneurie;* article *le* (17) for *la; çou* (7) for *ce; vo* (8, 9) for *vostre;* conj. *u* (1, 20) for *ou;* 2nd-pers. pl. verbs in *-(i)és*, as in *faciés* (10); cond. *saroit* (16) for *savroit.*
TN: On Blanche de Castille's authorship of this song, see "Introduction to the Authors: What We Know, What We Can Surmise," in the introduction to this book. Coldwell (1986: 50 and 61) accepts the manuscript attribution, but she admits in a note that there is some doubt as to its validity and that some think the piece was written by the queen's admirer, Thibaut de Champagne; she cites Maillard's patronizing acceptance of the attribution to Blanche and lets the manuscript attribution to the queen stand. — 17 The noun *joie* could be either masculine or feminine in the thirteenth century; it was often masculine in northern and eastern dialects. Use of the article *le* for *la* could also be a dialectal trait. — 20 Instead of sounding the mute *e* in *dame*, Bédier (1910) and others emend *Espris* to *Esp[e]ris* (−1).

37

Chanson pieuse
Ballette or Rotrouenge

An paradis bel ami ai,
Tout deduisant en chanterai.

I have a handsome friend in heaven,
Merrily I will sing of Him.

I Et pour mes maus a oublïer
   N'ai autre raison de chanter
   Quant il en est sans moi aleir,
   Li biax, li dous qui m'amour at.
   An paradis bel ami ai,
   Tout deduisant en chanterai.

To forget my woes   3
Is my only reason for singing
Since He went off without me,
The handsome, sweet one who has my love.
I have a handsome friend in heaven,
Merrily I will sing of Him.

II An mon païs ai bel ami,
   Sage et cortois et bien apris:
   C'est li maistres d'amour sans fin.
   Sa tres grans biauteis sospris m'at.
   En paradis bel ami ai.
   E! tres dous Diex, quant vous verrai?

In my land I have a handsome friend,   9
Wise and noble and refined:
He is the master of eternal love.
I am smitten by His great beauty.
I have a handsome friend in heaven.
Oh! Dear sweet Lord, when will I see You?

III Diex! ou querrai .i. mesagier
    Preu et cortois, bien ensaingnié,
    C'a mon ami puisse envoier
    Que j'ains par amours de cuer vrai?
    En paradis bel ami ai.
    E! tres dous Diex, quant vous verrai?

God! Where will I find a messenger,   15
Worthy, noble, and well taught,
I could send to my beloved
Whom I love with all my heart?
I have a handsome friend in heaven.
Oh! Dear sweet Lord, when will I see You?

IV E! dous Diex, con j'ai bien choisit!
    Si haut m'at fine Amours assis:
    Ce est li rois de paradis
    Qui par amour languir me fait.
    En paradis bel ami ai.
    E! tres dous Diex, quant vous verrai?

Oh! Sweet Lord, what a good choice I made!   21
True Love has set me in such a high place:
It is the king of heaven
Who makes me languish lovingly.
I have a handsome friend in heaven.
Oh! Dear sweet Lord, when will I see You?

RS 47a, L 265-651, MW 362, B 679

Manuscript: Metz, Bibliothèque Municipale 535, fol. 166 (destroyed 1944)

Editions: Långfors 1932: 154; Picot 1975, 1: 116 (French translation); Bec 1978: 67

Text: Långfors 1932: 154

DF: Lorraine, including *an* (1, 9) for *en; ei* for tonic *e,* as in *aleir* (5), *biauteis* (12); preservation of final *t,* as in *choisit* (21); 3rd-pers. sing. pres. ind. *at* (6, 12, 22) for *a.* Picard, including *s* for *ss,* as in *mesagier* (15); final *s* for *z,* as in *grans* (12); *biax* (6) for *beaus.*

TN: We have modified Långfors' text as follows: we give *at* instead of *ast* in line 6 and *.i.* instead of *.j.* in line 15; we have altered the punctuation of lines 2 and 22.

38

Chanson pieuse
Rotrouenge

I   Je plains et plors come feme dolente,   I lament and weep like a sorrowful woman,

     Quar j'ay perdu ce que plus m'atalente;   For I have lost what I care for most;

     A grant tristour fuïe [est] ma jouvente.   In great sadness my youth has fled.

     Sans nul confort   *Devoid of all comfort*

     Triste sera ma vie jusque a la [mort].   *Sad will be my life till the day I die.*

6   II   Beau dous cher fis, simple vis, bele bouche,   Dear sweet beloved son, beautiful face, lovely mouth,

     La vostre mort, beau fis, au cuer me touche;   Your death, dear son, touches me deeply;

     Des ores mais vivray come une souche.   From this day forward, I shall live like a stump.

     Sans nul confort   *Devoid of all comfort*

     Triste sera ma vie jusque a la [mort].   *Sad will be my life till the day I die.*

11   III   Beau dous cher fis, vos deinaistes decendre   Dear sweet beloved son, You deigned to descend

     Dou ciel en moy et char umaine prendre;   From heaven into me and take on human flesh.

     Por vostre mort bien me doit li cuer fendre.   Your death was bound to break my heart.

     Sans nul confort   *Devoid of all comfort*

     Triste sera ma vie jusque a la [mort].   *Sad will be my life till the day I die.*

16   IV   Beau dous cher fis et beau sire et beau pere,   Dear sweet beloved son, dear lord and father,

     Quant vos de moi feïstes vostre mere,   Because You chose me for your mother,

     Por vostre mort doi ge avoir bouche amere.   Your death was bound to leave a bitter taste in my mouth.

     Sans nul confort   *Devoid of all comfort*

     Triste sera ma vie jusque a la [mort].   *Sad will be my life till the day I die.*

21   V   Beau dous cher fis, a la vostre naisance   Dear sweet beloved son, at Your birth

     Remés virge sans mal et sans grevance,   I remained a virgin without sin and without wrong,

     Que en pren trop nature sa vengance.   For which nature now amply takes its revenge.

     Sans nul confort   *Devoid of all comfort*

     Triste sera ma vie jusque a la [mort].   *Sad will be my life till the day I die.*

26   VI   Beaus dous cher fis, que grant joie j'avoie   Dear sweet beloved son, what great joy I felt

     . . . .

RS 746a, L 265-919, MW 304, B 1659

Manuscript: Florence, Biblioteca Medicea Laurenziana XVII, 16, fol. 1

Editions: Heyse 1856: 60; Meyer 1877: 374; Bartsch 1920: 106; Contini 1977: 230; Bec 1978: 65

Text: Edited by ED-Q

RR: 2 je ay *(+1)* — 3 *(–1) (em. Meyer)* — 5 cera; jusques; mort *missing (em. Meyer)* — 8 viveray *(+1)* — 10 cera; mort *missing* — 12 umain *(–1) (em. Meyer)* — 15 mort *missing* — 17 fistes *(–1) (em. Meyer)* — 18 a. la b. *(+1) (em. Meyer)* — 20 mort *missing* — 22 Be mest *(em. Heyse)* — 23 sans v. *(em. Bartsch)* — 25 jusques; mort *missing.*

DF: Lorraine, including *dou* (12) for *del; c* for *s,* as in RR (5, 10); pret. *deinaistes* (11) for *deignastes.* Picard *s* for *ss,* as in *naisance* (21).

TN: 3 Contini (1977) sees a faint interlinear abbreviation for *est.* — 5 Contini (1977) reads the second line of the refrain as a decasyllable, emending *jusques a* (RR 5, 25) and *jusque a* (10, 15, 20) to *jusqu'a.* — 23 Contini (1977) emends *Que* to *Or.* — 26 This line is followed by a blank space large enough to accommodate several more stanzas.

39

Chanson pieuse
Ballette

	Li debonnaires Dieus m'a mis en sa prison.	*The gracious Lord has put me in His prison.*

I | Vous ne savez que me fist | You do not know what Jesus Christ,   2
| Jhesucrist, li miens amis, | My beloved, did to me,
| Qu[ant] jacobine me fist | When He made me a Jacobin
| Par grant amours. | Through His great love.
| *Li debonnaires [Dieus m'a mis en sa prison].* | *The gracious Lord has put me in His prison.*

II | Il m'a si navré d'un dart, | He has struck me with His arrow,   7
| M[ais que] la plaie n'i pert. | Though the wound cannot be seen.
| Ja nul jour n'[en] guariré | I will never be cured
| Se par li non. | If not by Him.
| *Li debonn[aires Dieus m'a mis en sa prison].* | *The gracious Lord has put me in His prison.*

III | Dieus, son dart qui m'a navré, | God, the arrow that struck me,   12
| Comme il est dous et souefz! | How sweet and gentle it is!
| N[uit] et jour mi fait penser | Night and day it reminds me of
| Con Dieus [est] douz. | How sweet God is.
| *Li debonnaires [Dieus m'a mis en sa prison].* | *The gracious Lord has put me in His prison.*

39. *Li debonnaires Dieus m'a mis en sa prison*
i 253r

Li de - bon - nai - res Dieus m'a mis en sa pri - son.

Vous ne sa - vez que me fist

Jhe - su - crist, li miens a - mis,

Qu[ant] ja - co - bi - ne me fist

Par grant a - mours.

Li de - bon - nai - res Dieus m'a mis en sa pri - son.

IV	Quant regart par paradis,	When I look toward heaven,	17
	Dont [li] rois est mes amis,	Where my beloved is king,	
	De larmes [et] de soupirs	My whole heart melts	
	Mes cuers font to[us].	Into tears and sighs.	
	Li debonnaires [Dieus m'a mis en sa prison].	*The gracious Lord has put me in His prison.*	
V	Se je souvent plouroie	If I were to weep often	22
	Et tre[s] bien Dieu amoie,	And love God perfectly,	
	Il me donr[oit] sa joie,	He would give me His joy,	
	Autrement non.	Otherwise not.	
	Li debo[nnaires Dieus m'a mis en sa prison].	*The gracious Lord has put me in His prison.*	
VI	Quant je pense a Marie,	When I think of Mary,	27
	Qui fu [de] nete vie,	Who led a pure life,	
	J'ai une jalousie	I am jealous	
	Que [. . .] bon.	That [. . .] good.	
	Li debonn[aires Dieus m'a mis en sa prison].	*The gracious Lord has put me in His prison.*	
VII	Prions [a] la pucele,	Let us pray to the maiden,	32
	Qui fu saint[e et] honneste,	Who was holy and honorable,	
	Qu'en paradis nous [mete]:	To lead us to paradise:	
	C'est mout biau don.	It's a glorious gift.	
	Li debonn[aires Dieus m'a mis en sa prison].	*The gracious Lord has put me in His prison.*	

RS 1646, L 265-1746, MW 311, B 1223

Manuscript: *i* 253r♪

Editions: Bartsch 1884: 581; Jeanroy 1889: 483; Järnström and Långfors 1927: 189; Rosenberg and Tischler 1981: 7♪; Dufournet 1989: 64 (French translation); Rosenberg, Tischler, and Grossel 1995: 86♪ (French translation); Tischler 1997, 11: no. 949♪

Text: Rosenberg and Tischler 1981: 7

RR: With the exception of refrain lines and of line 32, square brackets indicate conjectures necessitated by mutilation of the manuscript. — 7 nauree *(+1)* — 32 P. la p. *(−1)*.

TN: 1 The refrain is probably inspired by a secular one, *"Sa bochete vermoillete / M'a mis an prixon"* (B 1641). — 4 A *jacobine* is a Dominican nun (from the location of the first Dominican convent on the Rue St.-Jacques in Paris). According to Järnström and Långfors (1927: 30-31), this song was composed for a sisterhood affiliated with the order of Saint Dominic, to which the compiler of manuscript *i* belonged. — 7 Descriptions of the onset of love in Old French literature drew on imagery found in the works of the Latin poet Ovid. The God of Love shoots an arrow into the heart of the hapless victim, who is then bound to obey Love's commands. This secular imagery was often adapted, as in this poem, to describe one's love for God. — 30 Bartsch 1884 gives *Que ne m'est bon.* Järnström and Långfors (1927) offer *Qu'art con charbon.* — 32 Bartsch 1884 gives *Prions donc la pucelle;* Jeanroy 1889 offers *[Or] prions la pucele.*

40
Chanson pieuse
Rotrouenge

Li solaus qui en moy luist est mes deduis,	*The sun that shines within me is my delight,*
Et Diex est mes conduis.	*And God is my guide.*

3 I Et que me deman[dez vous], amis mi[gnoz]? — What do You ask of me, gracious friend?

[Quar a vous] ai tout donné, et cuer et cors. — For I have given my all to You, both heart and body.

Et que voulez vous de moy? Voulez ma mort, — And what do You want from me? Is it my death,

Savoreus Jhesucrist? — Sweet Jesus Christ?

Li soulaus [qui en moy luist est mes deduis, — *The sun that shines within me is my delight,*
Et Diex est mes conduis]. — *And God is my guide.*

9 II Je li feray une tour a mon cuerçon, — I will build Him a tower in my little heart,

Ce sera ou plus biau lieu de ma maison; — It will be in the finest place in my house;

Il n'en istra ja nul jour, mon ami douz, — My sweet beloved will never leave it,

Ains sera en deduit. — Rather, He will live there in delight.

Li soulaus [qui en moy luist est mes deduis, — *The sun that shines within me is my delight,*
Et Diex est mes conduis]. — *And God is my guide.*

15 III Diex! or ardent cilz bisson par paradis; — God! How these bushes are burning in paradise;

Amours les font jubiler et tressaillir. — Love makes them exult and sparkle.

Fins amans ont tout le temps en Jhesucrist, — Their true love is ever Jesus Christ,

Quar c'est tout leur desir. — For He is all they long for.

Li solaus [qui en moy luist est mes deduis, — *The sun that shines within me is my delight,*
Et Diex est mes conduis]. — *And God is my guide.*

21 IV Hé mi, lasse! que feray? N'i puis aler. — Oh, wretched me! What will I do? I cannot get there.

40. *Li solaus qui en moy luist est mes deduis*
i 266v

Li so - laus qui en moy luist est mes de - duis,

Et Diex est mes con - duis.

Et que me de - man - [dez vous], a - mis mi - [gnoz]

[Quar a vous] ai tout don - né, et cuer et cors.

Et que vou - lez vous de moy? Vou - lez ma mort,

Sa - vo - reus Jhe - su - crist?

Li so - laus [qui en moy luist est mes de - duis,

Et Diex est mes con - duis].

Esperance et fine amour, quar m'i portez,   Hope and true love, please carry me there,
Qu'aprez ceste mortel vie i puisse aler: So that after this mortal life I may go there:
Ce sont tous mes deduis.   That is all my delight.
Li solaus [qui en moy luist est mes deduis,   *The sun that shines within me is my delight,*
Et Diex est mes conduis].   *And God is my guide.*

27   V   Dame Marie, priez a vostre fil   Lady Mary, entreat your Son
Qe tant com vivons en ce mortel essil,   That, as long as we live in this mortal exile,
Sa grace nouz doint, par quoy soion si fil,   He grant us His grace, by which we may be His children,

Et en son livre escrit.   And be written in His book.
Li solauz [qui en moy luist est mes deduis,   *The sun that shines within me is my delight,*
Et Diex est mes conduis].   *And God is my guide.*

RS 1936a=2076, L 265-691, MW 348, B 1238

Manuscript: *i* 266v♪

Editions: Bartsch 1884: 584; Jeanroy 1889: 485; Gennrich 1918: 41♪; Gennrich 1921: 259♪; Gennrich 1932: 76♪; Pauphilet 1952: 834; Woledge 1961: 142 (English translation); Bec 1978: 68; Tischler 1997, 12: no. 1103♪

Text: Edited by ED-Q

RR: 3-4 Square brackets indicate conjectures necessitated by mutilation of the manuscript. The conjectured readings are for the most part the same as those found in previous editions. — 5 V. vous *(+1)* — 12 *followed by supernumerary lines* cil doit bien estre esbaudis qui sert tousdis en fais en dis le roy de paradis — 21 Hé] Je *(em. Jeanroy)* — 28 com nouz v. *(+1)* — 29 Qe sa g. *(+1)*.

TN: 5 In Jeanroy 1889 emended to *Est-ce ma m.* — 7 *Li soulaus* added later. — 13 *Li soulaus* added later. The supernumerary lines (see RR 12) may constitute the beginning of another strophe, or the scribe may have intended to cite a different refrain (B 361) at the end of this stanza. — 31 *Li solauz* followed by *et cetera*.

ME: 4/1-4/5 The notes of line 4 are identical to those of line 3, but the notator distributed them among the syllables differently, so that the music of line 4 is hypometric: g-d-d-cd-e-d-c-de-fede-d. To make the two lines identical and to accommodate the conjectured text (see TN), we have split the two-note neume (cd) over *tout* into single notes. — 5/8 To accommodate the proposed reading of the text of line 5 (see RR), we have combined two single notes originally over the two syllables of *voulez* into a two-note neume over the syllable *vou-*.

MC: Marginal trimming caused the loss of a few pitches and clefs, all of which can be reconstructed by comparing repeated music.

A Circle of Voices

Rondeaux

The rondeau, also commonly designated *rondel* and *rondet a carole,* is a lyric form characterized by its density and circularity. Typically, it consists of a single eight-line stanza, which normally opens and closes with a two-line refrain that comprises two rhymes corresponding to two melodic phrases; in addition to framing the rondeau, the refrain is also partially interpolated within it and thus constitutes five of the song's eight lines. A rondeau's melody and rhyme scheme are those of its refrain; hence, the metric scheme of a rondeau can be represented by the formula *ABaAabAB,* its melody by *ABAAABAB.* This structure was not codified and did not stabilize until the end of the thirteenth century. In its earliest manifestations, the form often consists of only six lines (*aAabAB*), whereas multi-strophic and polyphonic rondeaux are typical of the fourteenth century.

The earliest Old French rondeaux are found among the lyric insertions in Jean Renart's *Roman de la rose ou de Guillaume de Dole,* which has been variously dated from ca. 1200 to ca. 1228. There is ample evidence of the collective and choreographic execution of rondeaux; they were meant to accompany the chain dance known as the *carole* and other forms of divertissement. Some indication can be found in romances staging the performance of rondeaux that singing might have alternated between a chorus and a soloist, the chorus voicing the refrain in response to the soloist, who interpreted the rondeau's three additional lines. This alternation underscored the dancers' movements and gestures (Doss-Quinby 1984: 62–70; Page 1989: 110–33).

Although the refrains of several of the rondeaux given here are cited elsewhere, notably as lyric insertions in narratives, we give the melody only if it is found in the same manuscript as the full rondeau text.

41
Rondeau

Ainssi doit on aler
A son ami.

So must one go
To one's beloved.

Bon fait deporter,	It is good to play,
—Ainssi [doit on aler].—	*—So must one go.—*
Baisier et acoler,	To kiss and embrace,
Pour voir le di.	Truly I say so.
Ainssi doit [on aler	*So must one go*
A son ami].	*To one's beloved.*

L 265-19, MW 266, G rond. 87, B rond. 168, B 65

Manuscript: *k* 77r

Editions: Raynaud 1883: 94; Gennrich 1921: 75♪; Boogaard 1969: 82

Text: Edited by ED-Q

TN: 3 (−1) Raynaud 1883 gives *Don fait [le] deporter;* in Gennrich 1921, emended to *Bon fait [a] deporter.*

MC: Gennrich (1921) reconstructs a melody for this rondeau by expanding the music of the two-verse refrain inserted after verse 349 in the *Court de Paradis* transmitted in Paris, Bibliothèque Nationale de France, fr. 25532, fol. 333v: *"Ensi doit on aler / A son ami."* These two verses with the same melody appear also as the second half of the motetus (Mot 435) of a two-voice motet over the tenor "HODIE" in manuscripts *M* (fol. 209v) and *T* (fol. 191v).

42

Rondeau

Amours sont perdues,	*Love is gone,*
Seulete demour.	*I remain all alone.*
Il n'en est mes nules,	There is no trace of it left,
—Amors [sont perdues].—	*—Love is gone.—*
Je.s ai maintenues	I sustained it
Jusqu'a icest jour.	Up to this day.
Amors sont perdues,	*Love is gone,*
[Seulete demour].	*I remain all alone.*

L 265-127, MW 281, G rond. 86, B rond. 167, B 179

Manuscript: *k* 77r

Editions: Raynaud 1883: 94; Gennrich 1921: 75; Boogaard 1969: 82

Text: Edited by ED-Q

43
Rondeau

E, mesdixans, Dieus vos puixe honir!	Ah, slanderers, may God curse you!
A tort m'aveis grevee.	Wrongly have you grieved me.
Tollut m'aveis la riens ke plus desir,	You have taken from me what I most desire,
—E, mesdixans, Dex vos puxe honir!—	—Ah, slanderers, may God curse you!—
Mais jai de lui je ne quier departir	I wish never to distance from him
Mon cuer ne ma pancee.	My heart or thought.
E, mesdixans, Dex vos puxe honir!	Ah, slanderers, may God curse you!
A tort m'aveis grevee.	Wrongly have you grieved me.

(line 5 marked at right)

L 265-766, MW 135, G rond. 93, B rond. 131, B 863

Manuscripts: *I* 248v (260v) (base), *k* 78r

Editions: Raynaud 1883: 29; Gennrich 1921: 78; Boogaard 1969: 71

Text: Edited by ED-Q

TV: 2 Car trop m'a. grevé — 3 rien — 4 Hé *(rest missing)* — 5 Ne ja de li ne q. mais d. — 7-8 Hé *(rest missing)*.

DF: Lorraine, including *ai* for *a*, as in *jai* (5); *an* for *en*, as in *pancee* (6); *ei* for tonic *e*, as in *aveis* (2, 3); *u* for *ui*, as in *puxe* (4, 7); *c* for *s*, as in *pancee* (6); *x* for *s(s)*, as in *mesdixans* (1, 4, 7), *puixe* (1), *puxe* (4, 7); preservation of final *t*, as in *Tollut* (3).

44
Rondeau

Hé, Diex! quant vandra	Oh, God! When will he come,
Mes tres douz amis?	My dear sweet friend?
Ne le vi pieça.	I have not seen him for a while.
Hé, Diex! quant ven[dra]?	Oh, God! When will he come?
Oublïee m'a,	He has forgotten me,
Si m'en esbaïs.	So I am distraught.
Hé, Diex! quant [vandra	Oh, God! When will he come,
Mes tres douz amis]?	My dear sweet friend?

(line 5 marked at right)

L 265-758, MW 276, G rond. 105, B rond. 184, B 822

Manuscript: *k* 80r

Editions: Raynaud 1883: 102; Gennrich 1921: 83; Toja 1966: 158; Boogaard 1969: 87

Text: Edited by ED-Q

45

Rondeau

Hé! que me demande li miens amis?
Velt il guerroier a moi?
Il a bien .vij. anz que je ne le vi.
Hé! que me demande [li miens amis]?
S'il a fait amie, je ferai ami
Qui guerroiera por moi.
Hé! que me demande li miens [amis?
Velt il guerroier a moi]?

Oh! What does my lover want from me?
Does he want to battle with me?
It has been seven years since last I saw him.
Oh! What does my lover want from me?
If he has found another lover, I will too,
One who will battle for me.
Oh! What does my lover want from me?
Does he want to battle with me?

L 265-768, MW 134, G rond. 113, B rond. 191, B 868
Manuscript: *k* 82r
Editions: Raynaud 1883: 106; Gennrich 1921: 87; Boogaard 1969: 90
Text: Edited by ED-Q
RR: 3 le] la *(em. Raynaud).*

46

Rondeau

J'ai ameit et amerai
Trestout les jours de ma vie
Et plus jolive an serai.
J'ai bel amin, cointe et gai,
—J'ai ameit et amerai.—
Il m'ainme, de fi lou sai;
Il ait droit, je suis s'amie,
Et loialtei li ferai.
J'ai ameit et amerai
Trestout les jors de ma vie
Et plus jolive en serai.

I have loved and will love
All the days of my life,
And I will be merrier for it.
I have a handsome lover, charming and lively,
—I have loved and will love.—
He loves me, I know this well;
He has the right, I am his love,
And I will be faithful to him.
I have loved and will love
All the days of my life,
And I will be merrier for it.

L 265-796, MW 115, G rond. 141, B rond. 143, B 905
Manuscript: *I* 249v (261v)
Editions: Raynaud 1883: 34; Gennrich 1921: 98; Boogaard 1969: 75; Rosenberg and Tischler 1981: 150; Rosenberg, Tischler, and Grossel 1995: 322
Text: Edited by ED-Q
DF: Lorraine, including *an* (3) for *en; ei* for tonic *e,* as in *loialtei* (8); preservation of final *t,* as in *ameit* (1); *amin* (4) for *ami; lou* (6) for *le;* 3rd-pers. sing. pres. ind. *ait* (7) for *a.*

47
Rondeau

Jai ne lairai por mon mari ne die
Li miens amins jeut aneut aveucke moi.
Je li dis bien ainz qu'il m'eüt plevie:
—Jai ne lairai por mon marit ne die—
S'il me batoit ne faixoit vilonie,
Il seroit cous, et si lou comparroit.
Jai ne lairai por mon mari ne die
Li miens amins jeut aneut avecque moi.

Never on account of my husband will I stop saying
That my lover lay with me last night.
I said it clearly before he was betrothed to me:
—Never on account of my husband will I stop saying—
If he beat me and treated me badly,
He would be a cuckold and thus would pay.
Never on account of my husband will I stop saying
That my lover lay with me last night.

L 265-826, MW 132, G rond. 147, B rond. 149, B 1004
Manuscript: *I* 250r (262r)
Editions: Bartsch 1870: 21; Raynaud 1883: 37; Aubry 1909: 224♪; Gennrich 1921: 100♪; Boogaard 1969: 77; Lea 1982: 68 (German translation); Tischler 1997, 14: no. R22♪
Text: Edited by ED-Q
RR: 5 S'il] C'il.
DF: Lorraine, including *ai* for *a,* as in *Jai* (1); preservation of final *t,* as in *marit* (4); *amins* (2) for *amis; c* for *s,* as in RR; *x* for *s,* as in *faixoit* (5); *aneut* (2) for *anuit; lou* (6) for *le.*
TN: 2 Aubry 1909 and Gennrich 1921 emend *aveucke* to *aveuc,* whereas Tischler 1997 gives *avoec.* — 8 Aubry 1909 emends *avecque* to *aveuc,* whereas Gennrich 1921 and Tischler 1997 give *avec.*
MC: Aubry (1909), Gennrich (1921), and Tischler (1997) reconstruct melodies for this rondeau using music of the refrain inserted after verse 6941 of *Renart le nouvel.* Three distinct melodies for the refrain are preserved in three manuscripts: Paris, Bibliothèque Nationale de France, fr. 372 (fol. 52r), fr. 1593 (fol. 50v), and fr. 25566 (fol. 167r).

48
Rondeau

Je ne [li] deffendrai mie
Qu'il ne m'aint,
Et si ne l'amerai mie.
Tiex dist: "[Je] vos aing, [a]mie,"
Qui se faint.
Je ne li deffendrai [mie
Qu'il ne m'aint].
Mainte dame est engignie

I will not forbid him
To love me,
But I will not love him.
Some who say: "I love you, dear,"
Are lying.
I will not forbid him
To love me.
Many a woman is deceived

Par tel plaint;	By such a plea;
10 Cele est fole qui s'i fie.	She is crazy to put faith in it.
[Je ne li deffendrai mie	*I will not forbid him*
Qu'il ne m'aint,	*To love me,*
Et si ne l'amerai mie].	*But I will not love him.*

L 265-905, MW 720, G rond. 85, B rond. 166, B 1081
Manuscript: *k* 77r
Editions: Raynaud 1883: 94; Gennrich 1921: 75; Boogaard 1969: 82
Text: Edited by ED-Q
RR: 1 *(–1) (em. Raynaud)* — 4 *(–2) (em. Raynaud)* — 10 est] en *(em. Raynaud).*
DF: Picard *ie* for *iee,* as in *engignie* (8).

49

Rondeau

Or n'i serai plus amiete	*Now I will no longer be Robin's friend,*
Robin, trop ai demoré;	*I have lingered too long;*
Ainz irai ou bois violete cuillir.	Instead I will go pick violets in the woods.
Or n'i serai [plus amiete].	*Now I will no longer be his friend.*
5 S'il a fet amie, je ferai	If he has found a friend, I shall
Autresi ma volanté.	Likewise do my will.
Or n'i serai [plus amiete	*Now I will no longer be Robin's friend,*
Robin, trop ai demoré].	*I have lingered too long.*

L 265-1283, MW 169, G rond. 88, B rond. 169, B 1454
Manuscript: *k* 77v
Editions: Raynaud 1883: 95; Gennrich 1921: 76; Boogaard 1969: 83
Text: Edited by ED-Q
TN: 2 Boogaard (1969) suggests the possibility of emending *ai* to *a* or *ait,* following the text of the refrain as it appears in Mot 1129. — 3 In Raynaud 1883, emended to *Ains prendrai ou b. v.;* in Gennrich 1921, emended to *Ains cueudrai ou b. v.* — 5 In Raynaud 1883, emended to *Je ferai si amie a fete;* in Gennrich 1921, emended to *Je ferai s'il amie a fete.*

50

Rondeau

Soufrés, maris, et si ne vous anuit,	*Be patient, husband, and may it not irk you,*
Demain m'arés et mes amis anuit.	*Tomorrow you will have me and my lover will tonight.*

50. *Soufrés, maris, et si ne vous anuit*
a 108v

Sou - frés, ma - ris, et si ne vous a - nuit,

De - main m'a - rés et mes a - mis a - nuit.

Je vous def - fenc k'un seul mot n'en par - lés.

–Sou - frés, ma - ris, et si ne vous mou - vés.–

La nuis est cour - te, a - par - mains me ra - rés,

Quant mes a - mis a - ra fait sen de - duit.

Sou - frés, ma - ris, et si ne vous a -. nuit,

De - main m'a - rés et mes a - mis a - nuit.

Je vous deffenc k'un seul mot n'en parlés.
— Soufrés, maris, et si ne vous mouvés.—
La nuis est courte, aparmains me rarés,
Quant mes amis ara fait sen deduit.
Soufrés, maris, et si ne vous anuit,
Demain m'arés et mes amis anuit.

I forbid you to speak one word of it.
—Be patient, husband, and do not move.—
The night is short, soon you will have me again,
When my lover has had his pleasure.
Be patient, husband, and may it not irk you,
Tomorrow you will have me and my lover will tonight.

L 265-1636, MW 352, G rond. 52, B rond. 193, B 1749
Manuscript: *a* 108v♪
Editions: Laborde 1780, 2: 362 (French translation); Bartsch 1870: 20; Raynaud 1883: 129; Gennrich 1921: 40♪; Toja 1966: 156; Boogaard 1969: 90; Lea 1982: 68 (German translation); Tischler 1997, 14: no. R38♪
Text: Edited by ED-Q
DF: Picard, including *sen* (6) for *son;* 1st-pers. sing. pres. ind. in *-c,* as in *deffenc* (3); 2nd-pers. pl. verbs in *-(i)és,* as in *Soufrés* (1), *parlés* (3), *mouvés* (4); fut. *arés* (2) for *avrez, ara* (6) for *avra.*
TN: 1 and 7 Gennrich (1921), followed by Tischler (1997), emends *anuit* to *mouvés.* — 4 Raynaud (1883) emends *mouvés* to *anuit.*

51

Rondeau

Toute seule passerai le vert boscage,
Puisque compaignie n'ai.
Se j'ai perdu mon ami par mon outrage,
— Toute seule [passerai le vert boscage].—
Je li ferai a savoir par .i. mesage
Que je li amenderai.
[Toute seule passerai le vert boscage,
Puisque compaignie n'ai].

All alone I will walk through the green woods,
Since I have no companion.
If I have lost my love by my fault,
—All alone I will walk through the green woods.—
I will send a message to let him know
I will make amends to him.
All alone I will walk through the green woods,
Since I have no companion.

L 265-1673, MW 124, G rond. 95, B rond. 175, B 1789
Manuscripts: *k* 78v (base); Rome, Biblioteca Apostolica Vaticana, Regina 1543, no. 3, fol. I^{a}v♪ (incipit only)
Editions: Raynaud 1883: 98; Gennrich 1921: 79♪; Woledge 1961: 209 (English translation); Toja 1966: 157; Boogaard 1969: 85; Tischler 1997, 14: no. R39♪
Text: Edited by ED-Q
DF: Picard, including *c* for *ch,* as in *boscage* (1); *s* for *ss,* as in *mesage* (5).
TN: Cited in Johannes de Grocheio's *De musica* as an example of the rondeau: "There are indeed many who call any *cantilena* a 'rotunda' or 'rotundellus' because it turns back on itself in the manner of a circle, beginning and ending in the same way [that

is, with a refrain]. However, I only call the kind of song a 'rotunda' or 'rotundellus' whose parts have the same music as the music of the response or refrain. When it is sung it is drawn out in an expansive way like the *cantus coronatus*. The French song *Toute sole passerai le vert boscage* is of this kind. This kind of song is customarily sung toward the West—in Normandy, for example—by girls and by young men as an adornment to holiday celebrations and to great banquets" (Page 1993b: 26).

MC: Gennrich (1921) and Tischler (1997) reconstruct a melody for this rondeau using the first and last verses of the motetus (Mot 846) of our motet no. 68, "*Toute soule passerai li bois ramé . . . Puis que compaingnie n'ai, ai*," found in manuscript *Ba* (fol. 58r-v).

52
Rondeau

Vous arez la druerie,	*You will have your pleasure,*
Amis, de moi,	*My love, with me,*
Ce que mes mariz n'a mie.	*As my husband never has.*
Vos l'avez bien deservie	You have well deserved it,
En bone foi.	In good faith.
Vos [arez la druerie,	*You will have your pleasure,*
Amis, de moi].	*My love, with me.*
Mesdissant sont en agait	Slanderers are waiting in ambush
Et main et soir	Both morning and night
Por nos faire vilonie.	To do us harm.
Vous [arez la druerie,	*You will have your pleasure,*
Amis, de moi,	*My love, with me,*
Ce que mes mariz n'a mie].	*As my husband never has.*

L 265-1742, MW 719, G rond. 90, B rond. 171, B 1853

Manuscript: *k* 77v-78r

Editions: Raynaud 1883: 96; Aubry 1909: 223♪; Gennrich 1921: 77♪; Boogaard 1969: 83; Tischler 1997, 14: no. R43♪

Text: Edited by ED-Q

DF: Picard, including *s* for *ss*, as in *deservie* (4); *ss* for *s*, as in *Mesdissant* (8); fut. *arez* (1) for *avrez*.

TN: 8 Raynaud (1883), Aubry (1909), Gennrich (1921), and Tischler (1997) emend *agait* to *envie*.

MC: Aubry (1909), Gennrich (1921), and Tischler (1997) reconstruct a melody for this rondeau by expanding a refrain inserted after verse 6828 in *Renart le nouvel* in Paris, Bibliothèque Nationale de France, fr. 25566, fol. 168v: "*Vous arés la singnourie, / Amis, de moi, / Che que mes maris n'a mie.*"

Voices in Polyphony

Motets

The Old French polyphonic motet is a complex genre whose individual parts, both text and music, maintain a certain amount of independence, even while they are woven together by counterpoint and an overall triple meter. This metrical regularity is based on the rhythmic "modes" described by thirteenth-century music theorists. These regular patterns of long and short notes prevail throughout a piece and help give it its structure, and the tenors adhere to them more strictly than the upper voices. Mode 1 (as in the tenors of motet nos. 55, 56, 59, and 68) consists of a simple alternation of quarter notes and eighth notes (the modern equivalent of longae and breves; a rest could substitute for a note of the same duration): ♩♪♩♪. Mode 2 (as in the tenors of motet nos. 53, 57, 61, and 64) reverses the order: ♪♩♪♪. Mode 3 (as in the motetus of motet no. 67 and the quadruplum of motet no. 71) is slightly more complex, with three different note values, a dotted quarter note followed by an eighth note and a quarter note: ♩.♪♩♩.♪♩♩. Mode 4 is the same as mode 3 without the initial dotted quarter note. Mode 5 (as in the tenors of motet nos. 58, 62, and 65), which consists of a series of dotted quarter notes—♩. ♩. ♩.—and mode 6 (as in the triplum and motetus of motet no. 61), a series of eighth notes—♪♪♪♪♪♪— have a different feel from the other modes, in that each consists of a single rhythmic value and thus is not "patterned" by the alternation of values.

Sometimes a tenor will combine two different short modal patterns to create a new one, as in motet nos. 54, 60, and 66 (which blend modes 1 and 5), motet no. 69 (which combines modes 1, 5, and 6), and motet nos. 67 and 71 (which shift between modes 3 and 5). The regularity of these modes was increasingly obscured as shorter rhythms were combined into longer ones (when, for instance, a quarter note and an eighth note were melded into a dotted quarter note) or, more strikingly, long notes were split into several short ones (for example, when a dotted quarter note was divided into three eighth notes). The tenors of motet nos. 69 and 70 seem almost free of modal structure because of this.

The upper voices also follow a mode, although not necessarily the same one as the tenor, but the modes were even more loosely applied in these parts than in the tenor, in order to accommodate the text. While for the tenor the pitches (usually taken directly from a pre-existing melody, either from plainchant or from a secular song) and the rhythmic mode provide a framework, in the upper voices the controlling element is the text. Although intricately constructed, most of these texts are heterometric, that is, they are not strophic, nor do they follow set versification patterns (lines vary in length and number, and rhymes repeat unpredictably). As the poems of the upper voices increased in length, the notes became more numerous and hence of shorter duration. Motet no. 53, for example, seems to begin in mode 2, but the many extra eighth notes and even sixteenth notes cause the melody to lose any feeling of rhythmic regularity; in motet no. 69, the mode of the upper voices is nearly impossible to discern. Sometimes the tenor was repeated, especially if the upper voices were particularly long: see motet nos. 53, 55, 59, 60, 63, 65, 67, 68, and 71.

As so many of the elements of a motet are reworkings of borrowed materials, the upper voices often incorporate texts or music (or both) that are also found in other contexts, such as verses from monophonic chansons (as in song no. 16 = Mot 820), and especially refrains that are found independently in other sources, such as the refrain of a rondeau (motet nos. 60, 63 [motetus], 68 [motetus], 69 [triplum and motetus], 70, and 75), the refrain of another type of song with a fixed or variable refrain (motet nos. 54, 58, 59, 60, 63 [motetus], 68 [triplum], 71 [quadruplum, triplum, and motetus], and 73), a lyric insertion in a narrative, didactic, or other nonlyric work (motet nos. 58, 59, 60, 63 [motetus], 69, 71 [triplum and motetus], and 73), or even elements from other motets (motet nos. 58, 59, 60, 63 [triplum], 68 [motetus], and 69 [triplum and motetus]; see Doss-Quinby 1984: 117-33). In some motets the two lines of a refrain are separated and placed at the beginning and end of the part, respectively (motet no. 68); the term *motet enté* has been applied to such pieces, although in the Middle Ages the few contexts in which this expression occurs do not correspond to the phenomenon of a "divided refrain," which is probably best viewed as a compositional technique rather than as a subgenre of the motet (see Everist 1994: 75-89, 162). Gennrich and Boogaard identified many "refrains" in the motet repertoire (on the basis of content, semantic elements, location in the poem, or other criteria—although not, significantly, musical criteria, as there appears to be nothing distinct about the musical features of these "refrains"), which are not extant in any independent source (see Everist 1994: 54-71). The search for possible concordances continues, and whereas in this book we have not italicized postulated but as yet unattested refrains in the texts, we do provide Boogaard's index number for them.

Each upper part of a motet was sung by a soloist, and the overall tempo of the piece depended on the contrapuntal and textual interplay among these parts. Scholars disagree as to whether the singer or singers of a tenor part sang the liturgical text (which seems unlikely because this text is often extracted from the middle of a plainchant text and has no semantic value by itself) or simply intoned the notes on a neutral sound, or whether the lowest part was played on an instrument; the sources give no performance instructions to clarify the issue. French tenors, like those in motet nos. 70 and 71, might well have been sung with the text of the complete poem, although as with Latin tenors only an incipit is given in the manuscripts, and the singer would have had to supply the words either from memory or from another source, as we have done in this book.

MOTETS FOR TWO VOICES

53
Motet

Mot	Cil bruns ne me meine mie	This dark-haired man is not leading me off
	Por rendre en .i. abaïe,	To enter a convent,
	Mes pour mener bone vie,	But to lead the good life,
	Que que l'en die.	Whatever people may say.
5	Pour folie	In their madness
	En ont envie	Slanderers
	Mesdisant;	Are spreading rumors;
	Que qu'il en voisent disant,	Whatever they are saying about it,
	Bien voi	I see clearly
10	Et bien aperçoi	And fully realize
	Qu'il ne m'a mie	That he has not
	Ravie	Ravished me
	Por fere nounain de moi.	To make me a nun.

T   IN SECULUM

Mot 156; L 265-373; MW 67,1; B 357
M13
Manuscripts: *Mo* 268r-268v♪ (base), *W2* 224v-225r♪
Editions: Jacobsthal 1880: 286; Raynaud 1881: 206; Rokseth 1935-39, 3: 74♪; Tischler 1982: no. 165♪; Tischler 1985: no. 249♪ (English translation)
Text: Edited by JTG
RR: Mot 13 de moi *missing (reading from W2).*

53. Cil bruns ne me meine mie/IN SECULUM
Mo 268r-v

Motetus

Cil bruns ne me mei - ne mi - e Por

Tenor

IN SECULUM

rendre en *une* a - ba - i - e, Mes pour me - ner bo-ne vi - e,

Que que l'en di - e. Pour fo - li - e En ont en - vi - e Mes-di - sant;

Que qu'il en voi - sent di - sant, Bien voi Et bien a - per - çoi

Qu'il ne m'a mi - e Ra - vi - e Por fe - re nou nain de moi.

TV: Mot 1 Cist brunez — 4 Q. qu'on en — 8 voisant — 10 aperçoit.

ME: Mot 1/8 L emended to B after Rokseth 1935-39 — 3/8 L emended to B after Rokseth 1935-39 — 6/4-6/5 2li-B-R=fe-d-R emended without R from *W2* — 7/3 d emended to c from *W2* — T 4-5 B-R-B=d-R-c emended to 3li=dec from *W2* — 14 L emended to B after Rokseth 1935-39 — 18 L emended to B after Rokseth 1935-39 — 20 L emended to B after Rokseth 1935-39 — 34 L emended to B after Rokseth 1935-39 — 44 L emended to B after Rokseth 1935-39.

MV: Mot 1/7 3li=ede — 6/4-6/5 3li=fed — 7/3 c — 8/3 e^p — 9/1 e — 10/1 e^p — 10/3 e^p — 13/3 N=e — 13/6 3li=gfe — T 13-14 N-2li=a-ac — 43-46 2li-2li=cg-gf.

54

Motet

Mot	*A tort sui d'amours blasmee:*	Wrongly am I blamed for loving:
	Hé, Diex! si n'ai point d'ami.	Oh, God! I have no lover!
	Pour ce me sui ge a celle donee	So I have given myself
	Qui mere est celui	To the mother of Him
5	Qui por noz en la crois mort souffri:	Who for us suffered death on the Cross;
	De touz doit estre henouree.	She should be honored above all others.
	Si li cri	So I cry out to her
	Merci	For mercy
	A jointes mains, et pri	With hands joined, and pray
10	Qu'el ne me mete en oubli,	That she not forget me,
	Si qu'a s'amour n'aie failli.	For I have not failed in my love for her.

T	LATUS

Mot 241; L 265-146; MW 934,1; B 189

M14

Manuscript: *Mo* 232v–233r♪

Editions: Jacobsthal 1880: 63; Raynaud 1881: 162; Rokseth 1935-39, 3: 4♪; Tischler 1985: no. 180♪ (English translation)

Text: Edited by ED-Q

TN: Mot Tischler 1985 designates only the first line as a refrain.

ME: Mot 3/5-3/6 The notator gave a single ligature of two notes over the words *ge a,* evidently assuming an elision. We have split the ligature into two separate notes for the two words.

54. *A tort sui d'amours blasmee*/Latus
Mo 232v-233r

Motetus

A tort sui d'a-mours blas-me - e: Hé Diex! si n'ai point d'a-

Tenor

Latus

mi. Pour ce me sui ge a cel-le do-ne - e Qui mere est ce-lui

Qui por noz en la crois mort souf-fri: De touz doit estre he-nou-re-e.

Si li cri Mer-ci A join-tes mains, et pri Qu'el ne me mete en ou-

bli, Si qu'a s'a-mour n'ai-e fail-li.

55

Motet

Mot	Je les ai tant quises	I have so desired
	Les loiaus amours,	True love,
	Et tant ai aprises	And known
	Joies et dolours,	Its joys and sorrows,
5	Ke d'amours sui senee;	That I am wise in the ways of love;
	Et si sui, Dieu merchi, bien amee.	And so I am, thank God, well loved.
	Des or ai jus mises	Henceforth I have chased away
	Toutes mes pauours,	All my fears,
	Car se j'ai desiree	For if ever I wished
10	Amour a maintenir a tous jors,	To sustain love forever,
	Or i sui assenee.	Now I am ready for love.

T   VITAM

Mot 426; L 265-879; MW 1151,1

M32

Manuscripts: *T* 195v-196r♪ (base), *StV* 291v♪ (music and text incipit only)

Editions: Raynaud 1883: 88; Tischler 1982: no. 326♪

Text: Edited by ED-Q

RR: Mot 8 The scribe wrote *dolours* for *pauours,* then skipped back to the end of line 5 and wrote *Sui senee, / Et si sui, Dieu merchi, bien amee. / Des or ai jus mises / Toutes mes* again, concluding correctly with *pauours.* The music of the repeated *dolours* is the same as for the later *pauours,* while the music of the repeated text is identical to the music of the same text earlier. The unacceptable dissonances between motetus and tenor confirm that this repetition is an error. We have emended following Tischler 1982.

DF: Picard *ch* for *c,* as in *merchi* (Mot 6). Lorraine *our* for *eur,* as in *dolours* (Mot 4), *pauours* (Mot 8).

TN: Mot Tischler (1982) designates lines 1-2 and 11 as a refrain. This postulated refrain is not listed in Boogaard 1969.

ME: Mot 5/4 b emended to a from *StV* — T 21 The tenor in *T* is written out only once and must be repeated from this point. — 6-8 2li-4li=gb-afga emended to 3li-2li=gba-ga from *StV* — 9-10 3li=afg emended to fde from *StV* — 39-41 final ligature (3li) lengthened to end with the motetus, following *StV* in which the middle note of the final ligature is elongated.

MC: The reading in *StV* is an untexted clausula with the incipit "Je les ai tant quises" in the margin. *StV* gives b♭ at the beginning of several staves.

55. Je les ai tant quises/VITAM
T 195v-196r

Motetus

Je les ai tant qui - ses Les loi - aus a - mours, Et tant ai a -

Tenor

VITAM

pri - ses Joi - es et do - lours, Ke d'a - mours sui se - ne - e;

Et si sui, Dieu mer - chi, bien a - me - e. Des or ai jus

mi - ses Tou - tes mes pau - ours, Car se j'ai de - si - re - e

A - mour a main - te - nir a tous jors, Or i sui as - se - ne - e.

56
Motet

Mot	J'ai fait ami a mon chois,	I have found a sweetheart to my liking,
	Preu et sage et cortois;	Worthy and wise and refined.
	Si me tieg por amie,	He considers me his sweetheart,
	S'alongera ma vie.	So my life will be prolonged.

T   GAUDETE

Mot 436; L 265-808; MW 381,8; B 933
M34
Manuscripts: *M* 210r♪ (base), *T* 191v–192r♪
Editions: Raynaud 1883: 61; Tischler 1982: no. 314♪
Text: Edited by ED-Q
MV: Mot 3/3 L=c.

57
Motet

Mot	A vos vieg, chevalier sire,	I come to you, sir knight,
	Del pié me traiez l'espine;	Remove the thorn from my foot.
	El sentier d'amors l'ai prise:	I was pricked by it in the path of love;
	S'en sui malade.	I am ailing from it.
5	S'on ne la me trait, ja morrai, lasse.	If someone does not remove it, I will soon die, alas.

T   ET FLOREBIT

Mot 528; L 265-202; MW 192,21
M53
Manuscripts: *M* 209v–210r♪ (base), *T* 191v♪
Editions: Raynaud 1883: 60; Tischler 1982: no. 312♪
Text: Edited by JTG
TV: Mot 1 vieng chevalliers — 3 d'amour — 5 S'on le me t. je.
TN: Mot 2 This image may well have reminded listeners of the fable of the Lion and the Shepherd. In this fable, retold many times in the Middle Ages, a lion steps on a thorn, a shepherd removes the thorn from his paw, and the two part; when they meet again, the lion remembers the earlier good deed by the shepherd and spares his life. The morals attached to the fable all speak of the importance of remembering good deeds; however, the moral of the version found in Brussels, Bibliothèque Royale, lat. 536, reads: "Bonum est benefacere et beneficii meminisse quia mutuis

56. J'ai fait ami a mon chois/GAUDETE
M 210r

Motetus

J'ai fait a - mi a mon chois, Preu et sage et cor-

Tenor

GAUDETE

tois; Si me tieg por a - mi - e, S'a - lon - ge - ra ma vi - e.

57. A vos vieg, chevalier sire/Et FLOREBIT
M 209v-210r

Motetus: A vos vieg, che - va - lier si - re, Del pié me trai - ez l'es - pi - ne;

Tenor: Et FLOREBIT

El sen - tier d'a - mors l'ai pri - se: S'en sui ma - la - de. S'on ne la me

trait, ja mor - rai, las - se.

beneficiis amicicia fovetur et mutuis maliciis crescit discordia" ("It is good to do favors and to recall favors, because friendship is nurtured by mutual favors and strife grows from mutual acts of malice"; Romuli Anglici Cunctis, *Exortæ fabulæ,* Hervieux 1893–99, 2: 583). This moral applies particularly well to this motetus because of its reference to fostering friendship. In Middle French, the expression "tirer l'espine du pied" was a commonplace (Di Stefano 1991, s.v. "epine"). — 5 Tischler (1982) designates this line as a refrain. This postulated refrain is not listed in Boogaard 1969.
ME: T 5 c-c-b missing, supplied from *T* — 14 rest missing, supplied from *T.*
MV: Mot 1/4-1/6 2li-N-2li=ba-g-af — 2/4-2/6 2li-N-2li=ba-g-af.

58
Motet

Mot	Biaus douz amis, or ne vouz anuit mie	Dear sweet friend, do not be distressed	
	Se d'estre ensamble fesons tel demouree,	If we delay so long being together,	
	Car on dit: *"Qui bien aime a tart oublie."*	For it is said: *"He who loves well does not soon forget."*	
	Pour ce n'iert ja nostre amor desevree,	So never will our love be severed,	
	Ne n'ai aillors ne desir ne pensee	And I have no desire or thought	5
	Fors seulement qu'ensamble estre puissomes!	Save that we may be together!	
	Hé, biau cuers doz, je voz aim seur tous homes:	Oh, fair, sweet heart, I love you above all men;	
	Aiez pitiés de vo loial amie,	Take pity on your faithful friend,	
	Et si pensés que par tans i soiomes,	And think that in time we will be together,	
	Pour mener joie, com amans a celee.	Having joy, as secret lovers.	10
	Diex! quar noz herberjomes.	God! Let us find shelter.	

T   DOMINE

Mot 814; L 265-234; MW 1044,1; B 1585
Tenor unidentified
Manuscript: *Mo* 240r-241r♪
Editions: Jacobsthal 1880: 279; Raynaud 1881: 172; Rokseth 1935-39, 3: 21♪; Woledge 1961: 200 (English translation); Tischler 1985: no. 196♪ (English translation)
Text: Edited by ED-Q
DF: Picard, including *iau* for *eau,* as in *Biaus* (Mot 1); *vo* (Mot 8) for *vostre;* 2nd-pers. pl. verbs in *-(i)és,* as in *pensés* (Mot 9); 1st-pers. pl. pres. subj. and imperative in *-omes,* as in *puissomes* (Mot 6), *soiomes* (Mot 9), *herberjomes* (Mot 11).
TN: Mot 3 Cited in Morawski 1925: no. 1835. This proverb is found in numerous

58. Biaus douz amis, or ne vouz anuit mie/Domine
Mo 240r-241r

Motetus: Biaus douz a - mis, or ne vouz a - nuit mi - e Se d'estre en-

Tenor: Domine

sam - ble fe - sons tel de - mou-re - e, Car on dit: *"Qui bien aime a*

tart ou - bli - e." Pour ce n'iert ja nostre a - mor de-se - vre - e,

Ne n'ai ail-lors ne de-sir ne pen-se - e Fors seu - le - ment qu'en-

samble es - tre puis - so - mes! Hé, biau cuers doz, je voz aim seur tous ho -

mes: Ai - ez pi - tiés de vo loi - al a - mi - e, Et si pen-

sés que par tans i soi - o - mes, Pour me - ner joi - e, com a - mans a ce -

le - e. Diex! quar noz her - ber - jo - mes.

contexts, from motets to lyric songs, even in a lai by Guillaume de Machaut. There is no particular musical phrase uniquely associated with the proverb.

ME: Mot 2+ L=R emended to B=R after Rokseth 1935-39 — 8/1-8/2 L-L emended to B-B after Rokseth 1935-39 — T 25 f missing, emended after Rokseth 1935-39 — 31 d emended to g after Rokseth 1935-39.

59

Motet

Mot	Amis, vostre demoree	Beloved, your absence
	Me feit d'amours a celee	Makes me feel the pains
	Sentir les dolours,	Of secret love,
	Car vostres est toz	For my heart is yours
5	Mes cuers, s'il tant voz agree,	Entirely—if it should please you—
	Et sera tous jors;	And always will be;
	Ne ja se ce n'est par voz	And never unless it is by you
	N'en voel estre desevree,	Do I wish to be parted from it,
	Puis qu'a vos me sui donee.	Since I have given myself to you.
10	Et biax cuers douz,	And fair, sweet heart,
	Quant plus me bat et destraint li jalous,	*The more the jealous one beats and oppresses me,*
	Tant ai ge miex en amor ma pensee.	*All the more do I have love in my thoughts.*

T   PRO PATRIBUS

Mot 829a; L 265-53; MW 424,1; B 1555
Tenor unidentified
Manuscript: *Mo* 249r♪
Editions: Jacobsthal 1880: 281; Raynaud 1881: 183; Rokseth 1935-39, 3: 36♪; Tischler 1985: no. 212♪ (English translation)
Text: Edited by JTG
ME: T 26 The tenor is written out only once, with the indication "iterum" here.
MC: Ludwig assigned the number Mot 404 to this motetus and located it with the Gradual "PRO PATRIBUS" tenor family (M30). But the tenor here does not correspond with that M30 tenor as found in other motets. It is identical to the tenor of another motet, "Un chant renvoisie et bel dirai de Sainte Ysabel / DECANTUR" (Mot 829b), found in a manuscript of the *Miracles de Nostre Dame* of Gautier de Coinci, Paris, Bibliothèque de l'Arsenal, 3517 (fol. 14r). No source for either this "PRO PATRIBUS" or "DECANTUR" has been identified. See van der Werf 1989: 135.

59. Amis, vostre demoree/PRO PATRIBUS
Mo 249r

Motetus

A - mis, vos - tre de - mo - re - e Me feit d'a - mours a ce - le - e

Tenor

PRO PATRIBUS

Sen - tir les do - lours, Car vos - tres est toz Mes cuers, s'il tant voz a - gre - e,

Et se - ra tous jors; Ne ja se ce n'est par voz N'en voel es - tre de - se -

vre - e, Puis qu'a vos me sui do - nee. Et biax cuers douz, *Quant plus me*

bat et des - traint li ja - lous, Tant ai ge miex en a - mor ma pen - se - e.

MOTETS FOR THREE VOICES

60
Motet

Tr	Diex! de chanter maintenant	God! Why am I seized
	Por quoi m'est talant pris,	By the desire to sing now,
	Qu'au cuer ai un duel dont sui peris	When I feel in my heart an ache from which I will perish
	Se cele que j'aim ne me soit confortans?	If the woman I love does not comfort me?
5	Et quant je remir et pens	And when I recall and reflect
	A sa simplece	On her sincerity
	Et son semblant,	And her countenance,
	Son cler vis,	Her bright face,
	Ses ieuz dous regardans,	The tender gaze in her eyes,
10	Il n'est mal qui me blece;	No harm can injure me;
	Por ce l'amera	So my heart will love her
	Mes cuers, a son comant l'avra.	And be at her command.
	Or me doinst Diex que m'amor bien emploie!	May God grant that my love be well placed!
	Cele part vois, car tart m'est que la voie.	I am headed toward her, for I long to see her.

Mot	Chant d'oisiaus et fuelle et flors	Birdsong and foliage and flowers
	Et tans joli	And the joyful season
	Mi font ramembrer d'amors,	Bring love to mind,
	Si que je ne pens aillors	So that I think of nothing else
5	Qu'a vos, amis.	But you, beloved.
	Tant avés, ce m'est avis,	It seems to me, you have such
	Biauté et valour et pris	Beauty and worth and merit
	Que vostre serai toudis	That I will always be yours,
	Sans nule mesproison.	Rightfully.
10	*Qui donrai je mes amors,*	*To whom shall I give my love,*
	Douz amis,	*Sweet friend,*
	S'a vos non?	*If not to you?*
	Ja vers vos ne faussera	Never will my heart be untrue,
	Mes cuers qui a vos s'otroie;	For it is pledged to you;

Por bien amer avrai joie	*From loving well, I will have joy*
Ou ja nule ne l'avra.	*Or no woman ever will.*

15

T   IN SECULUM

Tr 176; L 265-516; MW 1330,1

Mot 177; L 265-516; MW 599,1; B 387/1027/1494

M13

Manuscripts: *Mo* 125v-127r♪ (base), *Cl* 388r-v♪

Editions: Jacobsthal 1880: 39; Raynaud 1881: 62; Rokseth 1935-39, 2: 179♪;
Anderson and Close 1975: no. 47♪ (English translation); Tischler 1982: no. 235♪;
Tischler 1985: no. 87♪ (English translation); Smith 1997: 131 (English translation)

Text: Edited by ED-Q

RR: Tr 4 que] qui *(reading from Cl)* — 7 son] som — 11 amerai — Mot 1 flors] flor
(reading from Cl).

TV: Tr 1 chante — 3 perit — 4 Se une riens — 9 douz euz — 11 amerai — 13 enplaiee
— Mot 2 chans jolis — 4 puis allous — 6 Tant *missing* — 8 touz jourz — 10 Cui — 13
Et quant vers vous fauserai — 15 avrai je j.

DF: Picard, including *iau* for *eau,* as in *oisiaus* (Mot 1), *biauté* (Mot 7); 2nd-pers. pl.
verbs in *-(i)és,* as in *avés* (Mot 6).

TN: Tr 14 Tischler (1982 and 1985) designates this line as a refrain. This postulated
refrain is not listed in Boogaard 1969. — Mot 13-14 Only Boogaard (1969) identifies
these lines as a refrain.

ME: Tr 9/2 3li not c.o.p., emended after Rokseth 1935-39 — 12/4 3li not c.o.p.,
emended after Rokseth 1935-39 — 13/2 3li not c.o.p., emended after Rokseth 1935-39
— Mot 8/5 3li not c.o.p., emended after Rokseth 1935-39 — 10/5 3li not c.o.p.,
emended after Rokseth 1935-39 — 14/3 3li not c.o.p., emended after Rokseth 1935-39
— 14/7 4li not c.o.p., emended after Rokseth 1935-39 — 14/8-14+ B-R, emended
after Rokseth 1935-39 — T 17 L-R, emended after Rokseth 1935-39.

MV: Tr 3/2 a_p — 4/4 B=c — 4/8 a_p — 4/10 B=f — 5/4 B=b — 7/3 f_p — 9/2 3li not
c.o.p. — 10/4 B=c — 11/1-11/3 B-L-B=a-b-a — 12/4 3li not c.o.p. — 13/2 3li not
c.o.p. — 13/3 B=a — 13/5-13/6 B-L=e-g — 14/5 B=e — Mot 1/6 c_p — 3/1-3/2 L-L=e-
e — 3/4 L=c — 5/3 B=e — 7/4-7/7 B_p-2li-B-L=c_p-ag-f-g — 8/5 3li not c.o.p. — 8+
R — 9/2-9/3 B^p-B=c^p-d — 10/5 3li not c.o.p. — 10+ R — 14/1 a_p — 14/3 3li not c.o.p.
— 14/7 4li not c.o.p. — 14/8-14+ B-R — 15/5 3li=bcb — 16/5 2li=ag — T 26 a — 27
B-L=g-g — 29-end, tenor not repeated.

60. Diex! de chanter maintenant/Chant d'oisiaus et fuelle et flors/IN SECULUM
Mo 125v-127r

Triplum: Diex! de chan- ter main- te- nant Por quoi m'est ta- lant

Motetus: Chant d'oi- siaus et fuelle et flors Et tans jo- li

Tenor: IN SECULUM

pris, Qu'au cuer ai un duel dont sui pe- ris Se ce- le que

Mi font ra- mem- brer d'a- mors, Si que je ne pens ail- lors Qu'a

j'aim ne me soit con- for- tans? Et quant je re- mir et pens A

vos, a- mis. Tant a- vés, ce m'est a- vis, Biau- té et va-

sa sim- plece Et son sem- blant, Son cler vis, Ses ieuz dous

lour et pris Que vos- tre se- rai tou- dis Sans nu- le mes-

61. Qu'ai je forfait ne mespris/Bons amis, je vos rendrai/In SECULUM
Mo 213v-215r

61
Motet

Tr Qu'ai je forfait ne mespris,   How have I wronged
    Dame, envers voz?   Or failed you, my lady?
    Vostre amor mi destraint si   Your love tortures me so
    Que je languis et muir toz.   That I languish and am dying.
    Haro! je voz pri merci,   Help! Have mercy on me,   5
    Biaus fins cuers doz.   Dear true, sweet heart.

Mot Bons amis, je vos rendrai   Dear friend, I will compensate you
    Les deperz et les corros   For the scorn and chagrin
    Que vos avés endurés   You have endured
    Comme loiaus amorous: As a loyal lover:
    Si me rent et doins a voz.   I surrender and give myself to you.   5

T IN SECULUM

Tr 192; L 265-1401; MW 673,12; B 783
Mot 193; L 265-1401; MW 850,3
M13
Manuscript: *Mo* 213v-215r♪
Editions: Jacobsthal 1880: 59; Raynaud 1881: 145; Rokseth 1935-39, 2: 290♪; Tischler
1985: no. 163♪ (English translation); Smith 1997: 222 (English translation)
Text: Edited by JTG
TN: Tr 5-6 Only Boogaard (1969) identifies these lines as a refrain. — Mot 2
Raynaud (1881) emends to *Le despit et le corros.*

62
Motet

Tr Quant se depart li jolis tans,   When the joyful season ends,
    Que froidure revient,   As cold returns
    Qu'oisel laissent leur chant,   And birds leave off their singing,
    Adonc me vient   Then I am stirred
    Si grant   By such a great   5
    Talent   Desire
    De chanter que faire un chant me couvient,   To sing that I must compose a song,
    Quant de ma dame me souvient,   For I recall my lady,

62. Quant se depart li jolis tans/Hé! cuer joli/IN SECULUM
Mo 374r-375r

Triplum: Quant se de-part li jo-lis tans, Que froi-du-re re-vient,

Motetus: Hé! cuer jo-li, trop m'a-vés lais-sié en do-

Tenor: IN SECULUM

Qu'oi-sel lais-sent leur chant, A-donc me vient Si

lour, Dont ja n'is-trai A nul jour, Bien sai! Hé

grant Ta-lent De chan-ter que faire un chant me cou-vient,

Diex! dus-qu'a-donc que je vous ra-vrai? Trop sui ma-

Quant de ma-da-me me sou-vient, Qui mon cuer en joi-e

ri-e De vou com-pai-gni-e Que je n'ai. Biaus si-re

tient. Ja de li ne par-ti-rai, Ains la ser-vi-rai, Et se-

Diex, quant vous ver - rai? Trop m'est tart Que je vous re-

rai Pour li jo-lis tant com je vi-vrai, Car j'ai Si

voi - e, se Diex me gart! Je-sus vous ra - maint Et si saint!

tres grant de-duit, Quant je i pens jour et nuit, Que de tant me puis je

U je mor-rai a ce mot: E! e! o!

bien van - ter Que trop tart com-men-chai a a - mer.

biaus dous a-mis, o-re de-mo-rés vous trop!

Qui mon cuer en joie tient.	Who keeps my heart joyful.
10 Ja de li ne partirai,	Never will I leave her;
Ains la servirai,	Rather, I will serve her
Et serai	And will be
Pour li jolis tant com je vivrai,	Joyful for her as long as I live,
Car j'ai	For I have
15 Si tres grant deduit,	Such great delight,
Quant je i pens jour et nuit,	When I think of her day and night,
Que de tant me puis je bien vanter	That this much I can claim indeed:
Que trop tart commenchai a amer.	I began to love too late.

Mot	Hé! cuer joli, trop m'avés laissié en dolour,	Oh, tender heart! You have left me in such woe,
	Dont ja n'istrai	From which I will never emerge,
	A nul jour,	Ever,
	Bien sai!	I am sure!
5	Hé, Diex! dusqu'adonc que je vous ravrai?	Oh, God! When will I have you again?
	Trop sui marie	I am so terribly sad
	De vou compaignie	For I do not have
	Que je n'ai.	Your company.
	Biaus sire Diex, quant vous verrai?	Dear Lord God, when will I see you again?
10	Trop m'est tart	I am so impatient
	Que je vous revoie, se Diex me gart!	To see you again, so help me God!
	Jesus vous ramaint	May Jesus and His saints
	Et si saint!	Keep you!
	U je morrai a ce mot:	Or I will die singing this song:
	E! e! o! biaus dous amis, ore demorés vous trop!	*Ah! ah! oh! Dear sweet friend, you stay away too long.*
15		

T   IN SECULUM

Tr 207; L 265-1480; MW 653,1
Mot 208; L 265-1480; MW 1058,1; B 804/814/844/1141/1810
M13
Manuscript: *Mo* 374r-375r♪
Editions: Jacobsthal 1880: 311; Raynaud 1881: 280; Rokseth 1935–39, 3: 231♪;
Tischler 1985: no. 324♪ (English translation)
Text: Edited by ED-Q
RR: Tr 13 com *repeated.*

DF: Picard, including *an* for *en,* as in *tans* (Tr 1); *iau* for *eau,* as in *Biaus* (Mot 9); *ch* for *c,* as in *commenchai* (Tr 18); conj. *u* (Mot 14) for *ou; vou* (Mot 7) for *vostre;* 2nd-pers. pl. verbs in *-(i)és,* as in *avés* (Mot 1), *demorés* (Mot 15).

TN: Tischler (1985) does not recognize any refrains in the motetus. — Mot 14 The term *mot* is commonly used to designate a refrain cited in a narrative or lyric context; the term *motet* (a diminutive form of *mot*) first referred to brief lyrics we now label *refrains* before being applied to polyphonic compositions (Doss-Quinby 1984: 164-66). — 15 We italicize this postulated refrain because it is introduced by the term *mot,* which can be taken as an indication of exogenous discourse.

ME: Tr 10/5-11/5 Tischler (1985) emends by raising all pitches by a third; Rokseth (1935-39) raises only pitches of 11/1-11/5. The R after 10/7 suggests that if an error of placement occurred it more likely followed this stroke, so we have adopted Rokseth's less interventionist interpretation.

63
Motet

Tr	*Mout me fu grief li departir*	Bitterly painful was the separation
	De m'amïete	From my beloved,
	La jolie au cler vis,	The beauty with the radiant face,
	Qui est blanche et vermellete	White and rosy
	Comme rose par desus lis,	Like a rose against a lily,	5
	Ce m'est avis;	It seems to me;
	Son tres douz ris	Her ever-so-sweet laughter
	Mi fait fremir	Makes me quiver,
	Et si oell vair riant languir.	And her sparkling, cheerful eyes, languish.
	Ha, Diex! com mar la lessai!	Oh, God! Woe that I left her!	10
	Blanchete comme flour de lis,	Lily-white maiden,
	Quant vous verrai?	When will I see you?
	Dame de valour,	Worthy lady,
	Vermelle comme rose en mai,	Rosy as the rose in May,
	Pour vous sui en grant dolour.	Because of you I am in great pain.	15

Mot	*Robin m'aime, Robin m'a,*	Robin loves me, Robin has me,
	Robin m'a demandee,	Robin asked for me,
	Si m'avra.	So he will have me.
	Robin m'achata corroie	Robin bought me a belt
	Et aumonniere de soie;	And a silk purse;	5
	Pour quoi donc ne l'ameroie?	Why then would I not love him?

63. *Mout me fu grief li departir/Robin m'aime, Robin m'a/*PORTARE
Mo 292r-293r

Aleuriva!	*Aleuriva!*
Robin [m'aime, Robin m'a,	*Robin loves me, Robin has me,*
Robin m'a demandee,	*Robin asked for me,*
Si m'avra].	*So he will have me.*

10

T   PORTARE

Tr 297; L 265-1179; MW 614,1; B 1346
Mot 298; L 265-1179; MW 400; B 1633/1879
M22
Manuscripts: *Mo* 292r-293r♪ (base), *Ba* 52v♪
Editions: Coussemaker 1865: no. 28♪; Coussemaker 1872: 423♪; Jacobsthal 1880: 291; Raynaud 1881: 226; Stimming 1906: 68; Aubry 1908, 2: 182♪; Gennrich 1921: 71♪; Rokseth 1935-39, 3: 108♪; Gleason 1942: 65♪; Wilkins 1967: 73♪; Anderson 1977: no. 81♪ (English translation); Tischler 1985: no. 265♪ (English translation); Badel 1995: 206 (French translation); Smith 1997: 254 (English translation)
Text: Edited by JTG
TV: Tr 1 gries li departirs — 4 et *missing* — 7 Ses — 9 vair ieull — 10 Hé; mal — 14 vermeilete — 15 en si g. — Mot 1 Robins m. Robins — 2 Robins — 4 Robins — 6 Et p. — 8 Robin et cetera *Mo.*
TN: Tr Anderson (1977) designates lines 1-2, but not line 3, as a refrain. He also identifies line 15 as refrain; this postulated refrain is not listed in Boogaard 1969. Tischler (1985) recognizes only line 15 as a refrain. — Mot 1-3 Adam de la Halle cites a rondeau with the same refrain in his *Jeu de Robin et Marion* (ll. 1-7). — 7 Tischler (1985) does not designate this line as a refrain.
ME: T 34 final note missing, supplied from *Ba.*
MV: Tr 2/1 f$^\sharp$ — 3/5 SSS=edc — 4/5 B^p=e^p — 4/7 SSS=edc — 5/6 f$^\sharp$ — 9/1 2li s.perf.=ab — 9/3 SSS=agf$^\sharp$ — 9/6 no sharp — 10/1 B$_p$=f$^\sharp_p$ — 11/5 f$^\sharp$ — 13/4 B=g — 15/4 SS=gf — 15/6 L — Mot 4/3 SSS=edc — 5/3 SSS=edc — 8/3 SSS=edc — 10/2 2li c.perf. — T 2-3 BLBL not ligated — 7 BSSB not ligated — 12-13 BLBL not ligated — 16-17 BLBL not ligated — 19 BL not ligated — 21 BSSB not ligated — 26-27 BLBL not ligated — 29 BL not ligated — 31 BSSB not ligated.

64
Motet

Tr	Je me doi bien doloseir	Rightly must I grieve
	Et de chanchon faire reposeir	And cease composing song
	Cant celle ki mun cuer at pris at mari,	When she who has stolen my heart has taken a husband,
	Dont trop ai le cuer mari!	Which saddens my heart so!

Nonporcant raison pieche at	Nonetheless it is right that for a long while 5
N'ous de chanteir.	I do not dare sing.
Melhour bien m'en puis vanteir,	I can take pride in a greater good,
Car la belle mandeit m'at	For my beauty has revealed to me
K'ultre sun greit	That, against her will,
Li at om marit doneit,	She was given a husband, 10
Et ke ja ne l'amerat,	And that she will never love him,
Ne por ce ne laisserat	Nor will she forsake
Le bien ameir,	Passionate love,
Car trop li seroit ameir.	For that would be too bitter.
Anchois ferat	Instead she will ensure 15
Tant k'ameit bien se porat	That the one who belongs to her
Li siens clameir.	Can claim to be loved passionately.

Mot	Por coi m'aveis vos doneit,	Why have you given me,
	Mere, mari?	A husband, mother?
	Cant ja par mun greit	For never willingly
	Ne fuist ensi	Would I have wished to be given
	K'a autrui fuisse doneie	To anyone other than 5
	K'a celi cui j'ai de moi saisit,	The one I have taken as my own,
	Ki tant m'at honoreie	Who has so honored me
	C'onkes mais nus mieus ne deservit	That no man has ever been more deserving
	K'amors li fuist graeie;	To have love granted to him;
	Et vos l'en aveis a tort parti!	And you have deprived him of it wrongly! 10
	Diex! j'astoie si bien assenneie,	God! I was so settled,
	Et vos m'aveis marïeie! aimi!	And you have married me off! Woe to me!
	Ja saviés vos bien k'avoie amis.	You knew I had a sweetheart.

T   DOCEBIT

Tr 354; L 265-1375; MW 473,1
Mot 353; L 265-1375; MW 1129,1; B 1514
M26
Manuscripts: *Tu* 27r-28r♪ (base), *Mo* 265v-266r♪, *StV* 288v-289r♪ (music and text incipit only)
Editions: Jacobsthal 1880: 286; Raynaud 1881: 203; Rokseth 1935-39, 3: 69♪; Auda 1953: no. 22♪; Tischler 1982: no. 86♪; Tischler 1985: no. 243♪ (English translation)
Text: Edited by WP
RR: Tr 14 tropl.

64. Je me doi bien doloseir/Por coi m'aveis vos doneit/DOCEBIT
Tu 27r-28r

Triplum: Je me doi bien do-lo-seir Et de chan-chon fai-re re-po-seir Cant cel-le ki mun cuer at pris at ma-ri, Dont trop ai le cuer ma-ri! Non-por-cant rai-son pieche at N'ous de chan-teir. Mel-hour bien m'en puis van-

Motetus: Por coi m'a-veis vos do-neit, Me-re, ma-ri? Cant ja par mun greit Ne fuist en-si K'a au-trui fuis-se do-nei-e K'a ce-li cui j'ai de moi sai-sit, Ki tant m'at ho-no-rei-e C'on-kes

Tenor: DOCEBIT

TV: Mot 3 Car — 5 autre — 6 c. qui — 8 onc m. nus hom mieuz — 12 assenee — 13 bien *missing;* ami.

DF: *Tu* is a Walloon manuscript, and this song displays traits peculiar to that dialect, such as *Melhour* (Tr 7) for *meilleur,* as well as ones characteristic of both Walloon and Lorraine, including *ei* for tonic *e,* as in *doloseir* (Tr 1), *mandeit* (Tr 8), *doneie* (Mot 5); preservation of final *t,* as in *greit* (Tr 9), *saisit* (Mot 6), *deservit* (Mot 8); 3rd-pers. sing. pres. ind. *at* (Tr 3) for *a;* 3rd-pers. sing. fut. in *-at,* as in *amerat* (Tr 11), *laisserat* (Tr 12), *ferat* (Tr 15). Picard *ch* for *c,* as in *chanchon* (Tr 2), *pieche* (Tr 5), *Anchois* (Tr 15). Anglo-Norman *mun* (Tr 3, Mot 3) for *mon, sun* (Tr 9) for *son.*

TN: There is no triplum in *Mo.* — Mot Tischler (1985) designates lines 12-13 as a refrain instead of lines 1-2 and 13, as postulated by Boogaard (1969).

ME: Mot 9/6-end, clef a fifth too high, emended from *Mo* and *StV.*

MV (*Mo*): Mot 2/2 g — 3/4 L=g — 4/3 2li c.perf. — 5/6-5/7 L-2li c.perf.=b^b-ag — 6/1 f — 7/7 L — 8/8 e^p — 9/1 no flat — 9/5 2li c.perf. — 9/7 L — 10/8-10/9 2li c.perf.-L — 11/2 2li c.perf. — 11/8 3li-b^{b}ag — 11/9-11/10 B-2li c.perf.-L — 12/4 2li c.perf.=cd — 12/8 2li c.perf.=cb — 12/9 L — 13/3 no flat — 13/7-13/8 4li c.perf.-3li c.perf.=gfga-agf — T 3-5 3li c.perf.-L=efg-d — 8-10 3li c.perf.-L=aca-a — 13-15 3li c.perf.-L=fge-g — 18-20 3li c.perf.-L=fdf-e — 23-25 3li c.perf.-L=gf(no sharp)a-c — 27-30 B-L-2li c.perf.-L-L=a-a-ca-a-g — 33-34 3li c.perf.=gef — 38-40 B-2li c.perf.-L=a-ag-a — 43-45 3li c.perf.-L=egb^b-a — 48-50 3li c.perf.-L=fed-a — 52 2li=gf (no sharp) — 53-55 3li c.perf.-R-L-L=aca-R-a-g.

MC: The motetus and tenor are given as an untexted clausula in *StV,* with the incipit "Pour coi m'avés vos doné mari" in the margin.

65

Motet

Tr	Je sui jonete et jolie:	I am young and pretty
	S'ai un cuer enamoré	And have an enamored heart
	Qui tant mi semont et prie	That so bids and entreats me
	D'amer par joliëté	To love ardently
5	Que tuit i sunt mi pensé.	That all my thoughts are of love.
	Mes mon mari ne set mie	But my husband does not know
	A qui j'ai mon cuer doné:	To whom I have given my heart.
	Par les sains que l'en deprie,	By the saints who hear our prayers,
	Il morroit de jalousie,	He would die of jealousy
10	S'il savoit la verité.	If he knew the truth.
	Mes, foi que je doi a Dé,	But by the faith I owe God,
	J'amerai!	I will love!
	Ja pour mari ne lairé:	Never will I stop loving because of my husband.

Quant il fait tout a son gré	When he does all he wishes
Et de mon cors sa volenté,	And has his will with my body, 15
Del plus mon plesir feiré.	All the more will I do as I please.

Mot Hé, Diex! je n'ai pas mari	Oh, God! I do not have a husband
Du tot a mon gré:	At all to my liking:
Il n'a cortoisie en li	There is no refinement in him
Ne joliveté!	Nor ardor!
Jone dame est bien traïe,	A young woman is indeed betrayed, 5
Par la foi que doi a Dé,	By the faith I owe God,
Qui a vilain est baillie	When she is handed over to a boor
Pour faire sa volenté;	For him to do his will;
Ce fu trop mal devisé.	This was very ill devised.
De mari sui mal païe:	I am poorly rewarded in my husband; 10
D'ami m'en amenderai,	I will compensate for it with a lover,
Et se m'en savoit mal gré	And if my husband resents me for it,
Mon mari, si face amie,	Let him find a mistress;
Car, voelle ou non, j'amerai!	For—whether he likes it or not—I will love!

T   VERITATEM

Tr 465; L 265-932; MW 908,1
Mot 466; L 265-932; MW 1126,1
M37
Manuscript: *Mo* 207v-209r♪

Editions: Jacobsthal 1880: 58; Raynaud 1881: 139; Rokseth 1935-39, 2: 282♪; Bec 1978: 13; Tischler 1985: no. 156♪ (English translation); Dufournet 1989: 60 (French translation); Smith 1997: 215 (English translation)

Text: Edited by ED-Q

DF: Picard, including *ie* for *iee,* as in *païe* (Mot 10); final *s* for *z,* as in *sains* (Tr 8); *mi* (Tr 5) for *mes.* Anglo-Norman, including *un* for *on,* as in *sunt* (Tr 5); *plesir* (Tr 16) for *plaisir;* 1st-pers. sing. fut. in -*é,* as in *lairé* (Tr 13), *feiré* (Tr 16).

ME: Tr 16/6 L emended to B after Rokseth 1935-39 — Mot 6+ B=R emended to L=R after Rokseth 1935-39 — 8+ B=R emended to L=R after Rokseth 1935-39 — 9+ B=R emended to L=R after Rokseth 1935-39 — 11+ B=R emended to L=R after Rokseth 1935-39 — 12+ B=R emended to L=R after Rokseth 1935-39 — 14/6 L emended to B after Rokseth 1935-39.

65. Je sui jonete et jolie/Hé Diex! je n'ai pas mari/VERITATEM
Mo 207v-209r

Triplum: Je sui jo - nete et jo - li - e: S'ai un cuer e - na - mo - ré Qui tant mi se - mont et pri - e D'a - mer par jo - li - e - té Que tuit i sunt mi pen - sé. Mes mon ma - ri ne set mi - e A qui j'ai mon cuer do - né: Par les sains que

Motetus: Hé, Diex! je n'ai pas ma - ri Du tot a mon gré: Il n'a cor - toi - sie en li Ne jo - li - ve - té! Jo - ne dame est bien tra - i - e, Par la foi que doi a Dé, Qui a vi - lain est bail -

Tenor: VERITATEM

l'en de-pri - e, Il mor-roit de ja-lou-si - e, S'il sa - voit la ve - ri - té.

li - e Pour fai - re sa vo - len - té; Ce fu trop mal de - vi - sé.

Mes, foi que je doi a Dé, J'a - me - rai! Ja pour ma - ri

De ma - ri sui mal pa - i - e: D'a - mi m'en a - men - de -

ne lai - ré: Quant il fait tout a son gré Et de mon

rai, Et se m'en sa - voit mal gré Mon ma -

cors sa vo - len - té, Del plus mon ple - sir fei - ré.

ri, si face a - mi - e, Car, voelle ou non, j'a - me - rai!

66. Je ne quier mais a ma vie/Dieus! trop mal mi pert que j'aie amé/MISIT

Ba 15r

Triplum

Je ne quier mais a ma vi-e Sou-le-te le bois pas-ser, Car mes a-mis n'i est mi-e, Qui tant mi soi-loit a-mer Et ser-vir et ho-nou-rer; Dieus! si n'i pour-roi-e mi-e Lon-gue-ment sans li du-rer. Ei-mi, Dieus, las-se! De

Motetus

Dieus! trop mal mi pert que j'aie a-mé, Quant par-mi le bois ra-mé Mon a-mi n'ai en-con-tré, Qui m'a-voit ci a-jour-né. Eyn-mi, Dieus! li mals d'a-mer Pein-ne mi fait en-du-rer Ci tout droit La ou je tieng mon doit;

Tenor

MISIT

li me vient trop grief pan - sé, Si ai tres bien

Las - se! de li mi vient Trop grief pan - sser; Bien me doit pe -

es - pro - vé Que la riens qui plus me grie - ve, C'est li mal d'a - mer.

ser Quant il mi cou - vient Sou - le - te le bois pas - ser.

66

Motet

Tr		
	Je ne quier mais a ma vie	Never again do I wish
	Soulete le bois passer,	To walk through the woods all alone,
	Car mes amis n'i est mie,	For my lover is not there,
	Qui tant mi souloit amer	He who once so loved
5	Et servir et honourer;	And served and honored me.
	Dieus! si n'i pourroie mie	God! I could not
	Longuement sans li durer.	Survive for long without him.
	Eimi, Dieus, lasse!	Alas, God, wretched me!
	De li me vient trop grief pansé,	He is the source of such bitter sadness;
10	Si ai tres bien esprové	Indeed, I know full well
	Que la riens qui plus me grieve,	That what torments me most
	C'est li mal d'amer.	Is the pain of love.

Mot		
	Dieus! trop mal mi pert que j'aie amé,	God! I have loved so foolishly, it seems to me,
	Quant parmi le bois ramé	Since in the lush woods
	Mon ami n'ai encontré,	I have not met with my lover,
	Qui m'avoit ci ajourné.	Who had summoned me here.
5	Eynmi, Dieus! li mals d'amer	Alas, God! The pain of love
	Peinne mi fait endurer	Makes me suffer anguish
	Ci tout droit	Right here,
	La ou je tieng mon doit;	Where I am pointing my finger.
	Lasse! de li mi vient	Alas! He is the source
10	Trop grief pansser;	Of such bitter sadness;
	Bien me doit peser	It should indeed distress me
	Quant il mi couvient	That I must
	Soulete le bois passer.	Walk through the woods all alone.

T   MISIT

Tr 573; L 265-911; MW 933,3; B 42/568
Mot 574; L 265-911; MW 143,1; B 43
M76
Manuscript: *Ba* 15r♪
Editions: Stimming 1906: 17; Aubry 1908, 2: 55♪; Anderson 1977: no. 27♪ (English translation)
Text: Edited by ED-Q
RR: Tr 1 quer *(em. Stimming)* — 7 lie — Mot 9 lie.

TN: Tr Anderson (1977) designates lines 1-2 and 11-12 as refrains, in addition to those postulated by Boogaard (1969).
ME: Mot 5/2 2li s.perf. emended to S-S.

67
Motet

Tr	Nus ne mi pourroit conforter	No one could ever comfort me	
	Ne donner joie et soulas,	Or bring me joy and pleasure	
	Se la bele non au vis cler,	Save the beauty with the radiant face,	
	Qui m'a dou tout mis en ses las.	Who has completely ensnared me.	
	Aymi! que ferai je, las!	Wretched me! What will I do, alas!	5
	Quant merci trouver ne puis?	Since I can find no mercy?	
	Hé! trop mi va de mal en pis!	Oh! It is going from bad to worse!	
	Que, s'osasse plaidier	For, if I dared plead	
	Et mon droit derraisnier,	And defend my right,	
	Lors fusse garis;	Then I would be cured;	10
	Mais riens ne mi puet aidier	But nothing can help me now	
	Fors mercis.	Except mercy.	

Mot	Nonne sui, nonne, laissiés m'aler,	I am a nun, a nun, let me go,	
	Je n'i [puis plus arester,	I can stay here no longer,	
	Ne ja n'i voudrai] vos matines sonner,	Nor do I ever wish to ring your matins,	
	Qui sovent mi font peinne et mal endurer.	Which often make me suffer pain and misery.	
	De froit trembler, tart couchier, main lever	Often I must—and it really annoys me—	5
	M'estuet sovent, qui mi fait mont grever;	Shiver from the cold, retire late, rise early;	
	De riens ne mi plaist tel vie a demener;	I find nothing pleasing in such a life;	
	Ces hores avec qu'il m'estuet recorder	These hours that I must repeat	
	Trop d'ennoi mi donnent,	Are so aggravating,	
	Et quant mi doi reposer,	And when I ought to be resting,	10
	Matines sonnent.	Matins ring.	

T   APTATUR

Tr 736; L 265-1221; MW 1085,1; B 53
Mot 737; L 265-1221; MW 38,1
O45
Manuscript: *Ba* 45v-46r♪

67. Nus ne mi pourroit conforter/Nonne sui, nonne, laissiés m'aler/APTATUR
Ba 45v-46r

Triplum: Nus ne mi pourroit con-for-ter Ne don-ner joie et sou-las, Se la be-le non au vis cler, Qui m'a dou tout mis en ses las. Ay - mi! que fe-rai je, las! Quant mer-ci trou - ver ne puis? Hé!

Motetus: Non-ne sui, non-ne, lais-siés m'a - ler, Je n'i [puis plus a-res-ter, Ne ja n'i vou-drai] vos ma-ti-nes son-ner, Qui so-vent mi font peinne et mal en-du-rer. De froit trem-bler, tart cou-chier, main le-ver M'es-tuet so-vent, qui mi fait mont gre-

Tenor: APTATUR

trop mi va de mal en pis! Que, s'o - sas - se plai - dier Et

ver; De riens ne mi plaist tel vie a de - me - ner; Ces ho - res a -

mon droit der - rais - nier, Lors fus - se ga - ris;

vec qu'il m'es - tuet re - cor - der Trop d'en - noi mi don - nent,

Mais riens ne mi puet ai - dier Fors mer - cis.

Et quant mi doi re - po - ser, Ma - ti - nes son - nent.

Editions: Stimming 1906: 62; Aubry 1908, 2: 157♪; Anderson 1977: no. 71♪ (English translation)

Text: Edited by ED-Q

RR: Mot 2–3 *text mostly illegible, taken from Stimming* — 11 Matinent.

TN: Mot 3 Matins is a liturgical night office, the first and chief of the canonical hours. It usually includes psalms, other scriptural and patristic readings, hymns, and prayers. — 8 "Hours" refers to times of the day ecclesiastically set for prayer and devotion.

68
Motet

Tr	Amours qui vient par mesage	A love conveyed by messenger
	Ne pourroit longues durer;	Could not last long;
	Pour coi ne li vuill mander,	That is why I do not wish to let her know—
	A la blondete, la sage,	My blond, my bright one—
5	La grant doulour ne la rage	The great sorrow and anger
	Qu'ele mi fait endurer.	She makes me suffer.
	Souvent souspirer	Often I must sigh
	M'estuet et mout grant malage	And overcome a great malaise
	Le mius que je puis passer;	As best I can;
10	Si n'i sai comment aler	So I do not know how
	Dire li tout mon courage	To tell her all I feel
	Et toute ma volenté.	And all I desire.
	Hé! se cil mals ne m'assouage,	*Ah! If this pain does not subside,*
	Je sui a la mort livrés.	*I am condemned to die.*
Mot	*Toute soule passerai li bois ramé,*	*All alone I will walk through the lush woods,*
	Puis que je n'i ai trové	Since here I have not found
	Mon tres dous loial ami,	My dear sweet faithful friend,
	En cui j'avoie tout mis	In whom I had placed
5	Mon pensé.	All my thoughts,
	Et il m'avoit creanté	And who had promised
	Qu'il venroit aveque mi	He would come with me
	El vert boscage;	Into the green woods;
	Si ne me tieng mie a sage,	So I do not consider myself wise
10	Quant tote sole i entrai.	To have gone in all alone.
	Hé! las! dous Dieus! que ferai?	*Alas! Dear God! What shall I do?*
	Je ne sai,	I do not know,

Mais soulete m'en rirai	But all alone I will walk once more
Tot le rivage,	Along the riverbank,
Puis que compaingnie n'ai, ai!	*Since I have no companion, alas!* 15

T   NOTUM

Tr 845; L 265-126; MW 1317,1; B 1662
Mot 846; L 265-126; MW 1492,1; B 824/1789
Tenor unidentified
Manuscripts: *Ba* 58r-v♪ (base); Rome, Biblioteca Apostolica Vaticana, Regina 1543, no. 3, fol. Iᵃv♪ (incipit only)
Editions: Stimming 1906: 75; Aubry 1908, 2: 204♪; Anderson 1977: no. 93♪ (English translation)
Text: Edited by WP
RR: Tr 9 mius] muis *(em. Stimming)* — Mot 8 El] Li *(em. Stimming).*
DF: Picard, including *iu* for *ieu,* as in *mius* (Tr 9); *c* for *ch,* as in *boscage* (Mot 8); *s* for *ss,* as in *mesage* (Tr 1); *mi* (Mot 7) for *moi;* cond. *venroit* (Mot 7) for *vendroit.*
MV: The Rome fragment (Regina 1543) has only the beginning of the piece; the initials were never added: Tr L-B-3li-B=c-b-cba-g over the text "[A]mours qui va," Mot L-B-L-B-L-SSS=f-g-a-a-a-agf over the text *"[T]oute seule passe-,"* T 3li-L-L-R=fed-d-c over the word "[N]EUMA."
MC: Gennrich (1921) and Tischler (1997) used the music of the first and last verses of the motetus to reconstruct a melody for the rondeau *"Toute seule passerai le vert boscage"* (song no. 51).

69
Motet

Tr	*S'on me regarde,*	*If someone is watching me,*
	S'on me regarde,	*If someone is watching me,*
	Dites le moi;	*Do tell me;*
	Trop sui gaillarde,	*I am too exuberant,*
	Bien l'aperchoi.	I see it clearly. 5
	Ne puis laissier que mon regard ne s'esparde,	I cannot keep my gaze from wandering,
	Car tes m'esgarde	For someone is looking at me
	Dont mout me tarde	Whom I am eager
	Qu'il m'ait o soi,	To be with,
	Qu'il a, en foi,	For in truth he has 10
	De m'amour plain otroi.	Full right to my love.
	Mais tel ci voi	But I see someone else here

68. Amours qui vient par mesage/*Toute soule passerai li bois ramé*/Notum
Ba 58r-v

Triplum: A - mours qui vient par me-sa - ge Ne pour - roit lon-

Motetus: *Tou - te sou - le pas-se-rai li bois ra - mé,*

Tenor: Notum

gues du - rer; Pour coi ne li vuill man - der, A la blon-de-

Puis que je n'i ai tro - vé Mon tres dous loi-al a - mi,

te, la sa - ge, La grant dou - lour ne la ra - ge

En cui j'a - voi - e tout mis Mon pen - sé.

Qu'e - le mi fait en - du - rer. Sou - vent sous-pi-

Et il m'a - voit cre - an - té Qu'il ven - roit a-

69. *S'on me regarde/Prenés i garde/*Hé! MI ENFANT
Mo 375v-376v

Triplum

S'on me re - gar - de, S'on me re - gar - de, Di - tes le moi;

Motetus

Pre - nés i gar - de S'on me re - gar - de; Trop sui gail - lar - de.

Tenor

Hé! MI ENFANT

Trop sui gail - lar - de, Bien l'a - per - choi. Ne puis lais - sier que

Di - tes le moi, Pour Dieu, vous proi, Car tes m'es - gar - de

mon re - gard ne s'es - par - de, Car tes m'es - gar - de

Dont mout me tar - de Qu'il m'ait o soi, Bien l'a - per - choi.

Dont mout me tar - de Qu'il m'ait o soi, Qu'il a, en foi,

Et tel chi voi Qui est, je croi—

	Qui est, je croi—	Who, I think—
	Feu d'enfer l'arde!—	May he burn in hell!—
15	Jalous de moi.	Jealously guards me.
	Mais pour li d'amer ne recroi,	But in spite of him I will not renounce love,
	Car, par ma foi,	For to tell the truth
	Pour nient m'esgarde;	He watches me in vain;
	Bien pert sa garde:	His surveillance is for naught:
20	J'arai rechoi.	I will find a hiding place.

Mot	*Prenés i garde*	*Please take note*
	S'on me regarde;	*If someone is watching me;*
	Trop sui gaillarde.	*I am too exuberant.*
	Dites le moi,	*Do tell me,*
5	Pour Dieu, vous proi,	In God's name, I beg you,
	Car tes m'esgarde	For someone is looking at me
	Dont mout me tarde	Whom I am eager
	Qu'il m'ait o soi,	To be with,
	Bien l'aperchoi.	I see him clearly.
10	Et tel chi voi	And I see someone else here
	Qui est, je croi—	Who, I think—
	Feu d'enfer l'arde!—	May he burn in hell!—
	Jalous de moi.	Jealously guards me.
	Mais pour li d'amer ne recroi.	But in spite of him I will not renounce love.
15	Pour nient m'esgarde;	He watches me in vain;
	Bien pert sa garde:	His surveillance is for naught:
	J'arai rechoi	I will find a hiding place
	Et de mon ami le dosnoi.	And have pleasure with my lover.
	Faire le doi:	I must do so,
20	Ne serai plus couarde.	And be a coward no longer.

T	HÉ! MI ENFANT	OH, MY CHILD

Tr 908; L 265-1627; MW 349,1; B 1531

Mot 909; L 265-1627; MW 204,1; B 1531

Manuscript: *Mo* 375v-376v♪

Editions: Coussemaker 1865: no. 19♪; Jacobsthal 1880: 311; Raynaud 1881: 282;
Rokseth 1935-39, 3: 233♪♪; Tischler 1985: no. 325♪ (English translation)

Text: Edited by JTG

DF: Picard, including *ch* for *c*, as in *aperchoi* (Tr 5), *rechoi* (Tr 20), *chi* (Mot 10); fut.
arai (Tr 20) for *avrai*.

TN: Tr Tischler (1985) designates only lines 1-3 as a refrain.
ME: Tr 16/6 B emended to L after Rokseth 1935-39 — 17/2 L^p emended to B^p after
Rokseth 1935-39 — Mot 14/6 B emended to L after Rokseth 1935-39 — T 46 B
emended to L after Rokseth 1935-39.

70
Motet

Tr	Dame que je n'os noumer,	Lady whom I dare not name,
	Quant porrai je a vous parler,	When will I be able to speak to you,
	Sade blondete?	Charming blond?
	Au cuer sent une amourete	I feel a love in my heart
	Qui souspirer	That makes me	5
	Me fait et colour muer.	Sigh and blush.
	Mais merveilles puis penser	But I think it a wonder
	Comment ce est que riens tant	That I desire nothing so much
	Ne desir qu'a vous aler;	As to go to you;
	Et si sent plus engrever	And I feel my pain	10
	Mon mal quant	Worsen when
	Plus prochaine estes de moi,	You draw closer to me.
	Et par ce sai je et voi	This is how I know and see
	Que du privé larron ne se puet on garder.	That one cannot guard against an intimate thief.

Mot	Amis, dont est engenree	Love, what generates
	En vo cuer tel volentés	In your heart such a conviction
	Qu'estre cuidiés refusés:	As to think you have been rejected:
	Pour ce que vous ai monstree	Because I have shown you
	Chiere autre que ne volés?	A demeanor other than you desire?	5
	Mais se bien saviés	But if only you knew
	Comment on doit retenir	How a woman should retain
	Amant c'on crient departir,	A lover she dreads to lose,
	Entendre porriés	You would understand
	Que le fis par tel desir	That I did it in the hope	10
	Qu'en aigrir	That by being harsh with you
	Vous feïsse en moi amer.	I might make you love me.
	Fins cuers, ne veulliés cesser,	True heart, do not cease to love me,
	Car aillours que vous chierir	For other than to cherish you
	Ne puis penser.	I can have no thought.	15

70. Dame que je n'os noumer/Amis, dont est engenree/LONC TANS A QUE NE VI M'AMIE
Mo 389r-390r

T	LONC TANS A	IT'S BEEN SO LONG
	QUE NE VI M'AMIE.	SINCE I LAST SAW MY BELOVED.
	[Trop me greva	It hurt me deeply
	Quant m'en covint partir,	When I had to part from her,
5	Car je l'aim et desir.	For I love and desire her.
	Trop m'aïr	It angers me greatly
	Quant pour li servir	That in order to serve her
	M'estuet languir,	I must languish;
	Et si ne m'en puis tenir.	When I think of her,
10	Quant la remir,	I cannot hold back
	De cuer souspir,	A heartfelt sigh
	Si que tout me fait fremir,	That makes me all ashiver,
	Car je l'aim de fin cuer sans mentir.	For I love her with a true heart, honestly.
	N'en puis joïr—	I cannot enjoy her—
15	Diex!—ne repentir:	Lord!—nor can I repent:
	Si m'estuet souffrir	So I must suffer
	Les maus dont je ne puis garir.]	The pains from which I cannot heal.

Tr 909c; L 265-422; MW 391,1

Mot 909d; L 265-422; MW 1395,1

T 512; L 265-290; MW 1463,1

Manuscript: *Mo* 389r-390r♪

Editions: Jacobsthal 1880: 37, 315; Raynaud 1881: 53, 290; Stimming 1906: 50; Aubry 1908, 2: 122♪; Rokseth 1935–39, 3: 254♪, 2: 167♪; Auda 1953: no. 27♪; Woledge 1961: 200 (English translation); Tischler 1973: no. 15♪ (English translation); Anderson and Close 1975: no. 10♪ (English translation); Anderson 1977: no. 57♪; Tischler 1982: no. 214♪; Tischler 1985: nos. 78♪, 337♪ (English translation)

Text: Edited by JTG

RR: Tr 14 se *repeated.*

TV: T 2 ne *missing Tu* — 4 convient *Ba* — 7 Car *Tu;* lui *Cl* — 11 Du *Cl* — 16 Ains *Tu* — 17 je *missing BaClTu.*

DF: Picard, including *c* for *qu,* as in *c'on* (Mot 8); *noumer* (Tr 1) for *nomer; engenree* (Mot 1) for *engendree; vo* (Mot 2) for *vostre;* 2nd-pers. pl. verbs in *-(i)és,* as in *cuidiés* (Mot 3), *volés* (Mot 5), *saviés* (Mot 6).

TN: Tr 14 *on* added later above the line. — T The full text of "LONC TANS A QUE NE VI M'AMIE" (T 512) appears in *Mo* 116v-118r♪ (our base manuscript) and *Ba* 35v-36r♪ as the motetus of a three-part motet that has "Cele m'a tolu la vie" (Tr 511) as the triplum and "ET SPERABIT" (M49) as the tenor. It also occurs in *Tu* 35r-36r♪ as the motetus of a three-part motet that has "Pulchra decens speciosa" (Tr 513) as the triplum and "ET SPERABIT" as the tenor. It is found as well in *Cl* 372r-v♪ as the motetus of a four-part motet that has "Cele m'a tolu la vie" as the triplum, "Ave,

deitatis templum mirabile" (Q 512a) as the quadruplum, and "ET SPERABIT,"
designated "ET SUPER," as the tenor. On this motet complex, see "Introduction to the
Music," in the introduction to this book. Note that Anderson and Close (1975)
recognize lines 16-17 as a refrain. Anderson (1977) identifies lines 1-4 and 16-17 as
refrains. Tischler (1982 and 1985) distinguishes lines 1-2, 9, and 16-17 as refrains.
These postulated refrains are not listed in Boogaard 1969.
ME: Tr 10/5-10/6 L-3li c.o.p.=d-cba for the three syllables of *engrever,* emended after
Tischler 1985.

MOTET FOR FOUR VOICES

71
Motet

Q	Jolïement en douce desirree	Gaily seized by sweet desire	
	Qui tant m'a souspris,	That has stolen over me,	
	J'aim la blondete	I am in love with the sweet	
	Doucete	Worthy	
	De pris,	Blond	5
	Comme celi ou j'ai mis ma pensee.	Who occupies my thoughts.	
	Hé! s'en chanterai doucement pour s'amistié.	Ah! So I will sing sweetly for the sake of her love.	
	Acoler et baisier	Embracing and kissing	
	M'a cousté et coustera.	Have and will cost me dearly.	
	Ja vilein part n'i avra:	Never will a rustic take an interest in it:	10
	Nostra sunt sollempnia,	*Nostra sunt sollempnia,*	
	Car trop biau deduit i a.	For there is such ardent pleasure in it.	
	C'est trop douce vie	It is such a sweet life—	
	Que que nus en die,	Whatever one may say—	
	De baisier, d'acoler,	Kissing, embracing,	15
	De rire et de jouer	Laughing and playing	
	A sa douce amie.	With one's sweet beloved.	
	Trop fait a proisier	He sets too great store by it	
	Qui l'a sans dansgier,	Who has it without resistance,	
	Mes l'amor devee	But may thwarted love	20
	Ait courte duree.	Be short-lived.	
	Mal ait amors ou pitié	*Cursed be the love in which mercy*	
	Et douçor n'est trovee.	*And sweetness are not found.*	

71. Jolïement en douce desirree/Quant voi la florete/Je sui jolïete/APTATUR
Mo 55v-58r

Quadruplum

Jo - lï - e - ment en dou - ce de - sir - re - e Qui

Triplum

Quant voi la flo - re - te Naistre en la pre - e,

Motetus

Je sui jo - li - e - te, Sa - de - te, plei - sans

Tenor

APTATUR

tant m'a sous - pris, J'aim la blon - de - te Dou - ce - te De

Et j'oi l'a - lo - ete A la ma - ti - ne - e Qui saut et ha -

Joi - ne pu - ce - le - te: N'ai pas quinze ans, Point ma ma - me -

pris, Com - me ce - li ou j'ai mis ma pen - se - e.

le - te, For - ment m'a - gre - e! S'en di - rai chan - ço - ne - te:

le - te Se - lonc le tans: Si de - usse a - pren - dre

l'a - mor de - ve - e Ait cour - te du - re - e. Mal ait a -

tieg ceste a - be - i - e: Trop u - se ma vie En grief tour -

car trop sui jo - ne - te. Je sent les doz maus de - soz ma cein - tu -

mors ou pi - tié Et dou - çor n'est tro - ve - e.

ment; Je ne vi - vrai mi - e Lon - gue - ment.

re - te: Hon - nis soit de Diu qui me fist non - ne - te!

Tr   Quant voi la florete

When I see the new flower

    Naistre en la pree,

Burgeon in the meadow,

    Et j'oi l'alöete

And I hear the lark

    A la matinee

In the morning

5   Qui saut et halete,

Hopping and fluttering,

    Forment m'agree!

It pleases me greatly!

    S'en dirai chançonete:

So I will sing a little song:

    Amouretes,

Love,

    Amouretes

Love

10 *M'ont navré.*

Has wounded me.

    En non Dé,

In the name of God,

    Li cuers mi halete

My heart is pounding

    En joliveté:

With joy,

    S'ai trové

For I have found

15 *Amouretes a mon gré;*

A love to my liking.

    Jolivement,

Gaily,

    Cointement,

Gracefully,

    Soutivment

Artfully,

    M'ont le cuer emblé

It has stolen my heart away

20 Et enamouré

And enraptured it

    Tant doucement.

So sweetly.

    Pour noient

For naught

    Maintieg ceste abeïe:

Does this nunnery confine me:

    Trop use ma vie

I am wasting my life

25 En grief tourment;

In bitter torment.

    Je ne vivrai mie

I will not live

    Longuement.

Long at all.

Mot Je sui jolïete,

I am a merry,

    Sadete, pleisans

Gracious, charming

    Joine pucelete:

Young girl,

    N'ai pas quinze ans,

Not yet fifteen.

5   Point ma mamelete

My little breasts are swelling

    Selonc le tans:

With time.

    Si deüsse aprendre

I should be learning

    D'amors et entendre

About love and turning my mind

    Les samblans

To its delightful

10 Deduisans;

Ways;

    Mes je sui mise en prison.

But I have been put in prison.

De Diu ait maleïçon	May God curse
Qui m'i mist!	The one who put me here!
Mal et vilanie et pechié fist	An evil, vile, and sinful thing he did
De tel pucelete	Sending such a young girl 15
Rendre en abïete.	To a nunnery.
Trop i mefist,	He did a wicked thing,
Par ma foi;	By my faith;
En relegion vif a grant anoi—	In the convent I live in great misery—
Diex!—car trop sui jonete.	God!—for I am too young. 20
Je sent les doz maus desoz ma ceinturete:	*I feel the sweet pangs beneath my little girdle:*
Honnis soit de Diu qui me fist nonnete!	*May God curse the one who made me a nun!*

T **Aptatur**

Q 720; L 265-949; MW 1551,1; B 253
Tr 721; L 265-949; MW 680,1; B 142/671/982/1105
Mot 722; L 265-949; MW 819,1; B 1126
O46
Manuscripts: *Mo* 55v-58r♪ (base), *Ba* 29v-30r♪, *I* 243v (256v), Ψ 36r-37r♪
Editions: Coussemaker 1865: no. 44♪; Jacobsthal 1879: 545; Raynaud 1881: 28; Stimming 1906: 37; Aubry 1908, 2: 105♪; Rokseth 1935-39, 2: 76♪; Woledge 1961: 198 (English translation); Anderson 1977: no. 49♪ (English translation); Bec 1978: 21; Tischler 1982: no. 379♪; Tischler 1985: no. 34♪ (English translation); Stanton 1986: 6 (English translation); Smith 1997: 112 (English translation)
Text: Edited by ED-Q
RR: Q 23 est] et — Tr 6 m'] gm' — Mot 5 moi malete *(reading from BaIΨ)*.
TV: Tr 3 Et voi Ψ — 5 chante et volete BaΨ — 9 Jolïetes BaΨ — 12 cuer Ba — 23 Mi tient BaΨ — 25 gries Ba — 26 n'i seroi (sere Ψ) BaΨ — Mot 1 Trop s. *I* — 2 Doucete et p. BaΨ, Doucette p. *I* — 3 Belle p. *I*Ψ — 7 Or d. *I* — 11 mis BaIΨ — 12 la m. *I* — 14 et vilenie pechié Ba*I* — 16 Mettre *I* — 17 mesprist BaIΨ — 19 r. vivre *I*; g. dollor *I* — 20 Diex *missing I* — 21 sans BaΨ — 21-22 *missing I*; De Dé soit honi Ψ — T Optatur Ba.
TN: Manuscripts Ba and Ψ include Tr 721 and Mot 722 only. Manuscript *I* includes Mot 722 only. — Q 11 "These are our solemn rituals." — Tr 7 Such terms as *chant, chançon,* or *chançonete* are commonly used to designate a refrain cited in a narrative or lyric context (Doss-Quinby 1984: 162-63). — 8-10 We italicize this postulated refrain because it is introduced by the term *chançonete,* which can be taken as an indication of exogenous discourse. — 12-13 Contrary to Boogaard (1969), Tischler (1982 and 1985) does not designate these lines as a refrain. — Mot 1-2 Anderson (1977) and Tischler (1982 and 1985) recognize a refrain; this postulated refrain is not listed in Boogaard 1969.
ME: Q 7/2 R after f here omitted — Tr 4+ R after 2li=ag here omitted — 13/4 2li c.perf. — Mot 4+ R after e$_p$ here omitted.

MV: Tr no flats in Ψ — 1/2 f$_p$ Ba — 2/2-2/3 L^p-2li=c^p-cb (no flat) Ba — 3/4 B$_p$=e$_p$ Ba — 4/6 3li=b♭ag Ba; L-R=g-R Ψ — 5/1 L=f Ψ — 5/2 L$_p$=f$_p$ Ba — 6/2-6/3 L^p-SSB=c^p-fed Ba — 7/7 L Ba — 8/2-9/2 3li-L-2li-L-3li=dcb♭-c-ab♭-c-dcb♭ Ba — 8+ no rest Ψ — 10/1-10/2 L-L=f-e Ba — 11/2 L=b (no flat) Ba — 13/1-13/4 B-B-L-2li=c-a-f-fg Ba — 14/2 L=b (no flat) Ba — 15/5-15/6 L^p-2li=e^p-ed Ba — 19/5 L-L^p-R=d-d^p-R Ψ — 20/2 f Ba — 20/5 LL=cc (no rest) Ba — 20+ L=c instead of R Ba — 21/3 no flat Ba — 22/1 e Ba — 24/5 L=f Ba — 25/3 L^p=a^p Ba — Mot 1/3-1/4 S-S=c-b (no flat) Ψ — 1/6 B=a Ψ — 2/3-2/4 B-B=e-d Ba — 2/4-2/5 f-g Ψ — 4+ R Ba — 6/2 L=c Ba — 6/3 no flat BaΨ — 7/6 L-R Ba — 8/6 3li=b♭ag Ba; L$_p$=a$_p$ Ψ — 9/1 B Ψ — 9/3-10/2 L-R-L-2li=g-R-c-b♭a Ba — 9+-10/2 R-L^p-2li=R-c^p-b♭a Ψ — 11/4 L$_p$=e$_p$ Ba — 11/6 no flat BaΨ — 14/3-14/4 B-B=e-d Ba — 14/6 L$_p$=c$_p$ Ψ — 14/8 L=b♭ Ba; 2li=ab (no flat) Ψ — 16/1-16/2 B-B-B=g-g-g for *rendre en* without elision Ψ — 17/4 LL^p-R=dd^p-R Ba — 19/1 e Ba — 19/9-20/1 3li-LL^p-LL-R=b♭ag-aa^p-cc-R Ψ — 20/1 LL$_p$-R=cc$_p$-R Ba — 20/2 f Ba — 20/5 no flat Ba — 20/6 L$_p$-L=a$_p$-f Ba — 21/6 B=a Ψ — 22/6-22/7 B-L^p=b♭-g^p Ba — 22/6 B=a Ψ — T no flats in Ψ — 5-7 4li=fgaf Ψ — 29-31 2li-2li=fg-gf Ψ — 37-39 4li=fgaf Ψ — 62-63 L-L=g-f Ba — 69-71 4li=fgaf Ψ — 94 L=g Ba — 101-3 4li=fgaf Ψ.

MC: The late thirteenth-century music theorist Magister Lambertus cited verses 7 and 24 of the triplum in his *Tractatus de musica.*

MOTET TEXTS WITHOUT MUSIC

These pieces are among the 101 compositions (37 rondeaux and 64 so-called motets entés) that constitute the last series of songs recorded in manuscript *I.* This compilation is known for its organization by genre and form, but unlike all other groups of lyrics in *I,* this section is not demarcated by an introductory rubric (such as "ci en comancent les balletes"), nor is it preceded by an *abecelaire,* or index. Four of the 64 compositions have concordances in the section of monophonic songs with the rubric "ci commencent li motet enté" in manuscript *N* (see Ludwig 1910: 307-13), and these works in *I* also have been labeled *motets entés* by modern scholars, even though the presence and use of attested refrains are not consistent in the collection in *I* (see Everist 1994: 14, 76-89). Fourteen of the texts are found in motets with music (in *Mo, W2,* and *T*), although because manuscript *I* does not preserve music, it records no tenors.

72
Motet

L'abe c'apeirt au jor,	The dawn that heralds the day,
Ki la nuit depairt,	Dispelling the night,
Mi fait soffrir grant dollor,	Makes me suffer great pain,

Can cilz de moi se depairt	Since the one I would fain love
Cui je tant amaixe.	Parts from me. 5
Pleüst ore a saint Jaike	May it now please Saint James
Ke nuns ne nos puist veoir ne reprandre	That no one see or reproach us
Et la nuit durast trante,	And that one night might last thirty,
S'avroit chascuns son desir!	So we each might have our desire!
Ne puet estre ke partir	It cannot be that 10
Vos covient, amins, de moi;	You must part from me, my love;
Et saichiés en bone foi,	And know in good faith
Ke malz nos fait, Dex li dont pix,	That he does us harm—may God give him worse!—
Ki moi et vous depart, dous amins!	Whoever separates me and you, sweet love!

Mot 1099; L 265-960; MW 1242,2; B 1207

Manuscript: *I* 244r-v (257r-v)

Editions: Raynaud 1883: 4; Hatto 1965: 375 (English translation); Bec 1978: 25; Lea 1982: 96 (German translation); Tischler 1982: no. 388

Text: Edited by WP

RR: 8 durait *(em. Raynaud)*.

DF: Lorraine, including *a* for *au* or *al* before consonant, as in *abe* (1); *ai* for *a*, as in *depairt* (2, 4), *Jaike* (6), *saichiés* (12); *an* for *en*, as in *reprandre* (7), *trante* (8); *ei* for tonic *e*, as in *apeirt* (1); *x* for *s(s)* as in *amaixe* (5), *pix* (13); *amins* (11, 14) for *amis*; *nuns* (7) for *nus*.

TN: 6 Possibly Saint James of Toul, who was born in Bertigny, Haute-Marne (Lorraine), and died in Dijon in 769. Prior to his elevation to the episcopacy in 756, Bishop James of Toul was a Benedictine monk in Hornbach Abbey in the diocese of Metz. Or, perhaps, Saint James the Less, also called the Younger, patron of the dying. His feast day was celebrated on May 1, a date associated with joyful festivities that in the Middle Ages included singing, dancing, and choosing a lover.

73
Motet

Osteis lou moi,	*Take it off,*
L'anelet dou doi!	*This ring on my finger!*
Avoir pas vilains ne me doit,	A boor should not have me,
Car, bien sai, cous en seroit	For I know well he would end up a cuckold
S'avocke moi	If he were with me 5
Longement estoit;	For long;
Departir m'an vuel orandroit,	I want to leave him right now,
Je ne suix pas mariee a droit.	*This marriage is not right.*

Mot 1100; L 265-1289; MW 4,9; B 1463
Manuscript: *I* 244v (257v)
Editions: Bartsch 1870: 367; Raynaud 1883: 5; Tischler 1982: no. 389
Text: Edited by WP
DF: Lorraine, including *ei* for tonic *e,* as in *Osteis* (1); *an* for *en,* as in *an* (7), *orandroit*
(7); *lou* (1) for *le; dou* (2) for *del.*

74

Motet

Trop suis jonette, maris,	I am too young for you, husband;
Por vos; trop fut anfantis	It was too foolish
K'il nos fist assembleir,	To join us together,
Car je ne poroie	For I could not
Teil vie meneir,	Lead such a life,
Ne si ne savroie	Nor could I
Ma joie oblïeir,	Forget my joy,
Ce seroit enfance,	That would be foolish,
Et si ne m'an sai	So I do not know
Coment deporteir:	How to behave.
S'an suis en doutance,	I am in doubt,
En dotance.	In doubt.

(line numbers 5 and 10 appear in the left margin)

Mot 1124; L 265-1713; MW 529,1; B 1818
Manuscript: *I* 246v (258*bis*v)
Editions: Raynaud 1883: 17; Tischler 1982: no. 415
Text: Edited by WP
DF: Lorraine, including *an* for *en,* as in *anfantis* (2), *an* (11); *ei* for tonic *e,* as in
assembleir (3), *Teil* (5), *meneir* (5), *oblïeir* (7), *deporteir* (10).

75

Motet

Je ne serai plus amiette	*I will no longer be Robin's*
Robin, car il ne lou desert;	*Friend,* since he does not deserve it,
Car il fait tout en apert	For he does openly
Chose dont il me corrouce.	Something that angers me.
Cuide il je ne voie goute	Does he think I see nothing
Ou me welt il aveuleir?	Or does he mean to offend me?

(line number 5 appears in the left margin)

Je lou vix l'autrier ribeir	I saw him the other day fooling around,
Et escoler une gairce.	Seducing a girl.
De moi ait perdut la graice:	He has lost favor with me;
Voicet aillors flaioleir:	He can go play his flute elsewhere:
Ne revaigne plus ver mi,	He cannot come back my way,
Trop ait demoreit.	*He has stayed away too long.*

Mot 1129; L 265-914; MW 1508,1; B 1454

Manuscript: *I* 247r (259r)

Editions: Bartsch 1870: 212; Raynaud 1883: 19; Tischler 1982: no. 421

Text: Edited by WP

RR: 2 lou me d. *(em. Bartsch).*

DF: Lorraine, including *ai* for *a,* as in *gairce* (8), *graice* (9); *ei* for tonic *e,* as in *aveuleir* (6), *ribeir* (7), *flaioleir* (10); preservation of final *t,* as in *perdut* (9), *demoreit* (12); *w* for *vu,* as in *welt* (6); *c* for *s,* as in *Voicet* (10); *x* for *s,* as in *vix* (7); *lou* (2) for *le;* 3rd-pers. sing. pres. ind. *ait* (9, 12) for *a;* 3rd-pers. sing. pres. subj. *Voicet* (10) for *voise.* Picard *mi* (11) for *moi.*

CONCORDANCE OF SONG AND MOTET NUMBERS

Raynaud 1884 and Spanke 1955	This Book	Linker 1979	Mölk and Wolfzettel 1972	Boogaard 1969[a]	Ludwig 1910 and Gennrich 1958a
21	27	106-4	861	552	—
47a	37	265-651	362	679	—
59a=983	19	265-455	502	469	—
100	22	265-990	2024	1040	—
191	28	265-939	596	—	—
335	12	240-58	1279	—	—
365	10	265-52	2354	—	—
386	31	265-154	410	193	—
498	16	223-11	666	1427	820
517	14	265-973	801	—	—
746a	38	265-919	304	1659	—
747	35	265-978	78	123	—
856	24	265-1290	2364	1152	—
876=878	9	203-2	1802	—	—
931	4	53 & 84-31	685	—	—
944	6	242-2	1765	—	—
970	21	265-578	2210	802	—
1013	20	265-498	382	507	—
1029	30	265-665	2240	892	—
1054	8	242-4	1883	—	—
1074	5	265-380	2241	—	—
1112	3	246-1	1986	—	—
1283	13	265-534	923	—	—
1338	7	242-3	1921	—	—
1354	11	133-55	2084	—	—
1451	15	178-1	964	—	—
1481	29	65-12	369	1453	—
1564	33	265-1346	417	1515	—
1604a	36	265-117	371	1508	—
1640	18	57-1	2344	—	—
1646	39	265-1746	311	1223	—
1744	1	176-1	2286	—	—
1934	17	265-1326	1087	—	—
1936a=2076	40	265-691	348	1238	—
1937	23	265-1235	827	1716	—
1962	2	172 & 265-1100	—	2287	—

Raynaud 1884 and Spanke 1955	This Book	Linker 1979	Mölk and Wolfzettel 1972	Boogaard 1969[a]	Ludwig 1910 and Gennrich 1958a
1995	34	34-2	785	134, 1009, 1497, 1666, 377, 13	—
1999a	25	265-1528	489	1593	—
2048	32	265-1154	384	1325	—
2069	26	265-1703	542	1809, 1859	—
—	41	265-19	266	168; 65	—
—	42	265-127	281	167; 179	—
—	43	265-766	135	131; 863	—
—	44	265-758	276	184; 822	—
—	45	265-768	134	191; 868	—
—	46	265-796	115	143; 905	—
—	47	265-826	132	149; 1004	—
—	48	265-905	720	166; 1081	—
—	49	265-1283	169	169; 1454	—
—	50	265-1636	352	193; 1749	—
—	51	265-1673	124	175; 1789	—
—	52	265-1742	719	171; 1853	—
—	53	265-373	67,1	357	156
—	54	265-146	934,1	189	241
—	55	265-879	1151,1	—	426
—	56	265-808	381,8	933	436
—	57	265-202	192,21	—	528
—	58	265-234	1044,1	1585	814
—	59	265-53	424,1	1555	829a
—	60	265-516	1330,1	—	176
—	60	265-516	599,1	387, 1027, 1494	177
—	61	265-1401	673,12	783	192
—	61	265-1401	850,3	—	193
—	62	265-1480	653,1	—	207
—	62	265-1480	1058,1	804, 814, 844, 1141, 1810	208
—	63	265-1179	614,1	1346	297
—	63	265-1179	400	1633, 1879	298
—	64	265-1375	473,1	—	354
—	64	265-1375	1129,1	1514	353
—	65	265-932	908,1	—	465
—	65	265-932	1126,1	—	466
—	66	265-911	933,3	42, 568	573
—	66	265-911	143,1	43	574
—	67	265-1221	1085,1	53	736

Raynaud 1884 and Spanke 1955	This Book	Linker 1979	Mölk and Wolfzettel 1972	Boogaard 1969[a]	Ludwig 1910 and Gennrich 1958a
—	67	265-1221	38,1	—	737
—	68	265-126	1317,1	1662	845
—	68	265-126	1492,1	824, 1789	846
—	69	265-1627	349,1	1531	908
—	69	265-1627	204,1	1531	909
—	70	265-422	391,1	—	909c
—	70	265-422	1395,1	—	909d
—	70	265-290	1463,1	—	512
—	71	265-949	1551,1	253	720
—	71	265-949	680,1	142, 671, 982, 1105	721
—	71	265-949	819,1	1126	722
—	72	265-960	1242,2	1207	1099
—	73	265-1289	4,9	1463	1100
—	74	265-1713	529,1	1818	1124
—	75	265-914	1508,1	1454	1129

[a] In the case of rondeaux (our song nos. 41–52), the rondeau number appears first, followed by the refrain number.

Bibliography

Alvar, Carlos, ed. and trans. 1982. *Poesía de trovadores, trouvères, minnesinger (de principios del siglo XII a fines del siglo XIII)*. 2nd ed. Madrid: Alianza.

Anderson, Gordon, ed. 1977. *Compositions of the Bamberg Manuscript*. Corpus Mensurabilis Musicæ 75. [Stuttgart]: American Institute of Musicology.

Anderson, Gordon, and Elizabeth Close, eds. and trans. 1975. *Motets of the Manuscript La Clayette*. Corpus Mensurabilis Musicæ 68. [Rome]: American Institute of Musicology.

Anglès, Higini, ed. 1973. *Las canciones del rey Teobaldo*. Pamplona, Spain: Institución Príncipe de Viana.

Aubrey, Elizabeth. 1996. *The Music of the Troubadours*. Bloomington and Indianapolis: Indiana University Press.

———. 1997. "The Dialectic Between Occitania and France in the Thirteenth Century." *Early Music History* 16: 1-53.

———. 2000. "Sources, MS, §III, 3: Secular Monophony, French." In *The New Grove Dictionary of Music and Musicians*. 2nd ed. Ed. Stanley Sadie. London: Macmillan. Forthcoming.

Aubry, Pierre. 1909. "Refrains et rondeaux du XIIIᵉ siècle." In *Riemann-Festschrift*. Leipzig: Max Hesses Verlag. 213-29.

Aubry, Pierre, ed. 1908. *Cent motets du XIIIᵉ siècle, publiés d'après le Manuscrit Ed. IV.6 de Bamberg*. 3 vols. Paris: Rouart-Lerolle; Paris: Paul Geuthner. Reprint, New York: Broude Brothers, 1964.

Auda, Antoine. 1953. *Les "Motets Wallons" du manuscrit de Turin: Vari 42*. 2 vols. Brussels: Published by the author.

Badel, Pierre-Yves, ed. and trans. 1995. *Adam de la Halle, Œuvres complètes*. Paris: Librairie Générale Française.

Bagley, C[ynthia]. 1966. "*Cantigas de amigo* and *cantigas de amor*." *Bulletin of Hispanic Studies* 43: 241-52.

Baldwin, John. 1997. " 'Once There Was an Emperor . . .': A Political Reading of the Romances of Jean Renart." In *Jean Renart and the Art of Romance: Essays on Guillaume de Dole*. Ed. Nancy Vine Durling. Gainesville: University Press of Florida. 45-82.

Baret, Eugène. 1867. *Les troubadours et leur influence sur la littérature du midi de l'Europe*. 3rd ed. Paris: Didier.

Bartsch, Karl. 1884. "Geistliche Umdichtung weltlicher Lieder." *Zeitschrift für romanische Philologie* 8: 570-85.

Bartsch, Karl, ed. 1870. *Altfranzösische Romanzen und Pastourellen/Romances et pastourelles françaises des XIIe et XIIIe siècles*. Leipzig, Germany: Vogel. Reprint, Darmstadt, Germany: Wissenschaftliche Buchgesellschaft, 1967. Reprint, Geneva: Slatkine, 1973.

———. 1920. *Chrestomathie de l'ancien français (VIIIe–XVe siècles)*. 12th ed. revised by Leo Wiese. Leipzig, Germany: Vogel. Reprint, New York: Hafner, 1969. Reprint, New York: G. E. Stechert, 1988.

Baumgartner, Emmanuèle. 1990. *La harpe et l'épée: Tradition et renouvellement dans le Tristan en prose*. Moyen Âge. Paris: SEDES.

Baumgartner, Emmanuèle, and Françoise Ferrand, eds. and trans. 1983. *Poèmes d'amour des XIIe et XIIIe siècles*. Bibliothèque Médiévale 1581. Paris: Union Générale d'Éditions.

Bec, Pierre. 1969. "Quelques réflexions sur la poésie lyrique médiévale: Problèmes et essai de caractérisation." In *Mélanges offerts à Rita Lejeune*. 2 vols. Gembloux, Belgium: Duculot. 2: 1309-29.

———. 1977-78. *La lyrique française au moyen âge (XIIe- XIIIe siècles): Contribution à une typologie des genres poétiques médiévaux*. Vol. 1: *Études*. Vol. 2: *Textes*. Publications du Centre d'Études Supérieures de Civilisation Médiévale de l'Université de Poitiers 6-7. Paris: Picard.

———. 1979. " 'Trobairitz' et chansons de femme: Contribution à la connaissance du lyrisme féminin au moyen âge." *Cahiers de Civilisation Médiévale* 22: 235-62.

Bec, Pierre, ed. 1995. *Chants d'amour des femmes troubadours*. Paris: Éditions Stock.

Beck, Jean. 1927. *Les chansonniers des troubadours et des trouvères, publiés en facsimilé et transcrits en notation moderne*. Vol. 1, pt. 1: *Reproduction phototypique du Chansonnier Cangé, Paris, Bibliothèque Nationale, ms. français no. 846*. Vol. 1, pt. 2: *Transcription des chansons du Chansonnier Cangé, notes et commentaires*. Corpus Cantilenarum Medii Aevi I, 1. Paris: Honoré Champion; Philadelphia: University of Pennsylvania Press. Reprint, New York: Broude Brothers, 1964. Reprint, Geneva: Slatkine, 1976.

Beck, Jean, and Louise Beck. 1938. *Les chansonniers des troubadours et des trouvères*. Vol. 2, pt. 1: *Le Manuscrit du Roi, fonds français no. 844 de la Bibliothèque Nationale*. Vol. 2, pt. 2: *Analyse et description raisonnées du manuscrit restauré*. Corpus Cantilenarum Medii Aevi I, 2. Philadelphia: University of Pennsylvania Press. Reprint, New York, Broude Brothers, 1970.

Bédier, Joseph. 1896. "Les fêtes de mai et les commencemens de la poésie lyrique au moyen âge." *Revue des Deux Mondes* 135: 146-72.

———. 1910. "Un feuillet récemment retrouvé d'un chansonnier français du XIIIe siècle." In *Mélanges de philologie romane et d'histoire littéraire offerts à M. Maurice Wilmotte*. 2 vols. Paris: Honoré Champion. 895-922. Reprint, Geneva: Slatkine, 1972.

Bédier, Joseph, ed. 1912. *Les chansons de Colin Muset*. Paris: Honoré Champion.

———. 1938. *Les chansons de Colin Muset*. 2nd ed. Paris: Honoré Champion.

Bédier, Joseph, and Pierre Aubry, eds. and trans. 1909. *Les chansons de croisade avec leurs mélodies.* Paris: Honoré Champion. Reprint, New York: Burt Franklin, 1971. Reprint, Geneva: Slatkine, 1974.

Benskin, Michael, Tony Hunt, and Ian Short. 1992-95. "Un nouveau fragment du *Tristan* de Thomas." *Romania* 113: 289-318.

Benton, John. 1968. "Clio and Venus: An Historical View of Medieval Love." In *The Meaning of Courtly Love.* Ed. F. X. Newman. Albany: State University of New York Press. 19-42.

Berger, Roger. 1981. *Littérature et société arrageoises au XIIIe siècle: Les chansons et dits artésiens.* Mémoires de la Commission Départementale des Monuments Historiques du Pas-de-Calais 21. Arras: Commission Départementale des Monuments Historiques du Pas-de-Calais.

Bergner, Heinz, Paul Klopsch, Ulrich Müller, Dietmar Rieger, and Friedrich Wolfzettel. 1983. *Lyrik des Mittelalters: Probleme und Interpretationen.* Vol. 1: *Die mittellateinische Lyrik, die altprovenzalische Lyrik, die mittelalterliche Lyrik Nordfrankreichs.* Universal-Bibliothek 7896. Stuttgart: Philipp Reclam.

Bertoni, Giulio. 1917. "La sezione francese del manoscritto provenzale estense." *Archivum Romanicum* 1: 307-410.

———. 1919. "Le tenzoni del frammento francese di Berna A. 95." *Archivum Romanicum* 3: 43-61.

Blakeslee, Merritt. 1989. "La chanson de femme, les *Héroïdes,* et la *canso* occitane à voix de femme: Considérations sur l'originalité des *trobairitz.*" In *Hommage à Jean-Charles Payen, "Farai chansoneta novele": Essais sur la liberté créatrice au moyen âge.* Ed. Huguette Legros, Jean-Louis Backès, Jean Batany, Emmanuèle Baumgartner, Michel Rousse, and Michel Zuinghedau. Caen: Université de Caen. 67-75.

Bloch, Marc. 1939-40. *La société féodale.* 2 vols. Paris: Albin Michel.

Boer, C[ornelis] de, ed. 1909. *Philomena, conte raconté d'après Ovide par Chrétien de Troyes.* Paris: Librairie Paul Geuthner.

———. 1921. *Piramus et Tisbé: Poème du XIIe siècle.* Classiques Français du Moyen Âge 26. Paris: Honoré Champion.

Boogaard, Nico van den. 1969. *Rondeaux et refrains du XIIe siècle au début du XIVe.* Bibliothèque Française et Romane D, 3. Paris: Klincksieck.

Bossuat, Robert, Louis Pichard, and Guy Raynaud de Lage. 1964. *Dictionnaire des lettres françaises: Le moyen âge.* Paris: Arthème Fayard.

Boucherie, A[natole]. 1872. "Fragment d'une anthologie picarde (XIIIe siècle)." *Revue des Langues Romanes* 3: 311-36.

Boulton, Maureen. 1993. *The Song in the Story: Lyric Insertions in French Narrative Fiction, 1200-1400.* Philadelphia: University of Pennsylvania Press.

———. 1997. "Lyric Insertions and the Reversal of Romance Conventions in Jean Renart's *Roman de la rose* or *Guillaume de Dole.*" In *Jean Renart and the Art of Romance: Essays on Guillaume de Dole.* Ed. Nancy Vine Durling. Gainesville: University Press of Florida. 85-104.

Brahney, Kathleen, ed. and trans. 1989. *The Lyrics of Thibaut de Champagne.* Garland Library of Medieval Literature A, 41. New York: Garland Publishing.

Brakelmann, Julius. 1867. "Die altfranzösische Liederhandschrift Nro. 389 der Stadtbibliothek zu Bern." *Archiv für das Studium der neueren Sprachen und Literaturen* 41: 339-76.

———. 1868a. "Die altfranzösische Liederhandschrift Nro. 389 der Stadtbibliothek zu Bern." *Archiv für das Studium der neueren Sprachen und Literaturen* 42: 241-392.

———. 1868b. "Die altfranzösische Liederhandschrift Nro. 389 der Stadtbibliothek zu Bern." *Archiv für das Studium der neueren Sprachen und Literaturen* 43: 241-394.

Brakelmann, Julius, ed. 1870-91. *Les plus anciens chansonniers français (XIIᵉ siècle).* Paris: Émile Bouillon.

Brittain, Fred, ed. 1951. *The Medieval Latin and Romance Lyric to A.D. 1300.* 2nd ed. Cambridge: Cambridge University Press.

Bruckner, Matilda Tomaryn. 1994. "Debatable Fictions: The *Tensos* of the *Trobairitz.*" In *Literary Aspects of Courtly Culture: Selected Papers from the Seventh Triennial Congress of the International Courtly Literature Society.* Ed. Donald Maddox and Sara Sturm-Maddox. Cambridge, England: D. S. Brewer. 19-28.

Bruckner, Matilda Tomaryn, Laurie Shepard, and Sarah White, eds. and trans. 1995. *Songs of the Women Troubadours.* Garland Library of Medieval Literature A, 97. New York: Garland Publishing.

Brumana Pascale, Biancamaria. 1975-76. "Le musiche nei jeux-partis francesi." *Annali della Facoltà di Lettere e Filosofia dell'Università di Perugia* 13: 509-72.

Bruneau, Charles. 1925. "Les parlers lorrains anciens et modernes: Bibliographie critique (1908-1924)." *Revue de Linguistique Romane* 1: 348-413.

Buffum, Douglas, ed. 1928. *Le Roman de la Violette ou de Gerart de Nevers par Gerbert de Montreuil.* Paris: Honoré Champion.

Burns, E. Jane, Sarah Kay, Roberta Krueger, and Helen Solterer. 1996. "Feminism and the Discipline of Old French Studies: *Une Bele Disjointure.*" In *Medievalism and the Modernist Temper.* Ed. R. Howard Bloch and Stephen Nichols. Baltimore: Johns Hopkins University Press. 225-66.

Carey, Richard, ed. 1972. *Jean de le Mote, Le parfait du paon.* Studies in the Romance Languages and Literatures 118. Chapel Hill: University of North Carolina Press.

Chambers, Frank. 1989. *"Las trobairitz soiseubudas."* In *The Voice of the Trobairitz: Perspectives on the Women Troubadours.* Ed. William Paden. Philadelphia: University of Pennsylvania Press. 45-60.

Chastel, André. 1959. *Trésors de la poésie médiévale.* Paris: Le Club Français du Livre.

Chaurand, Jacques. 1972. *Introduction à la dialectologie française.* Études 302. Paris: Bordas.

Coldwell, Maria. 1981. *"Guillaume de Dole* and Medieval Romances with Musical Interpolations." *Musica Disciplina* 35: 55-86.

———. 1986. *"Jougleresses* and *Trobairitz:* Secular Musicians in Medieval France." In *Women Making Music: The Western Art Tradition, 1150-1950.* Ed. Jane Bowers and Judith Tick. Urbana: University of Illinois Press. 39-61.

Collins, Fletcher, Jr., Robert Cook, and Roger Harmon, eds. and trans. 1982. *A Medieval Songbook: Troubadour and Trouvère.* Charlottesville: University Press of Virginia.

Contini, Gianfranco. 1977. "Una scheda curiosa." In *Studi filologici letterari e storici in memoria di Guido Favati.* Ed. Giorgio Varanini and Palmiro Pinagli. 2 vols. Medioevo e Umanesimo 28-29. Padua: Antenore. 1: 225-31.

———. 1978. "Fragments inconnus d'un ancien chansonnier français à Einsiedeln." In *Orbis mediaevalis: Mélanges de langue et de littérature médiévales offerts à Reto Radulf Bezzola à l'occasion de son quatre-vingtième anniversaire.* Ed. Georges Güntert, Marc-René Jung, and Kurt Ringger. Bern: Francke. 29-59.

Coussemaker, Edmond de. 1865. *L'art harmonique aux XIIe et XIIIe siècles.* Paris: A. Durand. Reprint, New York: Broude Brothers, 1964.

Coussemaker, Edmond de, ed. 1872. *Œuvres complètes du trouvère Adam de la Halle (poésies et musique) publiées sous les auspices de la Société des sciences, des lettres et des arts de Lille.* Paris: A. Durand et Pédone-Lauriel. Reprint, Ridgewood, N.J.: Gregg Press, 1965. Reprint, Geneva: Slatkine, 1970.

Crapelet, G[eorges] A[drien], ed. and trans. 1829. *L'histoire du Châtelain de Coucy et de la Dame de Fayel.* Paris: Imprimerie de Crapelet.

Crépet, Eugène, ed. 1861. *Les poëtes français: Recueil des chefs-d'œuvre lyriques de la poésie française depuis les origines jusqu'à nos jours.* Vol. 1: *Première période: Du XIIe au XIVe siècle.* Paris: Gide. Reprint, Paris: Quantin, 1863.

Curtis, Renée, ed. 1985. *Le Roman de Tristan en prose, tome III.* Cambridge, England: D. S. Brewer.

Delbouille, Maurice. 1933. "A propos des jeux-partis lorrains du chansonnier Douce 308 (I)." *Revue Belge de Philologie et d'Histoire* 21: 132-40.

Delbouille, Maurice, ed. 1932. *Jacques Bretel, Le Tournoi de Chauvency.* Bibliothèque de la Faculté de Philosophie et Lettres de l'Université de Liège 49. Paris: Droz.

Diez, Friedrich. 1863. *Über die erste portugiesische Kunst- und Hofpoesie.* Bonn: E. Weber.

Dijkstra, Cathrynke. 1995. *La chanson de croisade: Étude thématique d'un genre hybride.* Amsterdam: Schiphouwer en Brinkman.

Dinaux, Arthur, ed. 1836, 1839, 1843, 1863. *Trouvères, jongleurs et ménestrels du nord de la France et du midi de la Belgique.* Vol. 1: *Les trouvères cambrésiens.* Vol. 2: *Les trouvères de la Flandre et du Tournaisis.* Vol. 3: *Les trouvères artésiens.* Vol. 4: *Les trouvères brabançons, hainuyers, liégeois et namurois.* Paris: Tréchener. Reprint, Geneva: Slatkine, 1969-70.

Di Stefano, Giuseppe. 1991. *Dictionnaire des locutions en moyen français.* Bibliothèque du Moyen Français 1. Montreal: Éditions CERES.

Dittmer, Luther. 1960. *Paris 13521 and 11411: Facsimile, Introduction, Index and Transcriptions from the Manuscripts Paris, Bibl. Nat. nouv. acq. fr. 13521 (La Clayette) and lat. 11411.* Publications of Mediaeval Musical Manuscripts 4. Brooklyn: Institute of Mediaeval Music.

———. 1969. *Facsimile Reproduction of the Manuscript Wolfenbüttel 1099 Helmstadiensis- (1206) W2.* 2nd ed. Publications of Mediaeval Musical Manuscripts 2. Brooklyn: Institute of Mediaeval Music.

Doss-Quinby, Eglal. 1984. *Les refrains chez les trouvères du XIIe siècle au début du XIVe.* American University Studies 2, vol. 17. New York: Peter Lang.

———. 1994. *The Lyrics of the Trouvères: A Research Guide (1970–1990).* Garland

Medieval Bibliographies 17. Garland Reference Library of the Humanities 1423.
New York: Garland Publishing.

———. 1998. "Songs of the Women *Trouvères.*" *Metamorphoses: The Journal of the Five College Seminar on Literary Translation* 6.1: 132–43.

———. 1999. "*Rolan, de ceu ke m'avez / Parti dirai mon samblant:* The Feminine Voice in the Old French *jeu-parti.*" *Neophilologus* 83: 497–516.

Doutrepont, Auguste. 1890. *La clef d'amors: Texte critique avec introduction, appendice et glossaire.* Bibliotheca Normannica 5. Halle: Niemeyer.

Dragonetti, Roger. 1960. *La technique poétique des trouvères dans la chanson courtoise: Contribution à l'étude de la rhétorique médiévale.* Brugge: De Tempel. Reprint, Geneva: Slatkine, 1979.

Dronke, Peter, ed. 1984. *Women Writers of the Middle Ages: Critical Texts from Perpetua (†203) to Marguerite Porete (†1310).* Cambridge: Cambridge University Press.

———. 1996. *The Medieval Lyric.* 3rd ed. Woodbridge, Suffolk: D. S. Brewer.

Dubois, Raymond. 1957. *Le domaine picard: Délimitation et carte systématique dressée pour servir à l'inventaire général du picard et autres travaux de géographie linguistique.* Arras: Archives du Pas-de-Calais.

Dufournet, Jean, ed. and trans. 1989. *Anthologie de la poésie lyrique française des XIIᵉ et XIIIᵉ siècles.* Poésie 232. Paris: Gallimard.

Du Méril, Édélestand. 1850. *Mélanges archéologiques et littéraires.* Paris: Franck.

Earnshaw, Doris. 1988. *The Female Voice in Medieval Romance Lyric.* American University Studies 2, vol. 68. New York: Peter Lang.

Einhorn, E. 1974. *Old French: A Concise Handbook.* Cambridge: Cambridge University Press.

Epstein, Marcia, ed. and trans. 1997. *Prions en chantant: Devotional Songs of the Trouvères.* Toronto Medieval Texts and Translations 11. Toronto: University of Toronto Press.

Everist, Mark. 1989. *Polyphonic Music in Thirteenth-Century France: Aspects of Sources and Distribution.* Outstanding Dissertations in Music from British Universities. New York: Garland Publishing.

———. 1994. *French Motets in the Thirteenth Century: Music, Poetry, and Genre.* Cambridge: Cambridge University Press.

Faral, Edmond. 1924. *Les arts poétiques du XIIᵉ et du XIIIᵉ siècle: Recherches et documents sur la technique littéraire du moyen âge.* Bibliothèque de l'École des Hautes Études 238. Paris: Honoré Champion. Reprint, Geneva: Slatkine, 1982.

Fauchet, Claude. 1581. *Recueil de l'origine de la langue et poesie françoise, ryme et romans, plus les noms et sommaire des oeuvres de CXXVII. poetes François, vivans avant l'an M. CCC.* Paris: Mamert Patisson Imprimeur du Roy. Reprint, Geneva: Slatkine, 1972.

Ferrante, Joan. 1980. "The Education of Women in the Middle Ages in Theory, Fact, and Fantasy." In *Beyond Their Sex: Learned Women of the European Past.* Ed. Patricia Labalme. New York: New York University Press. 9–42.

———. 1989. "Notes Toward the Study of a Female Rhetoric in the Trobairitz." In *The Voice of the Trobairitz: Perspectives on the Women Troubadours.* Ed. William Paden. Philadelphia: University of Pennsylvania Press. 63–72.

Fiset, Franz. 1906. "Das altfranzösische Jeu-Parti." *Romanische Forschungen* 19: 407-544.

Foster, Genette. 1977. "The Iconology of Musical Instruments and Musical Performance in Thirteenth-Century French Manuscript Illuminations." Ph.D. diss., City University of New York.

Fotitch, Tatiana, and Ruth Steiner, eds. 1974. *Les lais du Roman de Tristan en prose d'après le manuscrit de Vienne 2542.* Münchener romanistische Arbeiten 38. Munich: Wilhelm Fink.

Foulet, Alfred, and Mary Blakely Speer. 1979. *On Editing Old French Texts.* Edward C. Armstrong Monographs on Medieval Literature 1. Lawrence: Regents Press of Kansas.

Foulet, Lucien. 1928. *Petite syntaxe de l'ancien français.* 3rd ed. Classiques Français du Moyen Âge 21. Paris: Honoré Champion.

Fresco, Karen, ed. 1988. *Gillebert de Berneville, Les poésies.* Textes Littéraires Français 357. Geneva: Droz.

Gally, Michèle. 1986. "Disputer l'amour: Les Arrageois et le jeu-parti." *Romania* 107: 55-76.

Gaunt, Simon. 1988. "Sexual Difference and the Metaphor of Language in a Troubadour Poem." *Modern Language Review* 83: 297-313.

———. 1995. *Gender and Genre in Medieval French Literature.* Cambridge: Cambridge University Press.

Gelzer, Heinrich, ed. 1953. *Altfranzösisches Lesebuch.* Heidelberg: C. Winter.

Gennrich, Friedrich. 1918. *Musikwissenschaft und romanische Philologie.* Halle: Niemeyer.

———. 1924-25. "Sieben Melodien zu mittelhochdeutschen Minneliedern." *Zeitschrift für Musikwissenschaft* 7: 65-98.

———. 1926-27. "Trouvèrelieder und Motettenrepertoire." *Zeitschrift für Musikwissenschaft* 9: 8-39 and 65-85.

———. 1932. *Grundriß einer Formenlehre des mittelalterlichen Liedes.* Halle: Niemeyer.

———. 1937. "Grundsätzliches zu den Troubadour- und Trouvèreweisen." *Zeitschrift für romanische Philologie* 57: 31-56.

———. 1958a. *Bibliographie der ältesten französischen und lateinischen Motetten.* Summa Musicæ Medii Aevi 2. Darmstadt, Germany: Published by the author.

———. 1958b. *Ein altfranzösischer Motettenkodex: Faksimile-Ausgabe der Hs La Clayette, Paris, Bibl. Nat. nouv. acq. fr. 13521.* Summa Musicae Medii Aevi 6. Darmstadt, Germany: Published by the author.

Gennrich, Friedrich, ed. 1921-27. *Rondeaux, Virelais und Balladen.* Vol. 1: *Texte.* Gesellschaft für romanische Literatur 43. Dresden: Gedruckt für die Gesellschaft für romanische Literatur. Vol. 2: *Materialien, Literaturnachweise, Refrainverzeichnis.* Gesellschaft für romanische Literatur 47. Göttingen: Gedruckt für die Gesellschaft für romanische Literatur.

———. 1925. *Die altfranzösische Rotrouenge.* Halle: Niemeyer.

———. 1955-56. *Altfranzösische Lieder.* 2 vols. Tübingen: Niemeyer.

———. 1958c. *Exempla altfranzösischer Lyrik: 40 altfranzösische Lieder.*

Musikwissenschaftliche Studien-Bibliothek 17. Darmstadt, Germany: Published by the author. Reprint, Langen bei Frankfurt, 1965.

Gérold, Théodore. 1932. *La musique au moyen âge*. Classiques Français du Moyen Âge 73. Paris: Honoré Champion. Reprint, 1983.

Gleason, Harold, ed. 1942. *Examples of Music Before 1400*. Rochester: Eastman School of Music of the University of Rochester.

Godefroy, Frédéric. 1880-1902. *Dictionnaire de l'ancienne langue française et de tous ses dialectes du IXe au XVe siècle*. 10 vols. Paris: Vieweg. Reprint, Paris: Librairie des Sciences et des Arts, 1937-38. Reprint, Nendeln, Liechtenstein: Kraus Reprint, 1969.

Goldin, Frederick, ed. and trans. 1973. *Lyrics of the Troubadours and Trouvères: An Anthology and a History*. Garden City, N.Y.: Anchor-Doubleday. Reprint, Gloucester, Mass.: Peter Smith, 1983.

Gossen, Charles Théodore. 1976. *Grammaire de l'ancien picard*. Paris: Klincksieck.

Greimas, A[lgirdas] J[ulien]. 1968. *Dictionnaire de l'ancien français jusqu'au milieu du XIVe siècle*. 2nd ed. Paris: Larousse.

Grimbert, Joan Tasker. 1999. "Diminishing the Trobairitz, Excluding the Women Trouvères." *Tenso* 14: 23-38.

———. 2001. "Songs by Women and Women's Songs: How Useful Is the Concept of Register?" In *The Court Reconvenes: Selected Proceedings of the Ninth Triennial Congress of the International Courtly Literature Society*. Ed. Chantal Phan, Barbara Altmann, and Carleton Carroll. Cambridge, England: D. S. Brewer. Forthcoming.

Grimm, Jacob. 1811. *Über den altdeutschen Meistergesang*. Göttingen: Heinrich Dieterich. Reprint, Hildesheim: Olms-Weidmann, 1993.

Grossel, Marie-Geneviève. 1994. *Le milieu littéraire en Champagne sous les Thibaudiens (1200-1270)*. 2 vols. Orléans: Paradigme.

Guida, Saverio, ed. and trans. 1992. *Canzoni di crociata*. Biblioteca Medievale 21. Parma: Pratiche Editrice.

Guiraud, Pierre. 1971. *Patois et dialectes français*. "Que sais-je?" 1285. Paris: Presses Universitaires de France.

Hasenohr, Geneviève, and Michel Zink, eds. 1992. *Dictionnaire des lettres françaises: Le moyen âge*. Encyclopédies d'Aujourd'hui. Paris: Livre de Poche.

Hatto, Arthur, ed. 1965. *Eos: An Enquiry into the Theme of Lovers' Meetings and Partings at Dawn in Poetry*. The Hague: Mouton.

Henry, Albert, ed. 1967. *Chrestomathie de la littérature en ancien français*. 4th ed. 2 vols. in 1. Bibliotheca Romanica 3-4. Bern: Francke.

Hervieux, Léopold. 1893-99. *Les fabulistes latins depuis le siècle d'Auguste jusqu'à la fin du moyen âge*. 5 vols. Paris: Firmin-Didot. Reprint, New York: Burt Franklin, 1965.

Heyse, Paul, ed. 1856. *Romanische Inedita auf italiänischen Bibliotheken*. Berlin: Wilhelm Hertz.

Hofmann, Konrad. 1867. "Eine Anzahl altfranzösischer lyrischer Gedichte aus dem Berner Codex 389." In *Sitzungsberichte der Königliche bayerischen Akademie der Wissenschaft zu München*. Munich: Weiss. 486-527.

Huchet, Jean-Charles. 1981. "Nom de femme et écriture féminine au moyen âge: Les *Lais* de Marie de France." *Poétique* 48: 407-30.

———. 1983. "Les femmes troubadours ou la voix critique." *Littérature* 51: 59-90.

Huizinga, Johan. 1950. *Homo ludens: A Study of the Play-Element in Culture.* Boston: Beacon Press.

Huot, Sylvia. 1987. *From Song to Book: The Poetics of Writing in Old French Lyric and Lyrical Narrative Poetry.* Ithaca: Cornell University Press.

———. 1989a. "Voices and Instruments in Medieval French Secular Music: On the Use of Literary Texts as Evidence for Performance Practice." *Musica Disciplina* 43: 63-113.

———. 1989b. "Polyphonic Poetry: The Old French Motet and Its Literary Context." *French Forum* 14: 261-78.

———. 1997. *Allegorical Play in the Old French Motet: The Sacred and the Profane in Thirteenth-Century Polyphony.* Stanford: Stanford University Press.

Jacobsthal, Gustav. 1879. "Die Texte der Liederhandschrift von Montpellier H. 196." *Zeitschrift für romanische Philologie* 3: 526-56.

———. 1880. "Die Texte der Liederhandschrift von Montpellier H. 196." *Zeitschrift für romanische Philologie* 4: 35-64 and 278-317.

Järnström, Edw[ard], and Arthur Långfors, eds. 1927. *Recueil de chansons pieuses du XIIIᵉ siècle.* Vol. 2. Annales Academiæ Scientiarum Fennicæ B, 20. Helsinki: Suomalaisen Tiedeakatemian Toimituksia.

Jeanroy, Alfred. 1889. *Les origines de la poésie lyrique en France au moyen âge.* Paris: Hachette. 4th ed., Paris: Honoré Champion, 1965.

———. 1918. *Bibliographie sommaire des chansonniers français du moyen âge.* Classiques Français du Moyen Âge 18. Paris: Honoré Champion. Reprint, Paris: Honoré Champion, 1965.

———. 1925. *Le chansonnier d'Arras: Reproduction en phototypie.* Société des Anciens Textes Français. Paris: Droz. Reprint, New York: Johnson Reprint, 1968.

Jeanroy, Alfred, and Pierre Aubry. 1909-12. *Le chansonnier de l'Arsenal (trouvères des XIIᵉ et XIIIᵉ siècles): Reproduction phototypique du manuscrit 5198 de la Bibliothèque de l'Arsenal.* 2 vols. in 3. Paris: Geuthner.

Jubinal, Achille. 1838. *Rapport à M. le Ministre de l'instruction publique, suivi de quelques pièces inédites tirées des manuscrits de la bibliothèque de Berne.* Paris: Librairie Spéciale des Sociétés Savantes.

Kasten, Ingrid, ed. and trans. 1990. *Frauenlieder des Mittelalters.* Universal-Bibliothek 8630. Stuttgart: Philipp Reclam.

Keller, Adelbert. 1844. *Romvart: Beiträge zur kunde mittelalterlicher Dichtung aus italiänischen Bibliotheken.* Mannheim: Friedrich Bassermann; Paris: Jules Renouard.

Kelly, Douglas. 1993. *Medieval French Romance.* New York: Twayne Publishers.

Kelly, Henry. 1985. "Gaston Paris's Courteous and Horsely Love." In *The Spirit of the Court: Selected Proceedings of the Fourth Congress of the International Courtly Literature Society (Toronto 1983).* Ed. Glyn Burgess and Robert Taylor. Cambridge, England: D. S. Brewer. 217-23.

Kendrick, Laura. 1988. *The Game of Love: Troubadour Wordplay.* Berkeley: University of California Press.

Kibler, William. 1984. *An Introduction to Old French.* New York: Modern Language Association of America.

Klinck, Anne. 1999. "The Oldest Folk Poetry? Medieval Woman's Song as 'Popular' Lyric." In *From Arabye to Engelond: Medieval Studies in Honour of Mahmoud Manzalaoui on His 75th Birthday.* Ed. A. E. Christa Canitz and Gernot Wieland. Ottawa: University of Ottawa Press. 229-52.

Kooijman, Jacques, ed. and trans. 1974. *Trouvères lorrains: La poésie courtoise en Lorraine au XIIIe siècle.* [Nancy, France]: Seurat.

Laborde, Jean-Benjamin de. 1780. *Essai sur la musique ancienne et moderne.* 4 vols. Paris: Ph.-D. Pierres. Reprint, New York: AMS Press, 1978.

Långfors, Arthur. 1932. "Notice des manuscrits 535 de la Bibliothèque municipale de Metz et 10047 des nouvelles acquisitions du fonds français de la Bibliothèque nationale, suivie de cinq poèmes français sur la parabole des quatre filles de Dieu." *Notices et extraits des manuscrits de la Bibliothèque nationale et autres bibliothèques* 42: 139-291. Paris: Imprimerie Nationale.

Långfors, Arthur, ed. 1926. *Recueil général des jeux-partis français.* Paris: Librairie Ancienne Édouard Champion.

La Ravallière, Lévesque de, ed. 1742. *Les poësies du Roy de Navarre, avec des notes et un glossaire françois.* 2 vols. Paris: Guerin.

La Villemarqué, Hersart de. 1856. "Rapport présenté à Son Excellence M. le Ministre de l'instruction publique et des cultes par M. le vicomte Hersart de la Villemarqué, sur une mission littéraire accomplie en Angleterre pendant les mois d'avril, mai et décembre 1855." *Archives des Missions Scientifiques et Littéraires,* série 1, 5: 89-116.

Lavis, Georges. 1991. "Le jeu-parti français: Jeu de réfutation, d'opposition et de concession." *Medioevo Romanzo* 16: 21-128.

Lazar, Moshé. 1964. *Amour courtois et fin'amors dans la littérature du XIIe siècle.* Paris: Klincksieck.

———. 1995. "Fin'amor." In *A Handbook of the Troubadours.* Ed. F. R. P. Akehurst and Judith Davis. Berkeley: University of California Press. 61-100.

Lea, Elisabeth, ed. and trans. 1982. *Altfranzösische Liebeslyrik.* 2nd ed. Universal-Bibliothek 802. Leipzig: Philipp Reclam. Reprint, 1990.

Lecoy, Félix, ed. 1979. *Jean Renart, Le Roman de la Rose ou de Guillaume de Dole.* Classiques Français du Moyen Âge 91. Paris: Honoré Champion.

Le Gentil, Pierre. 1963. "La strophe zadjalesque, les khardjas et le problème des origines du lyrisme roman." *Romania* 84: 1-27, 209-50, and 409-11.

Lepage, Yvan, ed. 1981. *L'œuvre lyrique de Richard de Fournival.* Publications Médiévales de l'Université d'Ottawa 7. Ottawa: Éditions de l'Université d'Ottawa.

Le Roux de Lincy, Antoine, ed. 1841. *Recueil de chants historiques français depuis le XIIe jusqu'au XVIIIe siècle.* Paris: Charles Gosselin.

———. 1859. *Le livre des proverbes français.* 2nd ed. 2 vols. Paris: Adolphe Delahays. Reprint, Geneva: Slatkine, 1968. Reprint, Paris: Hachette, 1996.

Lindelöf, U[no], and A[xel] Wallensköld, eds. 1901. *Les chansons de Gautier d'Épinal.* Mémoires de la Société Néophilologique de Helsingfors 3. Helsinki: Imprimerie Centrale de Helsingfors.

Linker, Robert. 1979. *A Bibliography of Old French Lyrics.* University, Miss.: Romance Monographs.

Lorenzo Gradín, Pilar. 1990. *La canción de mujer en la lírica medieval.* Monografías da Universidade de Santiago de Compostela 154. Santiago de Compostela, Spain: Servicio de Publicacións e Intercambio Científico da Universidade de Santiago de Compostela.

Lubinski, Fritz. 1908. "Die Unica der Jeux-partis der Oxforder Liederhandschrift (Douce 308)." *Romanische Forschungen* 22: 506-98.

Ludwig, Friedrich. 1910. *Repertorium organorum recentioris et motetorum vetustissimi stili.* Halle: Niemeyer. Revised by Luther Dittmer. 2 vols. in 3. Musicological Studies 7, 17, and 26. New York: Institute of Mediæval Music, 1964-78.

Maillard, Jean, ed. 1967a. *Anthologie de chants de trouvères.* Paris: Éditions Aug. Zurfluh.

———. 1967b. *Charles d'Anjou, Roi-trouvère du XIIIème siècle.* Musicological Studies and Documents 18. [Rome]: American Institute of Musicology.

Mary, André, ed. and trans. 1967. *Anthologie poétique française: Moyen âge.* 2 vols. Paris: Garnier-Flammarion.

Mätzner, Eduard. 1853. *Altfranzösische Lieder berichtigt und erläutert.* Berlin: Ferd. Dümmlers Verlag. Reprint, Bonn: Dümmlers, 1969.

Ménard, Philippe, ed. 1987. *Le Roman de Tristan en prose, tome I.* Geneva: Droz.

Menocal, María Rosa. 1987. *The Arabic Role in Medieval Literary History: A Forgotten Heritage.* Philadelphia: University of Pennsylvania Press.

Meyer, Paul. 1868. "Troisième rapport sur une mission littéraire en Angleterre et en Écosse." *Archives des Missions Scientifiques et Littéraires,* série 2, 5: 139-272.

Meyer, Paul, ed. 1874-77. *Recueil d'anciens textes bas-latins, provençaux et français.* 2 vols. Paris: F. Vieweg. Reprint, Geneva: Slatkine, 1977.

Meyer, P[aul], and G[aston] Raynaud. 1892. *Le chansonnier français de Saint-Germain-des-Prés (Bibl. nat. fr. 20050): Reproduction phototypique avec transcription.* Société des Anciens Textes Français. Paris: Firmin Didot.

Michel, Francisque, ed. 1830. *Chansons du Châtelain de Coucy.* Paris: Imprimerie de Crapelet.

Moignet, Gérard. 1973. *Grammaire de l'ancien français: Morphologie—syntaxe.* Paris: Klincksieck.

Mölk, Ulrich. 1988. "Die frühen romanischen Frauenlieder: Überlegungen und Anregungen." In *Idee, Gestalt, Geschichte: Festschrift Klaus von See. Studien zur europäischen Kulturtradition.* Ed. Gerd Wolfgang Weber. Odense, Denmark: Odense University Press. 63-88.

———. 1990. "Chansons de femme, trobairitz et la théorie romantique de la genèse de la poésie lyrique romane." *Lingua e Stile* 25: 135-46.

Mölk, Ulrich. ed. and trans. 1989. *Romanische Frauenlieder.* Klassische Texte des romanischen Mittelalters in zweisprachigen Ausgaben 28. Munich: Wilhelm Fink.

Mölk, Ulrich, and Friedrich Wolfzettel. 1972. *Répertoire métrique de la poésie lyrique française des origines à 1350.* 74 perforated cards. Munich: Wilhelm Fink.

Morawski, Joseph. 1925. *Proverbes français antérieurs au XVe siècle.* Paris: Librairie Ancienne Édouard Champion.

Nappholz, Carol, ed. and trans. 1994. *Unsung Women: The Anonymous Female Voice in Troubadour Poetry.* New York: Peter Lang.

Nelson, Deborah, and Hendrik van der Werf, eds. and trans. 1992. *The Songs Attributed to Andrieu Contredit d'Arras with a Translation into English and the Extant Melodies.* Faux Titre 59. Amsterdam: Rodopi.

Nissen, Elisabeth, ed. 1928. *Les chansons attribuées à Guiot de Dijon et Jocelin.* Classiques Français du Moyen Âge 59. Paris: Honoré Champion.

Noack, Fritz. 1898. *Der Strophenausgang in seinem Verhältnis zum Refrain und Strophengrundstock in der refrainhaltigen altfranzösischen Lyrik.* Greifswald, Germany: Druck von F. W. Kunike. Reprint, Marburg, Germany: Elwert, 1899.

Paden, William. 1992. "Some Recent Studies of Women in the Middle Ages, Especially in Southern France." *Tenso* 7: 94-124.

———. 2001. "The Lyric Lady in Narrative." In *Reassessing the Heroine in Medieval French Literature.* Ed. Kathy Krause. Gainesville: University Press of Florida. Forthcoming.

Page, Christopher. 1986. *Voices and Instruments of the Middle Ages: Instrumental Practice and Songs in France, 1100-1300.* London: J. M. Dent and Sons.

———. 1989. *The Owl and the Nightingale: Musical Life and Ideas in France, 1100-1300.* Berkeley: University of California Press.

———. 1993a. *Discarding Images: Reflections on Music and Culture in Medieval France.* Oxford: Clarendon Press.

———. 1993b. "Johannes de Grocheio on Secular Music: A Corrected Text and a New Translation." *Plainsong and Medieval Music* 2: 17-41.

Paris, Gaston. 1880. "La chanson du Pèlerinage de Charlemagne." *Romania* 9: 1-50.

———. 1883. "Études sur les romans de la Table Ronde: *Lancelot du Lac.*" *Romania* 12: 459-534.

———. 1891-92. Review of *Les origines de la poésie lyrique en France au moyen âge,* by Alfred Jeanroy. *Journal des Savants* 1891: 674-88 and 729-42; 1892: 155-67 and 407-29. Offprint, Paris: Bouillon, 1892.

Paris, Paulin. 1856. "Chansonniers des trouvères." In *Histoire littéraire de la France.* Vol. 23: *Fin du treizième siècle.* Paris: Firmin Didot. Reprint, Nendeln, Liechtenstein: Kraus Reprint, 1971. 512-831.

Paris, Paulin, ed. 1836-38. *Les grandes chroniques de France.* 6 vols. Paris: Tréchener.

Parisse, Michel. 1976. *La noblesse lorraine: XIe-XIIIe s.* Doctoral diss., Université de Nancy II, 1975. Lille: Atelier Reproduction des Thèses. Paris: Honoré Champion.

———. 1982. *Noblesse et chevalerie en Lorraine médiévale: Les familles nobles du XIe au XIIIe siècle.* Nancy, France: Service des Publications de l'Université de Nancy II.

Pauphilet, Albert, ed. 1952. *Poètes et romanciers du moyen âge*. Bibliothèque de la Pléiade 52. Paris: Éditions Gallimard.

Pelan, Margaret, ed. 1956. *Floire et Blancheflor, édition du ms. 1447 du fonds français avec notes, variantes et glossaire*. Publications de la Faculté des Lettres de l'Université de Strasbourg 7. Paris: Les Belles Lettres.

Pernoud, Régine. 1972. *La reine Blanche*. Paris: Albin Michel.

Pesce, Dolores. 1997. "Beyond Glossing: The Old Made New in *Mout me fu grief / Robin m'aime / Portare*." In *Hearing the Motet: Essays on the Motet of the Middle Ages and Renaissance*. Ed. Dolores Pesce. New York: Oxford University Press. 28-51.

Petersen Dyggve, Holger. 1934. *Onomastiaue des trouvères*. Annales Academiæ Scientiarum Fennicæ B 30, 1. Helsinki: Suomalaisen Tiedeakatemian Toimituksia. Reprint Bibliography and Reference Series 488. Music History and Reference Series 4. New York: Burt Franklin, 1973.

Petersen Dyggve, Holger, ed. 1951. *Gace Brulé, trouvère champenois*. Mémoires de la Société Néophilologique de Helsingfors 16. Helsinki: Société Néophilologique.

Pfeffer, Wendy. 1985. "The Riddle of the Proverb." In *The Spirit of the Court: Selected Proceedings of the Fourth Congress of the International Courtly Literature Society (Toronto 1983)*. Ed. Glyn Burgess and Robert Taylor. Cambridge, England: D. S. Brewer. 254-63.

———. 2001. "Complaints of Women, Complaints by Women: Can One Tell Them Apart?" In *The Court Reconvenes: Selected Proceedings of the Ninth Triennial Congress of the International Courtly Literature Society*. Ed. Chantal Phan, Barbara Altmann, and Carleton Carroll. Cambridge, England: D. S. Brewer. Forthcoming.

Picot, Guillaume, ed. 1975. *La poésie lyrique au moyen âge*. 2 vols. Nouveaux Classiques Larousse. Paris: Larousse.

Pillet, Alfred, and Henry Carstens. 1933. *Bibliographie der Troubadours*. Halle: Niemeyer.

Pope, M[ildred] K. 1934. *From Latin to Modern French with Especial Consideration of Anglo-Norman Phonology and Morphology*. Manchester: Manchester University Press.

Raynaud, Gaston. 1884. *Bibliographie des chansonniers français des XIIIe et XIVe siècles*. 2 vols. Paris: Vieweg. Reprint, Osnabrück, Germany: Biblio, 1971. Reprint, Bibliography and Reference Series 469. Music History and Reference Series 2. New York: Burt Franklin, 1972.

Raynaud, Gaston, ed. 1881-83. *Recueil de motets français des XIIe et XIIIe siècles*. 2 vols. Bibliothèque Française du Moyen Âge 1-2. Paris: Vieweg. Reprint, Hildesheim: Georg Olms, 1972. Reprint, Geneva: Slatkine, 1974.

Raynaud de Lage, Guy. 1972. *Introduction à l'ancien français*. 8th ed. Paris: Société d'Édition d'Enseignement Supérieur.

Reaney, Gilbert, ed. 1966. *Répertoire international des sources musicales/International Inventory of Musical Sources/Internationales Quellenlexicon der Musik*. Vol. B.IV.1: *Manuscripts of Polyphonic Music, 11th-Early 14th Century*. Munich-Duisburg: G. Henle Verlag.

Richter, Max, ed. 1904. *Die Lieder des altfranzösischen Lyrikers Jehan de Nuevile*. Halle: C. A. Kaemmerer.

Rieger, Angelica. 1985. " 'Ins e.l cor port, dona, vostra faisso': Image et imaginaire de la femme à travers l'enluminure dans les chansonniers de troubadours." *Cahiers de Civilisation Médiévale* 28: 385-415.

Rokseth, Yvonne. 1935-39. *Polyphonies du XIIIᵉ siècle: Le manuscrit H 196 de la Faculté de Médecine de Montpellier*. 4 vols. Paris: Éditions de l'Oiseau-Lyre.

Roques, Mario, ed. 1938. *Recueil général des lexiques français du moyen âge (XIIᵉ-XVᵉ siècles)*. Bibliothèque de l'École des Hautes Études 269. Vol. 1, 2: *Lexiques alphabétiques*. Paris: Honoré Champion.

Rosenberg, Samuel. 1983. "The Old French Lyric Death-Laments." In *Le Gai Savoir: Essays in Linguistics, Philology, and Criticism Dedicated to the Memory of Manfred Sandmann*. Ed. Mechthild Cranston. Studia Humanitatis. Madrid: José Porrúa Turanzas. 45-54.

———. 1995. "Women's Songs." In *Medieval France: An Encyclopedia*. Ed. William Kibler and Grover Zinn. Garland Encyclopedias of the Middle Ages 2. New York: Garland Publishing. 987.

Rosenberg, Samuel, Samuel Danon, and Hendrik van der Werf, eds. and trans. 1985. *The Lyrics and Melodies of Gace Brulé*. Garland Library of Medieval Literature A, 39. New York: Garland Publishing.

Rosenberg, Samuel, Margaret Switten, and Gérard Le Vot, eds. and trans. 1998. *Songs of the Troubadours and Trouvères: An Anthology of Poems and Melodies*. Garland Reference Library of the Humanities 1740. New York: Garland Publishing.

Rosenberg, Samuel, and Hans Tischler, eds. 1981. *Chanter m'estuet: Songs of the Trouvères*. Bloomington: Indiana University Press; London: Faber Music.

Rosenberg, Samuel, Hans Tischler, and Marie-Geneviève Grossel, eds. and trans. 1995. *Chansons des trouvères: Chanter m'estuet*. Paris: Librairie Générale Française.

Rosenstein, Roy. 1980. "Iocus amœnus: Love, Play and Poetry in Troubadour Lyric." Ph.D. diss., Columbia University.

Rychner, Jean, ed. 1966. *Les lais de Marie de France*. Paris: Honoré Champion.

Sadie, Julie, and Rhian Samuel, eds. 1994. *The Norton/Grove Dictionary of Women Composers*. New York: Norton.

Sadie, Stanley, ed. 1980. *The New Grove Dictionary of Music and Musicians*. 20 vols. London: Macmillan.

Sanders, Ernest. 1980. "Motet, §I,1: Medieval." In *The New Grove Dictionary of Music and Musicians*. Ed. Stanley Sadie. 20 vols. London: Macmillan. 12: 617-28.

Schläger, Georg. 1911. "Zur Rhythmik des altfranzösischen epischen Verses." *Zeitschrift für romanische Philologie* 35: 364-75.

Schreurs, Eugeen. 1995. *Anthologie van muziekfragmenten uit de Lage Landen: Polyfonie, monodie en leisteenfragmenten in facsimile*. Louvain, Belgium: Alamire Foundation.

Schultz, O. 1891. "Ein Lied von Gautier d'Espinau." *Zeitschrift für romanische Philologie* 15: 237.

Schultz-Gora, O. 1907. "Einige unedierte Jeux-partis." *Romanische Forschungen* 23: 497-516. *Mélanges Chabaneau*. Erlangen, Germany: Fr. Junge. 497-516.

Schutz, Richard, ed. 1976. "The Unedited Poems of Codex 389 of the Municipal Library of Berne, Switzerland." Ph.D. diss., Indiana University.

Schwan, E[duard], and D[ietrich] Behrens. 1932. *Grammaire de l'ancien français.* Trans. Oscar Bloch. 4th ed. Leipzig: O. R. Reisland.

Shapiro, Marianne. 1978. "The Provençal *Trobairitz* and the Limits of Courtly Love." *Signs* 3: 560-71.

Sigal, Gale. 1996. *Erotic Dawn-Songs of the Middle Ages: Voicing the Lyric Lady.* Gainesville: University of Florida Press.

Sinner, Jean. 1760-72. *Catalogus Codicum mss. Bibliothecæ Bernensis Annotationibus Criticis Illustratus.* 3 vols. Bern: Officina typogr. Brunneri & Halleri.

Sivéry, Gérard. 1990. *Blanche de Castille.* Paris: Fayard.

Smith, Lesley, and Jane Taylor, eds. 1997. *Women and the Book: Assessing the Visual Evidence.* London: British Library; Toronto: University of Toronto Press.

Smith, Norman. 1989. "The Earliest Motets: Music and Words." *Journal of the Royal Musical Association* 114: 141-63.

Smith, Robyn, ed. and trans. 1997. *French Double and Triple Motets in the Montpellier Manuscript: Textual Edition, Translation and Commentary.* Musicological Studies 68. Ottawa: Institute of Mediæval Music.

Spanke, Hans. 1929. "Zur Geschichte des altfranzösische Jeu-parti." *Zeitschrift für französische Sprache und Literatur* 52: 39-63.

Spanke, Hans, ed. 1925. *Eine altfranzösische Liedersammlung: Der anonyme Teil der Liederhandschriften KNPX.* Romanische Bibliothek 22. Halle: Niemeyer.

———. 1955. *G. Raynauds Bibliographie des altfranzösischen Liedes.* Musicologica 1. Leiden: Brill. Reprint 1980.

Stanton, Domna, ed. 1986. *The Defiant Muse: French Feminist Poems from the Middle Ages to the Present: A Bilingual Anthology.* New York: Feminist Press.

Steffens, Georg. 1897a. "Die altfranzösische Liederhandschrift der Bodleiana in Oxford, Douce 308." *Archiv für das Studium der neueren Sprachen und Literaturen* 98: 59-80 and 343-82.

———. 1897b. "Die altfranzösische Liederhandschrift der Bodleiana in Oxford, Douce 308." *Archiv für das Studium der neueren Sprachen und Literaturen* 99: 77-100 and 339-88.

Steffens, Georg, ed. 1905. *Die Lieder des Troveors Perrin von Angicourt.* Romanische Bibliothek 18. Halle: Niemeyer.

Stengel, Edmund. 1896. "Der Strophenausgang in den ältesten französischen Balladen." *Zeitschrift für französische Sprache und Literatur* 18: 85-114.

Stern, Samuel. 1948. "Les vers finaux en espagnol dans les muwaššaḥs hispano-hébraïques." *Al-Andalus* 13: 299-346.

Stimming, Albert, ed. 1906. *Die altfranzösischen Motette der Bamberger Handschrift nebst einem Anhang, enthaltend altfranzösische Motette aus anderen deutschen Handschriften, mit Anmerkungen und Glossar.* Gesellschaft für romanische Literatur 13. Dresden: Gedruckt für die Gesellschaft für romanische Literatur; Halle: Niemeyer.

Tarbé, Prosper, ed. 1850. *Les chansonniers de Champagne aux XIIe et XIIIe siècles.* Reims: Regnier. Reprint, Geneva: Slatkine, 1980.

———. 1851. *Chansons de Thibaut IV, comte de Champagne et de Brie, roi de Navarre.* Reims: Regnier.

Tavera, Antoine. 1978. "A la recherche des troubadours maudits." In *Exclus et systèmes d'exclusion dans la littérature et la civilisation médiévales. Senefiance 5.* Aix-en-Provence: CUER-MA. 135-62.

Thompson, Sally. 1978. "The Problem of the Cistercian Nuns in the Twelfth and Early Thirteenth Centuries." In *Medieval Women.* Ed. Derek Baker. Oxford: Basil Blackwell. 227-52.

Thurston, Ethel. 1959. *The Music in the St. Victor Manuscript, Paris Lat. 15139: Polyphony of the Thirteenth Century.* Studies and Texts 5. Toronto: Pontifical Institute of Mediaeval Studies.

Tischler, Hans, ed. 1973. *A Medieval Motet Book: A Collection of 13th Century Motets in Various Vocal and Instrumental Combinations.* New York: Associated Music Publishers.

———. 1978-85. *The Montpellier Codex.* 4 vols. Recent Researches in the Music of the Middle Ages and Early Renaissance 2-8. Madison, Wis.: A-R Editions.

———. 1982. *The Earliest Motets (to circa 1270): A Complete Comparative Edition.* 3 vols. New Haven: Yale University Press.

———. 1997. *Trouvère Lyrics with Melodies: Complete Comparative Edition.* 15 vols. Corpus Mensurabilis Musicae 107. Neuhausen, Germany: American Institute of Musicology and Hänssler-Verlag.

Tobler, Adolf, and Erhard Lommatzsch. 1925- . *Altfranzösisches Wörterbuch.* 11 vols. to date. Berlin: Weidmannsche Buchhandlung; Wiesbaden, Germany: Franz Steiner.

Toja, Gianluigi, ed. 1966. *Lirica cortese d'oïl, sec. XII–XIII.* Bologna: Pàtron.

Tyssens, Madeleine. 1992. "Voix de femmes dans la lyrique d'oïl." In *Femmes, mariages-lignages, XIIᵉ-XIVᵉ siècles: Mélanges offerts à Georges Duby.* Brussels: De Boeck Université. 373-87.

Ulrix, Eugène. 1921. "Les chansons inédites du ms. f. f. 844 de la Bibliothèque nationale, à Paris." *Leuvensche Bijdragen* 13: 69-79.

Ungureanu, Marie. 1955. *La bourgeoisie naissante: Société et littérature bourgeoises d'Arras aux XIIᵉ et XIIIᵉ siècles.* Mémoires de la Commission des Monuments Historiques du Pas-de-Calais 8. Arras: Commission Départementale des Monuments Historiques du Pas-de-Calais.

van der Werf, Hendrik. 1972. *The Chansons of the Troubadours and Trouvères: A Study of the Melodies and Their Relation to the Poems.* A. Oosthoek's Uitgeversmaatschappij NV. Utrecht: Oosthoek.

———. 1984. *The Extant Troubadour Melodies.* Rochester: Published by the author.

———. 1989. *Integrated Directory of Organa, Clausulae, and Motets of the Thirteenth Century.* Rochester: Published by the author.

———. 1997. "Jean Renart and Medieval Song." In *Jean Renart and the Art of Romance: Essays on Guillaume de Dole.* Ed. Nancy Vine Durling. Gainesville: University Press of Florida. 157-222.

Wackernagel, Wilhelm, ed. 1846. *Altfranzœsische Lieder und Leiche aus Handschriften zu Bern und Neuenburg.* Basel: Schweighauserische Buchhandlung.

Wahlgren, Ernst. 1925. "Sur la question de l'*i* dit parasite dans l'ancien français." In *Mélanges de philologie offerts à M. Johan Vising*. Göteborg, Sweden: N. J. Gumperts; Paris: Librairie Ancienne Édouard Champion. 290-335.

Waitz, Hugo. 1899. "Der kritische Text der Gedichte von Gillebert de Berneville mit Angabe sämtlicher Lesarten nach den Pariser Handschriften." In *Beiträge zur romanischen Philologie: Festgabe für Gustav Gröber*. Halle: Niemeyer. 39-118. Reprint, Geneva: Slatkine, 1975.

Wallensköld, Axel, ed. 1925. *Les chansons de Thibaut de Champagne, Roi de Navarre*. Paris: Librairie Ancienne Édouard Champion.

Walsh, P. G., ed. and trans. 1982. *Andreas Capellanus on Love*. Duckworth Classical, Medieval and Renaissance Editions. London: Duckworth.

Wartburg, Walther von. 1928- . *Französisches etymologisches Wörterbuch*. Bonn: Fritz Klopp.

Wilkins, Nigel, ed. 1967. *The Lyric Works of Adam de la Hale*. 2nd ed. Corpus Mensurabilis Musicæ 44. N.p.: American Institute of Musicology, 1984.

Wind, Bartina, ed. 1960. *Thomas, Les fragments du Roman de Tristan*. 2nd ed. Geneva: Droz; Paris: Minard.

Woledge, Brian, ed. and trans. 1961. *The Penguin Book of French Verse*. Vol. 1: *To the Fifteenth Century*. Harmondsworth: Penguin Books.

Wright, Craig. 1989. *Music and Ceremony at Notre Dame of Paris, 500-1550*. Cambridge Studies in Music. Cambridge: Cambridge University Press.

Yardley, Anne. 1986. " 'Ful weel she soong the service dyvyne': The Cloistered Musician in the Middle Ages." In *Women Making Music: The Western Art Tradition, 1150-1950*. Ed. Jane Bowers and Judith Tick. Urbana: University of Illinois Press. 15-38.

Zarifopol, Paul, ed. 1904. *Kritischer Text der Lieder Richards de Fournival*. Halle: E. Karras.

Zink, Michel. 1996. *Le moyen âge et ses chansons, ou Un passé en trompe-l'œil*. Paris: Éditions de Fallois.

Zink, Michel, ed. and trans. 1978. *Bele: Essai sur les chansons de toile*. Paris: Honoré Champion.

Zumthor, Paul. 1972. *Essai de poétique médiévale*. Paris: Seuil.

Index